The Cultural Crisis of the Firm

D1409983

*for my mother
and in memory of my father*

The Cultural Crisis of the Firm

Erica Schoenberger

For Bob
with admiration
and many thanks

Erica

B BLACKWELL
Publishers

First published 1997

2 4 6 8 10 9 7 5 3 1

Blackwell Publishers Inc.
238 Main Street
Cambridge, Massachusetts 02142
USA

Blackwell Publishers Ltd
108 Cowley Road
Oxford OX4 1JF
UK

Library of Congress Cataloging-in-Publication Data

Schoenberger, Erica J.
    The cultural crisis of the firm/Erica Schoenberger.
        p.   cm.
    Includes bibliographical references and index.
    ISBN 1-55786-637-6. – ISBN 1-55786-638-4 (pbk.)
    1. Corporate culture. I. Title.
HD58.7.S346 1997 96-24361
302.3'5–dc20   CIP

British Library Cataloguing in Publication Data

A CIP catalogue record for this book is available from the British Library.

Typeset in 10 on 12pt Sabon by Wearset, Boldon, Tyne and Wear.
Printed in Great Britain by Hartnolls Limited, Bodmin, Cornwall

This book is printed on acid-free paper

Contents

Acknowledgements

I've been working in this field for a long time, and I've had a lot of help. First, I would like to acknowledge the financial support of the National Science Foundation, the Spencer Foundation and the Renaissance Trust of England, without which, quite literally, this book wouldn't have been possible.

I should also like to thank Greenwood Press for permission to reproduce material in chapter 3, taken from an article previously published as 'Competition, time and space in industrial change,' in G. Gereffi and M. Korzeniewicz (eds), 1994, pp. 51–67. Similar thanks are due to Pion Limited, London, for permission to reproduce material in chapter 5, taken from an article previously published as 'Corporate strategy and corporate strategists: power, identity, and knowledge within the firm,' *Environment & Planning A*, 1994, 26, pp. 435–51.

I have also spent a great deal of time in the last decade or so talking with executives of a large number of American and European multinational corporations. For the most part, I promised them anonymity as a condition of the discussion, and I have held to that here, so I mostly can't thank anyone by name. But I do want them to know that I appreciated their willingness to have me around, their openness, their thoughtfulness, and the quality of their engagement with the issues I needed to talk about. I would also like to stress that although managers as a class come in for some pretty strong criticism in the text, my experience with managers as individuals has impressed me a great deal. I hope that their generosity toward me will seem to them in some small way repaid by this book. One person I can name in this context is Gerry Martin, who has provided a lot of encouragement, commentary, pointers, reality checks, and other kinds of help along the way. Another is Eric Wolman, who shared great stories, corrected my grammar and buoyed me up with his infectious enthusiasm at crucial moments. I'm very grateful to both.

Johns Hopkins has provided a very supportive institutional environment and a lot of terrific colleagues who have helped me in countless ways. Some central arguments in this book grew out of a research and teaching collaboration with Bill Leslie and Robert Kargon in the History of Science and Technology Department here. They have been very generous colleagues, with their time, their ideas, and their hard work. Emily Martin found a place for me in the Anthropology Department, my home away from home, and shared with me her ideas, her enthusiasms, and her wonderful courage. Katherine Verdery and Gillian Feeley-Harnik have both taught me a great deal, and have ever been staunch allies and friends. Lou Galambos, Ali Khan and Vicente Navarro have provided critical encouragement and friendship.

My colleagues in Geography and Environmental Engineering are, for the most part, quite removed from the content and style of my work, and yet have always been supportive of it. Just about the luckiest thing that ever happened in my life was coming into a program created and run by the incomparable Reds Wolman. I'm still hoping to be like him when I grow up. Hugh Ellis managed to keep me laughing while gently explaining why my ideas didn't hold water. Haydee Salmun has been my soulmate. Sabrina Linton and Isabel Miles have kept me going and kept me sane – or close enough.

The students that I've come to know here have been smart and funny and wise and have helped me in ways they can't even guess at. Out of many, I would have to name Kevin Archer, Patrick Bond, Sean Di Giovanna, Elizabeth Dunn, Michael Johns, Sarah Hill, Erik Swyngedouw, and Melissa Wright.

It is often alleged that academic life is full of petty quarrels, jealousies, and trivial inhumanities. My experience of it has been quite different. From graduate school on, I have been engaged with a group of scholars in various disciplines, universities, and countries who have contributed tremendously to my ideas and my professional development. Taken as a whole, they are an incredibly entertaining, yet serious, group who are struggling with a set of related issues and who have devoted a lot of time and effort to helping others, especially me, along. I want to thank in particular Gordon Clark, Peter Dicken, Meric Gertler, Amy Glasmeier, Norm Glickman, Ben Harrison, John Holmes, Hadjila Krifa, Ann Markusen, Flavia Martinelli, Doreen Massey, Anno Saxenian, Michael Storper, Mike Tietz, Dick Walker, and Neil Wrigley.

John Davey, of Blackwell Publishers, has been the editor of my dreams, trusting and enthusiastic when I most needed trust and enthusiasm, gently prodding at other times, but always hilariously funny.

Anyone who reads this book will recognize instantly my tremendous intellectual debt to David Harvey. But I would also want them to know how much he has meant to me, and done for me, as a colleague and a friend. He has watched out over the whole of my career, part guardian angel and part *nudge*, which was about what it took. He has accepted my alarming tendency to walk into immovable objects (literally and figuratively), and has always been there when I've needed him. Which, I'm happy to say, has been a lot.

Most of this book was written on the back deck of Kate Brady and Jim Smith's house in Berkeley, under the pear tree, amidst a tangle of puppies and kittens. I don't think it could have been written anywhere else. Kate is my oldest and best friend and I rely on her completely. Jim came on the scene a little bit later, but very generously accepted that being married to Kate included having me in the family. If we don't quite make beautiful music together, heaven knows it's not for want of trying.

Finally, my thanks to Christopher Paine, who got me started down this path, and to Che, who almost made it to the end.

Baltimore
April 1996

Part I

Competition, Time, and Space

1

The End of an Industrial Era

The Issue

Sometime between 1965 and 1975, the age of high mass production and the period of American hegemony in the global industrial economy came to an end. That these two events should occur together seems natural in some ways. American industrial dominance was based, after all, on the innovation and progressive development of the principles and processes of standardized mass production. As this system began to reach its productive and market limits, and as it began to encounter challenges based on rather different principles of production and competition, it seems perhaps inevitable that the firms involved in it – the firms which had, indeed, produced and consolidated the system to begin with – would be caught out.

Nor can we claim that this undermining of American hegemony was unequivocally a bad thing. While industrial supremacy was certainly good in significant ways for Americans, it would be hard to argue that this represented a morally right or self-justifying state of affairs. Why should such a tiny proportion of the world's population exercise such powerful sway over the rest, controlling such a vast amount of available resources, and influencing to a significant degree the possibilities of production and consumption, employment, wealth generation, and income in other regions of the globe?

It can also be argued that the situation was untenable economically, socially, and politically in very practical ways. Although the advantages of having been the first to elaborate the mass production system were very important in constraining the degree to which new competitors could enter the field, they could not indefinitely forestall the emergence of new sources of competition. Gramsci foresaw the problem with great clarity when he wrote in the early 1930s:

In reality American high-wage industry is still exploiting a monopoly granted to it by the fact that it has the initiative with the new methods. Monopoly wages correspond to monopoly profits. But the monopoly will necessarily be first limited and then destroyed by the further diffusion of the new methods both within the United States and abroad (compare the Japanese phenomenon of low-priced goods), and high wages will disappear along with enormous profits. (Gramsci, 1971:311)

Moreover, the system's stability and continued growth also *depended* on this diffusion. Its productive power was so great that the domestic economy alone couldn't absorb all the goods and surplus capital that it generated. Yet foreign markets could only serve as significant outlets for commodities and investment capital if they were built up and their wealth-generating capacities developed.

The dilemma was that this could only be accomplished through a process of industrialization that would eventually produce the challenge to American industrial hegemony. If the United States, through its postwar reconstruction activities in Europe and Japan, helped to create the conditions for its own industrial decline, it was nonetheless necessary that it did so. This necessity was also social and political, as the consequences of permanent economic subordination and fragility would have soon become unmanageable.

We can suppose, then, that the undermining of American industrial dominance was inevitable. It took place in a context of market saturation and stagnation, and was a product of macro-level political and economic processes. In this sense, the problem went beyond the power of firms and industries to fix or eliminate. But it doesn't follow from this that the unavoidable outcome was industrial decline and crisis. Yet that is what we saw in industry after industry: steel, automobiles, chemicals, semiconductors, computers, office equipment, consumer electronics, appliances, and more. Enormously wealthy and powerful firms in these industries found themselves beleaguered and on the brink of failure. Some disappeared. Others fought their way back to profitability, but painfully and with considerable losses. The fate of still others remains in doubt.

Why did this happen? The easy and true answer is that there were a lot of reasons, some general, some having to do with the specific predicaments of particular industries or individual firms. But it is both striking and sobering that at a particular historical moment and in a particular place, so many immensely powerful corporations were brought low.

True, the historical moment was a difficult one. After some decades of generally consistent growth, firms were faced with stagnating markets, excess capacity, and sharply intensified competition. In good times, life is undoubtedly easier, as even comparatively inefficient or backward firms can manage to hold on to a share of an expanding market. But even in bad times, some firms survive and indeed prosper – and this time was no exception. The firms which prospered, however, tended not to be those which had dominated their industries to that point and which accounted for a very large share of output, investment, and employment in those industries. Marx has an interesting take on this sort of situation, which he describes with characteristic relish:

> So long as things go well, competition effects an operating fraternity of the capitalist class ... so that each shares in the common loot in proportion to the size of his respective investment. But as soon as it no longer is a question of sharing profits, but of sharing losses, everyone tries to reduce his own share to a minimum and to shove it off upon another. ... How much the individual capitalist must bear of the loss, i.e., to what extent he must share in it at all, is decided by strength and cunning, and competition then becomes a fight among hostile brothers. (Marx, 1967c:253)

The problem that Marx doesn't raise here is why the outcome of this fight among hostile brothers has such a distinctive historical and geographical dimension: in other words, why, after decades of extraordinary success and nearly unchallenged dominance, do firms in the United States, say (or the frostbelt, or Detroit), seem generally lacking in the strength and cunning required to survive the shakeout and even flourish modestly at the expense of their brethren elsewhere.

It was certainly not for want of trying. These firms invested billions of dollars in new plant and equipment and billions more in research and product development. They restructured and refinanced, bought and sold divisions and companies, entered into joint ventures and strategic alliances with their competitors, closed plants and laid off thousands of workers and managers, extracted significant concessions from unions, reorganized administrative structures, moved production overseas, sought the advice of expensive consultants, lobbied for government protection or assistance in entering inaccessible markets, and more. Some firms did succeed in turning themselves around and strengthening their position in their markets. Ford, Xerox, Motorola, GE, and Intel are widely praised examples. But after two decades of frantic activity, many more still find themselves in serious difficulty.

So it is not quite accurate to say that the problem is that firms were resistant to change. It seems likely, though, that the kinds of change they were willing and able to undertake were constrained to run in certain channels and not others. In this way they failed to react appropriately to the new competitive conditions that they faced.

What structures this selective pattern of change and resistance? Again, there are many possible answers that are both plausible and accurate. But the central thesis of this book is that corporate cultures and managerial identities and commitments exerted a powerful force that structured the possibilities for change in ways that proved unavailing given the actual circumstances in which firms found themselves.

The Stakes

However much a part of our lives and consciousness firms such as GM, RCA, or IBM might have become, there is no reason to feel particularly sentimental about them. We can't want them to exist just because they are an important feature of a known and accepted industrial landscape. Moreover, even if they disappear as corporate entities, it is not necessarily the case that all of their assets – and the activities and employment connected to them – are simply vaporized. A great deal might be salvaged even from outright failure.

Still, there are important reasons to care about their fate. The principal one is that in a capitalist society, what happens to firms profoundly structures the life possibilities of huge numbers of people and bears heavily on the economic viability of entire communities, cities, and regions. In the normal course of events, the decline or failure of individual companies here and there can be absorbed reasonably well, although not without pain and serious dislocation for those most directly affected. But when significant numbers of the largest, most dominant firms are thrown into crisis at roughly the same time, then the possibilities for the absorption of these losses and the gradual reorganization of lives and activities are severely overmatched. This is all the more true when the decline of a leading firm puts an entire network of suppliers and subcontractors at risk. The result is acute and long-lasting hardship for large numbers of people and places.

Transformation and change are a normal feature of capitalist development, and change always implies loss as well as gain. Schumpeter had good reason to write of gales of creative destruction that are continually reshaping the landscape. But it is often the case that what is created is quite distant geographically from what is destroyed, and that those people tied to the wreckage will have little possibility of benefiting from the creative processes at work elsewhere. Thus, people in Detroit or Baltimore find their lives increasingly impossible even as the economies of Nashville or Silicon Valley, not to mention Tokyo, Munich, or the

Third Italy, forge ahead. So for this reason too, the fate of individual firms has considerable importance.

Finally, there is this. We have to acknowledge that any kind of significant corporate reorganization in the face of changed competitive circumstances is bound to involve serious dislocation and hardship for some. Chronic overcapacity, to cite one example, can only be resolved by cutbacks in production and employment somewhere. The introduction of new process technologies, which may be necessary for reasons having to do with productivity, product quality and performance, or yields, may unavoidably displace labor.[1] These, again, are normal features of capitalist developmental dynamics. Industrial competitiveness, in short, doesn't solve all problems. Indeed, becoming competitive can itself be a source of tremendous social and economic distress. On the other hand, not being competitive is still worse. By the same token, sudden and drastic corporate transformations driven by crisis are worse than gradual and continual adaptation to changing conditions.

So it is important to understand why leading firms, in case after case, found themselves on the very edge of the abyss before they were able to productively rethink themselves – and sometimes they couldn't do it even then. The underlying thesis here is that there is much to be learned from the failure of the powerful to react *appropriately* to new challenges.

Although this book is primarily concerned with the failure of American firms to act in their own best interest, some of the general lessons to emerge from this analysis should be more widely applicable. This would include in the first instance firms of other nationalities. But many other institutional agents – universities, hospitals, branches of government, etc. – are also faced with profoundly changing circumstances. They, too, are the arenas for powerful forces contesting and shaping patterns of change and resistance. Though the internal dynamics and external pressures that they experience may not be identical to those characteristic of large corporations, there are significant similarities. Not the least of the reasons for this is that these institutions are adopting many of the strategies and techniques currently favored by firms: total quality management, mission statements, experiential learning, decentralization and empowerment, and so on. As with firms, the degree to which these strategies and techniques provide an adequate response to their various predicaments will depend significantly on pervasive and highly conflictual cultural processes.

---

[1] We shouldn't, on the other hand, overlook the fact that many kinds of technology initiatives are misguided and counter-productive "solutions" to problems whose roots lie elsewhere.

The Setting

The claim that American industrial dominance was essentially about mass production needs some qualification. Important sectors in the manufacturing economy – aerospace, defense electronics, many kinds of industrial machinery, power generation equipment, and supercomputers are some – have never been organized as mass production industries. Tens of thousands of small job shops and small-scale, independent manufacturers might also be excluded, except for the fact that many of them are tied into mass production networks as suppliers and subcontractors.

Even if we accept that mass production was the dominant feature of the American industrial landscape, the concept still embraces extraordinary diversity across industries and firms. Process industries such as steel and chemicals apparently have little in common with manufacturing/assembly industries such as automobiles, personal computers, or appliances, and these are yet again different from textiles or books. Even within industries, Ford is a rather different place in important ways from GM, and the same is true for Apple compared to IBM, Westinghouse and GE, Kodak and Xerox or Polaroid, and so on.

It is important to address these sectoral and corporate specificities and the kinds of exception and idiosyncrasy associated with them. At the same time, it is useful to approach the problem at a higher level of abstraction in order to focus on certain patterns and tendencies that are broadly characteristic of American industrial practice in the twentieth century and that achieved their clearest expression in mass production.

The system of mass production represents, in effect, an ensemble of material practices, social relations, and understandings or ways of thinking. This ensemble is coherent and relatively stable in the sense that the different "pieces" are interrelated and work together so that the system can reproduce itself over time. At the same time, it is also contradictory and changeable; the system contains within itself significant tensions, pressures, and constraints that continually reproduce the conditions for conflict, dislocation, and change. At the limit, these tensions and constraints, combined with novel pressures from the outside, may exceed the capacity of the system for self-renewal and create the conditions for crisis.

Here I want to describe a stylized version of the key elements of the system.[2] Production was organized around standardized processes, often based on highly specialized or dedicated equipment that could

---

[2] For more detailed analyses of these various themes, see Harvey, 1982, 1989; Storper and Walker, 1989; Sayer and Walker, 1992; Schoenberger, 1988; Kochan et al., 1986; Piore and Sabel, 1984; Hounshell, 1984; Lipietz, 1982; Aglietta, 1979.

produce cheaply so long as volumes were high and product configurations relatively stable. Scale economies and capacity utilization rates had a tremendous, if sometimes contradictory, influence on unit output costs. Dominant producers tended to maintain capacity for market peaks, during which times scale economies could be exploited to the maximum. But the unavoidable market slumps, when capacity utilization rates fell, put strong pressures on costs and profits. A great deal of capital was in this way tied up in relatively inflexible plant and equipment and the system was intolerant of rapid product change.

Markets were conceived of as stratified according to product price and performance characteristics, but relatively homogeneous and stable within the various strata. Competition took place among a well-known and relatively small group of firms (Big Steel, the Big Three auto makers, the Big Four cereal producers, IBM and the BUNCH in typewriters and computers, etc.) and was oriented toward controlled product differentiation, brand loyalty, advertising, and distribution networks rather than all-out price competition.

Labor in this schema was treated as a cost to be minimized rather than as, say, a value-adding partner. Tasks were finely divided and specialized to the point that individual workers were the living counterparts of their machines, performing the same, repetitive motions throughout a shift. Moreover, a huge supervisory apparatus was put into place to manage the increasingly complex division of labor and to enforce work rhythms and performance. Workers were, in this sense, not only deskilled, but stripped of all responsibility for their own work.

The major mass production industries were unionized after long and bitter struggles, but however much they had resisted, the firms derived certain important benefits from the model of labor–management relations institutionalized here. Rights, responsibilities, and obligations were defined and codified in a way that unequivocally protected management's "right to manage." Given the utter importance of keeping the fixed capital stock in motion, union contracts were an important means of ensuring labor peace and uninterrupted production. These, however, were bought at the price of sharing productivity gains with workers in the form of steadily increasing real wages. In this way, wages were effectively taken out of competition while both wage trajectories and work rules became increasingly entrenched. This was, for the firms, a tolerable situation in a context of consistent market growth and productivity increases and in a world where all the major competitors played by the same rules and under the same constraints.

These practices and relations were associated with certain understandings about the way the world worked or should work, and the status of or value attached to different groups of people, kinds of activity, and outcomes. For example, the system implied certain ways of thinking about markets: how they were developed and how they behaved, the relationship of firms to them, even who "owned" particular segments of a market; and similarly for how competition was normally to be engaged in, who the competition was, and what the real sources of competitiveness were. Labor, as noted, was understood as a cost and had a very different status in the firm from management, say, or investors (compare this with current best-practice prescriptions that envision labor as an empowered, value-adding stakeholder in the firm). The technology and economics of production, combined with the specific understandings of markets, helped produce a world in which quantity ("getting metal out the door") was valued more than quality, for example, or product operating efficiencies. The system even produced very specific conceptions of time and space and how these could be managed. These practices, relations, and understandings, taken together, constitute what might be called the culture of mass production.

This system was, on the whole, extraordinarily successful for several decades – so much so that it took on an aura of naturalness and inevitability and the dominance of the dominant firms seemed incontestable. Nevertheless, the pressures and challenges were steadily building and their effects began to be felt more and more strongly from the late 1960s onwards.

An important source of pressure was that the system itself was so massively productive that it began consistently to exceed the capacity of even the richest markets to absorb the output. And, as Gramsci had foreseen, the tendency to chronic overcapacity was greatly worsened by the diffusion of the principles and practices of mass production to more and more areas of the globe.

What also mattered in this context was the particular form in which mass production diffused. The Western European versions of mass production, for example, were associated with rising wages and incomes, and the elaboration of important social welfare protections. As in the United States, this created the possibility for mass consumption of the goods produced. But this was less true of Japan at the time and not at all the case in many developing countries where employers had other ways of ensuring labor peace than sharing productivity gains with workers.

Two consequences followed from this state of affairs. First, many new sites of mass production were not also sites of mass consumption, so the output produced had to seek markets elsewhere – increasingly in the US and Western Europe – thus intensifying the problem of overproduction. Second, extremely low wages combined with rapidly rising productivity levels afforded these producers impressive cost advantages in their export markets. In this context, the cost rigidities characteristic of the core mass production regions, combined with the saturation and stagnation of their markets, put tremendous pressure on profits.

At roughly the same time, new kinds of competitive challenges were brewing from firms organized around different material practices, patterns of social relations, and ways of thinking about products, markets, competition, production processes, labor, time and space, and so on. This new competition emerged both domestically (for example, Apple, Sun, MCI, steel mini-mills, etc.) and abroad, notably in Japan and parts of Western Europe where divergent economic and social conditions fostered the development of these alternative models (cf. Piore and Sabel, 1984).

On the surface, this competition took the form of new product technologies and/or performance standards, and more rapid renovation of product lines. This already constituted a serious problem for mass production firms, which were hampered in their response by the enormous weight of specialized plant and equipment that could not easily be reallocated to new activities. But the challenge ran deeper than that. It was really a challenge to the entire culture of American mass production.

The Argument

I want in this book to target the culture of the firm as a way of understanding what happened when the tensions produced within the system of mass production, combined with the new sorts of competitive challenge it encountered, proved too great for the system to absorb. Through the analysis of corporate culture, I think we can better understand the processes underlying the selection of certain kinds of strategic response and the rejection of others. This may cast some light on why so many firms, despite all their efforts at change, failed to respond appropriately to the new conditions with the consequences we have seen.

Why the culture of the firm? In the first place because, within the general frame of the culture of mass production, the specificities of industries and firms are very important. Cultural processes work at various levels which, though interconnected, also allow for considerable diversity. Thus, we might plausibly speak of the culture of automobile production while understanding that the culture of GM is different in important ways from Ford or Chrysler.[3] The firm is a more concrete

---

[3] Even within firms, we should expect to find any number of divergent sites of cultural production, as between engineers and accountants, say, or line workers and management (cf. J. Martin, 1992).

arena of cultural production and in many ways more accessible to analysis than mass production culture as a whole. More importantly, however, the firm is also where strategies are produced, and one goal of the book is to show the connection between cultural processes and strategic trajectories.

At the most general level, the book needs to construct two rather different kinds of argument and then to show how they can be linked. The first task is to characterize the nature and meaning of the competitive predicament in which firms presently find themselves. The second task is to consider how the culture of firms is produced, and how this culture is centrally implicated in the production of corporate strategies – including strategies that may threaten the very existence of the firm and its culture.

The third task is to connect these arguments by showing how a drastically altered competitive environment may constitute, in effect, a cultural crisis for the firm, rendering it unable to respond effectively. In this way, I hope to show how a general and structural condition such as competition has historically and geographically specific results at the level of the firm. The organization of the book follows this tripartite form.

Part I: Competition, Time, and Space

Part I proposes that we can analyze the transformation of production systems by looking at the categories of competition, time, and space as interrelated strategic problems for the firm. Several claims are implicit in this statement. First is that the way competition works, and the competitive strategies available to firms, are different in different historical circumstances. Second is that control over time and space is always and centrally a problem for the firm, but that its specific character also varies, with changing repercussions for the character of production and competition. Third is that the ways the problems of competition, time, and space are constituted and resolved at different times are interconnected. Fourth is that while the character of the production system shapes the specific historical content of these categories, we must expect that this process goes two ways. In other words, the way competition takes place, and the way the problems of time and space are worked out, also feed back upon the constitution of the production system.

This section claims, in effect, that we can't learn everything we need to know about what drives change in the production system by looking only at production. By far the most useful tradition in the analysis of industrial change makes its approach through the study of the social relations of production (capital–labor relations, labor market analysis, etc.) and/or the forces of production (technology and organization of the production process).[4] This work has been of tremendous value and it is not my intent to argue otherwise.

But this approach has the effect of pushing the fact of competition into the background as a kind of general constraint that enforces the drive to, for example, improve labor control or raise productivity without entering directly into how these things will be accomplished. Competition becomes a category with very little theoretical weight or historical specificity.[5]

In parallel, time and space are normally considered as problems in the context of the production and circulation of commodities (such as struggles over the working day, spatial divisions of labor, the elaboration of the credit system, etc.).[6] They are the objects of a kind of general compulsion to minimize and cheapen enforced by the fact that firms which lag behind will be uncompetitive. What I will try to argue is that if we investigate them as historically specific strategic problems for the firm, we can learn something about the evolution of production systems that we would otherwise miss or misconstrue.

Chapter 2 elaborates the rationale for investigating change in production systems through the optic of competition, time, and space. The character and value of this approach are illustrated through the recounting of the first two of three episodes in industrial history. In effect, I want to retell familiar stories about production while changing the way the story is framed.

The first episode concerns the curiously delayed decline of the British cotton textile industry in the decades around the turn of the century. The recounting highlights the trade-offs between control over time and control over space in securing the competitive position of the industry despite its backward technology and organization. The second episode revisits the elaboration of the system of mass production in the American automobile industry in the twentieth century. It emphasizes

---

[4] The characterizations, of course, come from Marx, This literature is uncitably huge, but some crucial examples from within geography would include G. Clark, 1981; Massey and Meegan, 1982; Massey, 1984; G. Clark et al., 1986; Peet, 1984; A. Scott, 1988; Storper and Walker, 1989. Outside geography, classic works would include Piore, 1968; Marglin, 1974; Noble, 1986; Hymer, 1972; Burawoy, 1979; Edwards, 1979. For an excellent overview of the uneasy balance between the two emphases, see Lazonick, 1990.

[5] This is apart from the traditionally invoked dichotomy between competitive and monopoly capitalism. As with the other great dichotomy between markets and hierarchies (Williamson, 1975), the blurry ground between the two poles is where much of the interesting activity takes place.

[6] See Marx, 1967c; Harvey, 1982. N. Smith (1984) and Swyngedouw (1989) provide enlightening analyses of space as a force of production.

the relationship between the nature of competition, managed time in production, and spatial flexibility in producing a characteristic geographical allocation of production. It then shows how the logic of this temporal–spatial relationship was abruptly overthrown by the disruption of the competitive environment consequent on the advent of Japanese producers into the market.

In chapter 3, the third episode continues this story into the present. It argues that the transformed competitive environment entails a redefinition of the meaning of control over time and a recalibration of the relationship between time and space, undermining the viability of the old temporal–spatial strategy. The chapter considers the implications of this transformation for economic development processes in the industrial core as well as the periphery.

Part I closes with a consideration of theories that seek to explain the sources of industrial rigidity in an effort to understand why firms may fail to react appropriately to new conditions (chapter 4). Four different kinds of argument are evaluated. These focus on bureaucratic resistance to change, the economics of information and uncertainty, problems of capital–labor relations, and the issue of regional obsolescence. These theories all, in different ways, contribute to our understanding of the difficulties of corporate transformation and regional economic revitalization. But it is useful to interrogate the assumptions on which they are based and to specify their explanatory limits on theoretical and empirical/historical grounds. This will, I hope, provide the justification for the shift, in part II, to the analysis of corporate culture and strategy.

Part II: Corporate Culture, Strategy, and Change

Chapter 5 reviews the analysis of corporate culture prevalent in the management and business literature. It then proposes an alternative understanding of what corporate culture is, how it is produced, and how it changes. In this context, it is proposed that corporate cultures are not inherently resistant to change, but that cultural processes play a vital role in structuring patterns of selective change and resistance, and that these processes are inherently conflictual and power-laden.

The chapter also seeks to analyze the producers of the dominant culture of the firm – the highest-level managers who are involved in strategic decision-making. The aim is to show how the power of managerial identities and commitments also influences the kinds of knowledge that can be produced in the firm and the kinds of change that can be accepted. The chapter concludes by arguing that the problem facing firms is not so much how to *adapt* the corporate culture to a new strategy as to understand how culture *produces* strategy.

These propositions are illustrated and amplified through case studies of corporate transitions in chapter 6. The most detailed is a study of Lockheed's belated and traumatic move into missiles and space in the 1950s. Another case looks at the Xerox Corporation's almost fatally delayed response to Japanese competition in the 1970s.

Part III: *The Cultural Crisis of the Firm*

Chapter 7 starts out by exploring the rich literature which associates drastically altered material practices with a profound transformation in the experience of and the meanings surrounding time and space in different historical epochs (cf. Marx, 1967a; Thompson, 1967; Kern, 1983; Hareven, 1982; Harvey, 1989). Stress is placed on the degree to which these transformations in the experience and meaning of space and time are associated with tremendous social and cultural turmoil, the more so as the concepts of time and space are normally deeply internalized and naturalized in our experience of daily life.

Then attention shifts back to the firm and its top management. Returning to the argument from part I, it is proposed that the drastically altered competitive environment of firms has produced a new round of time–space compression. This, it is argued, is particularly traumatic for contemporary American firms and the people who run them, since their experience to date has been one of *control* of competitive environments (consequent on their extraordinary market power) and the associated ability to *manage* time and spatial relationships. These capacities have been suddenly and profoundly thrown into question with the advent of alternative models of competition, production, and temporal–spatial relations. Consequently, this competitive challenge constitutes, in effect, a cultural crisis for the firm, resulting in the inability to adopt appropriate strategies for change even where adequate knowledge concerning the kind of change required is available.

The next question, unavoidably, is what can be done in this circumstance to facilitate corporate transformations and, moreover, do so in a way that improves the position of people and places whose fates are tied closely to that of the firms involved. A clear-cut answer will be hard to come by, but I think the approach must be through questions of power in the firm – not only the perhaps obvious issue of how power is allocated (who has it, who doesn't), but what power is for, how it is experienced, and what it means.

The Approach

This book, quite obviously, is not an exercise in formal hypothesis testing. It is qualitative and interpretive, and in some places unavoidably speculative. If anything, it is an exercise in hypothesis building.

The kinds of question that it raises, and the answers that it tentatively sketches out, are derived in the first instance from my previous work on the competitive strategies of multinational corporations and the study of Lockheed which is reported on in detail here. This work has brought me much in contact with high-level executives of some sixty major industrial enterprises in various sectors, and it is this experience which informs much of the argument of the book. But it also draws on a wide range of secondary sources in the academic and management literature and the business press.

All of this means that there are no proofs, in the conventional sense, of the arguments proposed. At issue, rather, is the degree to which the interpretations offered are plausible and satisfying accounts of the events and processes described. Further, the interpretations must offer a persuasive way of linking the actions of a class of individuals (managers) to the general dynamics of the system taken as a whole. It's fair to say that the point is not to convince the reader that the specific interpretations offered are the unique and "true" explanations, but rather that this way of thinking can significantly aid us in understanding a very complicated puzzle.

2

Competition, Time, and Space in Industrial Change

Introduction

The aim of this chapter is to elaborate some ideas concerning how time, space, and competition work within the general framework of a capitalist space-economy, and how they are related to the conformation and operations of the production system. The first section reviews some theoretical arguments, largely derived from the Marxist literature, on the dynamics underlying the temporal and spatial characteristics of the production system. The central lesson of interest here is that, although we can readily identify very powerful general tendencies (for example, toward the progressive compression of time in production and circulation), these dynamics are inherently fraught with tensions and contradictions. This means that actual historical outcomes are highly indeterminate, and this indeterminacy has several important consequences for the discussion which follows.

In the first instance, the indeterminacy means that we have to look at how these processes and dynamics work themselves out historically and in different geographical, social, and political circumstances in order to understand why the production system looks the way it does. Further, this indeterminacy means that time and space are potentially strategizable. In other words, firms can attempt to obtain competitive advantages through the management of temporal and spatial dynamics. These points will be important later when we try to relate the meaning and the experience of time, space, and competition to cultural production and change within the firm. Finally, the pressures of competition and the contradictory tensions and trade-offs inherent in these categories mean that the strategic and operational problems associated with them can never be permanently resolved. Rather, they shift around or change their shape, continually reconstituting themselves as new problems that powerfully influence the trajectory of the production system.

This discussion is followed by an analysis of two episodes in industrial history in which the interplay among the categories of time, space, and competition and their relationship to the conformation of the production system are brought to the fore. These concern the delayed decline of the British cotton textile industry around the turn of the century and the rise and subsequent crisis of mass production of automobiles in the US.

Time, Space, and Competition: Theory and Practice

In conventional economic-geographic theory, the issues of time and space are rather neatly disposed of. Under the assumption of conditions of perfect competition, they are translated into a problem of cost minimization which allows one to calculate optimal locations. Variations in the problem may be associated with such features as the degree of labor intensiveness and, thus, the importance of minimizing labor as opposed to, for instance, transportation costs, the degree to which products gain or lose weight in processing, value-to-weight ratios (which, again, impinge on the role of transportation costs), and so on. But there are, in principle, optimal solutions and these are, moreover, stable outcomes (cf. Alonso, 1975; Webber, 1984). Marxist analyses, by contrast, operate at a different level of abstraction, but also identify very strong general tendencies which might seem to lead to determinate outcomes. Thus, for example, the general compulsion to compress time in production and circulation, powerfully enforced by the pressures of competition, would seem to mark out a single evolutionary trajectory for the production system.

A closer examination reveals, however, that each of these analytical dimensions of time, space, and competition should be seen rather as a field of conflicting and contradictory tensions. Moreover, the complexity and indeterminacy only increase as we try to trace the connections among them and to follow their evolution over time. Here I want to illustrate some of the contradictory pressures and trade-offs underlying the categories of time, space, and competition.

Temporal pressures

The problem of time arises in a number of contexts in Marxist analysis, but I want to focus here on the categories of turnover time and socially necessary labor time. In both cases, there is a strong *ceteris paribus* assumption that the general pressures of competition under capitalism promote and require continual reductions. The history of capitalism is, then, tendentially marked by a progressive compression of time in both these dimensions, and the key issues of historical interest would normally concern the mechanisms deployed to achieve these ends (such as new technologies in production or investments in transportation and communications infrastructure) and their economic and social effects. What we tend to see, however, are contradictory movements in which time is simultaneously compressed and expanded, depending on which part of the system one examines, so that the general progression is uneven and punctuated by more or less significant reverses. The possibility for this tension is inherent in the general theoretical framework.

The turnover time of capital comprises the time taken to produce a completed commodity (the production period) and the time taken to realize its embodied value through sale on the market (the circulation time) (Marx, 1967b:124–31; Harvey, 1982:62–4).[1] Compressing the time in which capital is tied up in production and circulation increases the rate at which money capital becomes available for reinvestment in further rounds of accumulation (Harvey, 1982:264; N. Smith, 1984:93). Harvey proposes the notion of "socially necessary turnover time," which he defines as "the average time taken to turn over a given quantity of capital within a particular sector, under the normal conditions of production and circulation prevalent at the time." Firms with a shorter-than-average turnover time will obtain excess profits; firms with above-average rates risk the devaluation of their capital. For this reason, there is a constant competitive struggle to accelerate turnover times (Harvey, 1982:186, 406).

Within this general compulsion to reduce turnover times, however, there are myriad opportunities for contradictory movements. The expansion of output associated with mechanization and increasing returns to scale, for example, is likely to necessitate a corresponding expansion of geographical markets, thus lengthening the time in circulation as commodities are transported over greater distances (Harvey, 1982:406). The multiregional or multinational corporation may sidestep this effect by implanting production in distant markets, but in doing so will tend to recreate the original problem.

By the same token, mechanization and the effort to capture scale economies, while they lead to increases in labor productivity (and,

---

[1] The circulation time also includes the time taken to convert money capital into productive capital through the purchase of labor and material inputs to production, but the sale of commodities on the market is arguably the more problematic and time-consuming (cf. Marx, 1967b:129).

hence, a reduction in socially necessary labor time), also tend to lengthen the time it takes to turn over the whole of the capital advanced, as the proportion of fixed capital (that tied up in durable plant and equipment) steadily increases. This kind of investment is normally depreciated over many years unless a significant shift in technology causes its sudden devaluation (Marx, 1967b:160–7). In this context, the turnover time of circulating capital (material and labor inputs consumed in the course of a given production period) may contract, but the price is that the turnover time of fixed capital lengthens. This would seem quite likely in the case of programmable automation, which often increases the speed of throughput; at the same time, it can be reprogrammed instead of retired (as is the case with dedicated machinery) when product configurations change (Schoenberger, 1989b).

The general compulsion to compress socially necessary labor times in production also encounters significant possibilities for reversals in practice. Again, this is not a consequence of mistakes in the system or in the theory; they are produced as the normal concomitant of the intricate workings of the system. The aggregate movement of socially necessary labor time in a sector or for the economy as a whole is likely to depend, for example, on the share of new products vs. old in a given sector, or of new industries vs. old in the economy. Newer products and industries are likely to have higher labor inputs than older ones whose production processes have been more thoroughly rationalized. Rapid technological change in an economy has, in this context, contradictory implications. Insofar as it is applicable to production processes, it tends to lower socially necessary labor times; as it is embodied in new products, labor times tend to increase.

It may also be the case that decreases in socially necessary labor time in one process or area of the economy may tend to produce increases elsewhere. This is the case, for example, in the production of many kinds of electronics goods. As functions are shifted from the hardware to the software, the labor time involved in the production and assembly of components decreases while expanding in the design of the increasingly complex software (Brooks, 1982; Schoenberger, 1989b).

Spatial tendencies

Spatial forms and dynamics are also conflicting and contradictory under capitalism. This can be seen clearly in the case of centralization vs. decentralization of production or in the tension between spatial mobility and fixity (Harvey, 1982; N. Smith, 1984; Storper and Walker, 1989).

The pressures in favor of geographical centralization and agglomeration of production grow out of the technology, organization, scale, and infrastructural requirements of production. Clustering together in space gives firms common (and therefore cheaper) access to large pools of labor, suppliers of inputs, customers, and the transportation and communications infrastructure that allows the efficient coordination of flows within, into, and out of the agglomeration. Further, the intricacies of the division of labor across and within firms can be more easily and surely managed under conditions of geographical proximity. At the same time, as the physical scale of production increases, more and more workers and activities are drawn together. And, as the population increases in this way, so do the activities and services that directly cater to the needs of these residents.

Yet there are equally strong pressures for spatial dispersal of productive activity, some of them produced by the negative effects of spatial concentration. These latter include the increased likelihood of unionization and wage drift across even unorganized firms, the costs of congestion, rising land costs or an actual lack of space suitable for large-scale production, the desire to escape outmoded and inefficient infrastructures, potential diseconomies of scale, or the inability to introduce important shifts in the technology or organization of production due to inherited rules and social norms of production. More "positive" reasons include the search for new (geographic) outlets for accumulated capital, the fight for access to or, in the best of the cases, control over distant markets for output or sources of material inputs, the drive to reduce time in circulation as noted above, the need to overcome protectionist barriers, and the like.

For all of these reasons, then, the "characteristic" spatial tendency of capitalism is toward *both* concentration and dispersal. The actual pattern at any given moment will depend on a variety of forces. As Harvey notes, "Capital is ... impelled sometimes towards simultaneous and sometimes towards successive phases of deepening and widening in the spatial configurations of productive forces and social relations" (Harvey, 1982:419).

Harvey has also been instrumental in showing us how the compulsion to eradicate spatial barriers to the free circulation of capital unavoidably produces spatial fixity and new spatial barriers which immobilize and/or channel capital geographically for considerable periods. Thus, for example, the laying down of transportation networks fixes capital for long periods of time in the form of roads, railways, ports, and the like. This infrastructure, expensive to create and long-lived, also channels the flow of commodity and productive capital, which is constrained to follow the existing route, as it were, until a new round of investments in the built environment frees it up to seek new routes (Harvey, 1982; cf. also N. Smith, 1984).

It should also be clear that the relationships between the categories of space and time are both intimate and filled with tension. There are very significant ways in which the problem of space *is* the problem of time, and vice versa. The costly investments in transportation infrastructure, for example, have as their primary aim not only the reduction of the monetary costs of movement over space, but the reduction of time in circulation. Distance, in this sense, is equivalent to time because, as Marx noted, "the important thing is not the market's distance in space but the speed with which it can be reached" (quoted in Harvey, 1982:377). This highlights an important tension as the compression of temporal rhythms is bought at the price of spatial fixity and the production of new spatial barriers.

We should expect, then, that time and space are frequently traded off against each other. Some ways in which this can happen, and the consequences for the production system, are illustrated below and in the next chapter.

Competition

Competition remains a relatively unproblematized category in both Marxist and mainstream economic-geographic analysis. It stands as a kind of stern enforcer of the rules of the game: those competitors who don't adhere to the rules (by, for example, minimizing costs or coming in at or below socially necessary labor times) will die. In the case of conventional economic theory, competition is the guarantor of efficiency and the promise of equilibrium. In Marxist theory, it guarantees only turbulence and constant change.

Within the Marxist literature, to be sure, there has been an effort to trace out an evolutionary trajectory of competitive forms. In this view, a period of early or competitive capitalism is succeeded by monopoly or late capitalism (cf. Baran and Sweezy, 1966; Mandel, 1974). Firm size and industrial organization are the principle axes of differentiation. Although helpful in some respects, there are ways in which these categories obscure as much as they reveal. For example, in the period of competitive capitalism, geographical fragmentation meant that even quite small firms could potentially benefit from a very powerful spatial monopoly. By contrast, the apparent stranglehold of large, oligopolistic firms can, as we have seen in recent decades, be exploded as global markets become more closely intertwined and new, large-scale competitors emerge seemingly overnight.

The product cycle theory, on the other hand, contained within it a cyclical theory of competitive form based on the degree to which technology is proprietary and products substitutable over the course of the product's life cycle. A new product, whose technology is proprietary to the innovating firm and whose functions are not easily substituted by other, existing products, enjoys a period of monopoly on the market, allowing competition to proceed on the basis of performance rather than price. This period is inevitably temporary, however, as more and more firms figure out how to make the same thing, and competition shifts to a cost basis more closely approximating the neoclassical model (Vernon, 1966; cf. also Markusen, 1985). This is helpful, as it shows how the same product can be implicated in entirely divergent market and competitive circumstances. Note, however, that outcomes here are wholly determined by position in the cycle, and competition is accordingly removed from the sphere of strategy.

The business studies literature, by contrast, is quite preoccupied with competition as strategy. Porter, for example, elaborates a set of variable circumstances in which a producer may find itself, and links these with a set of available strategies. The key variables turn on such factors as ease of entry into the market by potential new competitors, the relative power of buyers and suppliers, the potential for product substitution, and the actual and potential behavior of existing competitors. The particular values in each of these categories is not determined *a priori* (for instance, entry barriers may be high or low on the basis of a number of separate considerations), but once the values are revealed, the appropriate strategy follows more or less automatically (Porter, 1980). The analysis functions, in effect, as a kind of formula for deriving competitive strategies.

It could turn out that these are, in fact, the right sorts of calculation to make. Firms that fail would be deriving the values of the underlying variables incorrectly. And, indeed, there is considerable room for this, as some of them (such as the potential reactions of competitors) are difficult to predict accurately. There seems some reason to suppose, however, that if all firms followed the formula faithfully and got the values more or less right, the process would be self-cancelling. Some counter-formula move would be required to break the resulting stalemate.

In any case, one can see in this analysis that competitive strategies are, in some sense, produced by circumstances, and this seems to me helpful. On the other hand, the process by which this happens in this model seems excessively mechanistic and unidirectional. Ironically, this raises the question of what is really strategic about competitive strategy as Porter envisions it.

I think we need to move toward a notion of competition and competitive strategy that embraces the contradictions and tensions we saw at

work in the discussion on time and space. We should be able to anticipate that competition is constructed in different ways depending on circumstances while, at the same time, the kinds of competitive strategy
adopted act to change those circumstances, giving rise to new kinds of
competitive problem, and so on. The circumstances constrain but do
not determine the outcomes. The constraints at issue include the existing state of product and process technologies, the behavior of competitors, the history of the individual firm and its legacy of fixed and sunk
costs and institutionalized practices, the existing temporal rhythms and
spatial patterns of production and circulation, and the institutional and
political environment within which firms act.

This is a long list of constraints, but there are still important degrees
of freedom available to the firm. It can seek to position or reposition
itself in the more standardized or less standardized segments of any
given market. It can stake its success in the market variously on lowest
costs, highest quality, performance, service, reliability, design, distribution, or some combination of these. It can try to expand its geographical market or create new kinds of market altogether. It can collaborate
or merge with some erstwhile competitors or lobby for protection from
the state. In short, the list of available options is also long.

Again, the stress is on indeterminacy of outcome and the need to
understand how strategies and different models of competition are actually produced in different historical moments and geographical circumstances, and with what effect. Further, I think it important to emphasize
the inherent instability of outcomes, as the resolution of a particular
competitive problem or the elaboration of a more general competitive
model that embraces many firms inevitably produces new problems and
challenges.

This hints at the underlying contradictions whose working out produces perpetual turmoil in the system. Stability in the competitive
environment is much to be desired (at least by the existing competitors), most particularly because it allows the valorization of previous
investments (cf. Harvey, 1982). In a capital-intensive production
environment, it is of crucial importance in creating a context in which
both output and the retirement and renewal of the fixed capital stock
can be to some degree planned. But the sources of instability are too
numerous to control indefinitely. These include most obviously
changes in the constraining circumstances described above, such as the
innovation of new technologies which disrupt markets and the relationships among competitors. But they also include such factors as
innovations in the way firms envision their markets or their positioning
in different kinds of market, and this is really part of the field of competitive strategy proper.

When the stable competitive environment is disrupted, many things – including the organization of production, its temporal and spatial characteristics, and competitive strategies – must change. The question is how and with what effects. I try to trace through some of these processes in the historical episodes which follow.

Episode 1: The Delayed Decline of the British Cotton Textile Industry

In this section, I want to follow the argument of the economic historian William Lazonick as it concerns the apparently unwarranted, continued success of the English cotton textile industry in the late nineteenth and early twentieth centuries. In his book *Competitive Advantage on the Shop Floor* (Lazonick, 1990), he focuses on the persistence of craft control and the effect this had in blocking the uptake of more automated spinning and weaving technologies in Britain compared with the United States. Despite a growing productivity lag, however, the English industry remained competitive in key international markets until it entered a serious and permanent decline following World War I.

Lazonick's explanation emphasizes the different course of the social relations of production in Britain and the US. But the explanation also depends in crucial respects on different patterns of industrial organization and competitive environment in the two countries. Further, the delayed impact of the productivity lag in Britain is accounted for by the particular market orientation and competitive strategy of the British industry.

This case presents a particularly intriguing problem, as it challenges conventional views of what exactly constitutes industrial competitiveness and how this is maintained or destroyed. After reviewing Lazonick's argument, I want to retell the story in a way that emphasizes the relationships among competitive strategy, temporal and spatial control, and production organization. The aim is not to refute Lazonick's own approach, which I find quite illuminating, but to draw these themes to the fore to show how the ways in which the problems of competition, time, and space are posed and resolved in a particular historical context create an environment in which a particular approach to production can persist, and even flourish, although it is demonstrably inefficient and obsolete.

The institutionalization of craft control and its consequences

The crucial moment in the entrenchment of craft control in Britain comes in the transition to the self-acting mule in the 1830s and 1840s.

The advertised purpose of the self-actor was to eliminate the role of the skilled male craftworker – the minder – altogether. Yet this transformation did not occur, with implications that shadowed the British industry for well over a century (Lazonick, 1990:79).

That the persistence of craft control was not due to inherent technological requirements is made clear by a comparison with the US experience, in which the organization of work was quite different. In the US, capitalists were able to exert direct control over the labor process in its entirety.

Why did British capitalists, by contrast, pass up the opportunity afforded by the new technology both to reduce wages by displacing adult male workers and to exert control over the labor process? The key, according to Lazonick, lies neither in the minder's skill monopoly nor in the collective power of the craftworkers to defend their role in the labor process. He is quite explicit on this last count:

> For this transitional period, there is no evidence that the collective power of minders can account for the persistence of the minder–piecer hierarchical division of labor on the self-acting mule. During the 1830s and 1840s, the minders simply did not possess significant collective power. Moreover, there is no evidence that the minders had to put up a struggle to maintain the minder–piecer system. (Lazonick, 1990:95)

Rather, the internal division of labor, with the minder in control of his own work and that of his subordinates (piecers and others), remained in place because it functioned as a reasonably effective mode of labor management *given that the capitalists lacked the ability to undertake this function themselves.* This is an extraordinary statement to make about the leading capitalist power of the time and requires some elaboration.

The signal importance of the minder that allowed him to retain his craft status lay in his responsibility for the recruitment, training, and supervision of the workers further down the hierarchy. This continued supervisory role, according to Lazonick, sustained the position of the adult male craftworker despite the undermining of the physical strength and skill requirements for the job. Yet, since the impetus for the development of the self-actor was precisely the desire to bypass the male craftworker, additional parts of the story need to be filled in (Lazonick, 1990:88).

Lazonick offers two elements of an explanation. First, he argues that these supervisory requirements were exceptionally high. Constant attention, including at times physical discipline, had to be exerted to ensure that the piecers and other subordinate workers maintained an acceptable level of effort. Yet the organization of work in the US on the same technology was quite different. In New England, "top-down hierarchical authority prevailed and internal subcontract systems were virtually unknown" (Lazonick, 1990:98–9).

Second, Lazonick argues that British firms, as opposed to their American counterparts, lacked the managerial capacity to successfully appropriate this supervisory role. He links this inability to differences in industrial organization. In the US, a small number of large, vertically integrated firms controlled the business. The Lancashire industry, by contrast, was characterized by extreme vertical and horizontal disintegration and lack of coordination. This fragmentation meant that individual capitalists lacked the capacity to undertake the functions of recruitment and supervision that were, perforce, left to the minder. Nor, given the high degree of inter-firm competition, were they able to organize collectively to wrest control of the process from the craftworkers. The challenge was never made (Lazonick, 1990:99).

The minders, consequently, were able to use their craft status as a basis for organizing. By the last decades of the century, this collective power enabled them to resist attempts on the part of the still-fragmented capitalists to reclaim control of the work process and the relationship between effort and pay. The male minders' union, established in 1870, became one of the strongest unions in Britain and, by the end of the century, the minders were among the highest paid workers in Britain. Their shop-floor authority was confirmed in the district wage lists that had been adopted throughout Lancashire by the 1880s. These specified piece rates controlling for the speed of work. In this way, the minders (although not the subordinate workers, who were paid time wages) were compensated to a significant degree for intensification of effort and increased output. Many of these wage lists remained in force until 1945 (Lazonick, 1990:104–24).

Despite craft control and high wages, the British industry nevertheless remained competitive in the era of the self-acting mule. The reason, according to Lazonick, is that the wage lists, by ensuring that minders shared in the returns to increased effort, encouraged greater productivity on the existing technology. For this reason, Lazonick is able to claim that "craft control was consistent with, and perhaps even fundamental to, British industrial success" (Lazonick, 1990:113).

The problem in this scenario is that this institutionalized arrangement eventually blocked the uptake of the new, higher-throughput technologies of ring spinning and the automatic loom in the last decades of the nineteenth century. Yet the industry was able to adjust through recourse to a new competitive strategy which significantly delayed its decline.

Old technologies, new strategies

The productivity limits of the self-acting mule, effort notwithstanding, appear to have been reached by the 1890s (Lazonick, 1990:121, 162–3). Thereafter, for any given level of effort, output varied as a function of the quality of cotton inputs. Cheaper, low-quality cotton which broke easily required a greater intensity of effort. Yet because of the wage lists, the Lancashire capitalists were unable to reduce labor costs for any given level of output by using high-quality cotton. This simply allowed the minders and piecers to work less hard for the same earnings.

The workers were less protected, however, on the downside – the use of poor-quality cotton. According to Lazonick, the use of inferior cotton remained "the one key aspect of the production process never successfully regulated [by the workers]" (Lazonick, 1990:157). Accordingly, the Lancashire capitalists sought to reduce their unit costs of output through reducing the quality and cost of cotton inputs rather than through raising the productivity of labor. This was in sharp contrast to the situation in New England, where the productivity gains afforded by the use of high-quality, low-breakage cotton could be captured by the capitalists (Lazonick, 1990:128–34).

The British industry, then, staked its continuing competitiveness not on increasing output per worker, but on the manufacture of cheaper, lower-grade yarn and cloth. For this kind of production, the higher-yield technologies of the ring spindle and automatic loom were inappropriate, since they required high-quality cotton to be used effectively (Lazonick, 1990:152). In effect, the uptake of the new technology was blocked by the fact that the capitalists could not appropriate the productivity gains they yielded.

As the century closed, the new technologies transformed the American industry while leaving the British industry virtually untouched. Already by 1890, ring spindles constituted 62 percent of total spindles in the US (Lazonick, 1986:19). Even as late as 1913, ring spindles accounted for only about 25 percent of British capacity compared with over 90 percent in the US. At the same time, only 1–2 percent of British looms were automatic compared with 40 percent in the US (Lazonick, 1990:139).

While Lazonick estimates a productivity gap of only about 10 percent between mules and rings, the automatic loom seems to have been nearly twice as productive as the power loom (Lazonick, 1990:169). And, since spinning firms in Lancashire were producing low-quality output, weaving firms had to align their technology with the spinners.

In the long run, the productivity advantages of the automated equipment carried the day. In the interim, a strategy of cheapening output through degrading inputs managed to sustain and even enlarge the industry. But it was only possible for this strategy to be successful if there was a significant, uncontested market for cheap, low-quality output. Fortunately for the Lancashire textile capitalists, there was. A huge proportion of total output was exported, principally to the Middle East, South Asia, East Asia, and Latin America. India was particularly crucial, accounting for over 50 percent of so-called grey cloth exports (Lazonick, 1986:18).

Despite its growing technological and productivity lag, the British industry continued to expand rapidly until World War I, primarily to serve these growing markets. It is particularly striking that significant capacity expansion occurred on the basis of the outdated technology. After the war, however, the British were squeezed out of these markets by lower-cost competition, primarily in the form of exports from Japan or import-substituting production in such countries as India and Brazil.

To summarize Lazonick's analysis, British textile capitalists were never able to challenge craft control of the labor process or the relationship between effort and pay. This was not, initially, due to the collective strength of the craftworkers. Rather, it was due to the individual and collective weakness of the capitalists in a highly competitive, organizationally fragmented industry. Later, however, craft control provided the basis for collective worker organization that institutionalized and rigidified a characteristic pattern of relations of production that contrasted sharply with emerging competitor nations such as the US and, later, Japan and other developing countries.

The industry remained quite competitive for some decades despite this apparently crippling technological lag, however. This is so for two reasons. The first is that the minders were encouraged to increase their effort on the existing technology because they were assured of sharing in the gains resulting from intensification of work. The second is that the British firms were able to successfully specialize in low-quality products for developing-country export markets. But as the potential gains from increased effort hit their limits on the old technologies, and as new competitors vied for these key export markets, the British industry was progressively squeezed out.

Competitive strategy and control over time and space

I want here to recount this story in a somewhat different analytical frame, focusing on the trade-offs between control over time and control over space in the evolving competitive strategy of the British industry.

In Lazonick's story, it is clear that the British capitalists lost control over time in production and were able to compensate for this through their control over space (in the form of privileged access to colonial and quasi-colonial markets). But the nature of this loss of control over time and the eventual loss of control over space, which plunged the industry into irreversible decline, needs further elaboration.

As suggested, British textile capitalists lost their ability to keep pace with the reductions in socially necessary labor time realized by their key foreign competitors. Although productivity growth rates in spinning and weaving were modestly positive for most of the period from 1880 to 1913 (Farnie, 1979:199; Lazonick, 1990:157–62), this seems to be largely the product of significant intensification of work. Given the rigidity of wage levels and the social and physical limits to productivity increases of this kind, the position of the Lancashire capitalists appears fragile in the extreme.

There is, however, a further crucial distinction that sets the British industry apart. The unions were successful not only in preserving wage levels and work norms, but in resisting multiple shiftwork (Farnie, 1979:200). Compared with the foreign competition, this is a significant obstacle to the uptake of more capital-intensive technologies. Although spinning and weaving are not capital intensive compared with many other industries, as the weight of fixed capital in the sector increases, the pressure to keep it constantly in motion nevertheless becomes more acute. The inability to run multiple shifts is a serious problem in this context.

This can be defined as a problem of the turnover time of capital that peculiarly afflicts the British industry. Following Harvey, we can hypothesize that, had the new technologies been adopted, the Lancashire capitalists would have been operating above socially necessary turnover times, with all the consequences that this entails. It is true that foreign producers were turning over a larger volume of capital than their British competitors and this would tend to extend their turnover times. The extreme fragmentation of the British industry might have lent a certain advantage, as it reduces the turnover time for the individual, vertically disintegrated firm (Harvey, 1982:129–30). The highly developed system of factoring and rediscounting in Lancashire would have provided additional support in this line. But the combined advantages derived from productivity gains and multiple shiftwork on the new technology overseas would have gone far to tip the balance the other way.

In this context, it is also useful to consider the role of the British financial system, which seemed particularly ill suited to supporting the necessary investments in this period. Even as the finance sector underwent a process of centralization in the late nineteenth century, it remained heavily oriented to short-term lending and largely unavailable for the longer-term investments required for the renovation of the cotton textile industry. At the same time, competitive pressures for high-dividend payouts limited the industry's ability to reinvest earnings for longer-term purposes (Best and Humphries, 1986). Because of its limited time horizons, the credit system could not regulate the turnover time problem for the Lancashire capitalists (cf. Marx, 1967b; Harvey, 1982: ch. 9).

In any head-to-head competition with its overseas rivals, then, the Lancashire industry was already effectively out of the game well before World War I. But the industry didn't have to go head to head with the most advanced foreign producers. The British firms had an alternative competitive strategy available to them, involving different markets and products. In particular, they enjoyed privileged access to growing markets in less developed countries where competition from domestic producers remained inhibited until the war. This privileged access was rooted in the political, financial, and economic legacy of Britain's role as the leading industrial and colonial power of the nineteenth century. Famously in the case of India, this involved the prior dismantling of a flourishing local industry via the combined effects of the British industry's superior productivity, the monopsonistic position of the East India Company, and duties imposed on Indian textile exports. As a result, a quasi-monopoly over key geographical markets – spatial control – compensated for the Lancashire industry's loss of control over time.

Already by the 1870s, growing domestic competition and protectionism in the US and European markets had caused a progressive reorientation of British exports to unindustrialized countries (Matthews et al. 1982:452; Aldcroft, 1968:18–19; Farnie, 1979:181). Around the turn of the century, improved terms of trade for primary producers expanded their ability to consume the output of British textile mills. The bulk of the net increase in exports during this time went to these less developed markets, India primary among them. Other key growth markets included China, Turkey, the Dutch East Indies, and South America (Lazonick, 1990:144–51; Matthews et al., 1982:469; Aldcroft, 1968:118).

When Britain embraced free trade in the mid-nineteenth century, one of the principal objectives was precisely increasing access to foreign markets for its cotton textiles (Harley and McCloskey, 1981). At that time, the ability to enforce politically a free trade regime was all that was needed. The then-huge productivity advantage enjoyed by the Lancashire industry would do the rest. But British manufacturing exports, and cotton textiles above all, were dependent on the country's ability to maintain free access to uncontested foreign markets (Farnie, 1979:195). Writing in 1910, William Cunningham characterized free trade as "the fixing of Britain's monopoly of manufactures on the rest of the world for a few more decades than its natural term" (cited in Harley and McCloskey, 1981:57).

By the last quarter of the nineteenth century, this strategy had already failed in the most developed export markets of the US and Western Europe. And although protectionism was involved, the loss of these markets seems primarily a consequence of productivity gains in their domestic textile industries (Aldcroft, 1968:22).

In India and other developing countries, however, the story was different – at least until the war. Particularly within the empire, Britain had the political power to impose preferential market access and block import-substituting protectionist measures. In India, for example, imperial policy maintained low tariffs and countervailing domestic excise taxes on local production (Farnie, 1979:195; Drummond, 1981:294). The main threat to developing-country markets at this time came from Japan, which had become largely self-sufficient and a major supplier to the Chinese market. Brazilian import-substitution policies had also led to a shift of British exports to Argentina and Uruguay before the war (Tyson, 1968:105–14).

During the war, Britain lost this measure of spatial control, and was unable to reimpose it in the course of the 1920s. This was the case for several reasons. Not least among them, ironically, was Britain's continued commitment to the ideology of free trade – a commitment shared by the Lancashire industry. Even as its export position eroded, the industry did not organize to demand political efforts to defend it, and only insignificant attempts were made to enforce preferential access to empire markets (Farnie, 1979:195–6; Von Tunzelmann, 1981; Drummond, 1981:297).

During the war, of course, disruption of trade routes afforded a period of protected growth to manufacturers in less developed regions. It is what happened after the war that is particularly striking, as Britain failed to reimpose preferential access to these crucial markets, even within the empire. In the most important case of India, two problems were particularly at issue.

The first had to do with shifting British colonial objectives. The initial policy envisioned India strictly as a source of cheap raw materials and a market for manufactured exports with, in this context, a preference for a weak rupee. Eventually, however, the high costs of administering the empire led to a shift toward a policy in which the Indian administration was expected to support itself and provide a surplus to Britain. This second policy, which included the local development of manufacturing, protectionism, and a preference for a strong rupee, was in the ascendancy from the late nineteenth century, but especially after World War I. In particular, the growing cost burden led to permission for a temporary tariff on manufactured cotton goods as a source of revenue for the colonial administration. The tariff became permanent and, by 1925–6, customs revenues were the single largest source of income, accounting for over a third of the government of India's receipts (Fox, 1985:23).

Second, local political pressures in favor of domestic industrialization – especially with reference to cotton textiles – were increasingly acute. The imperial authorities acquiesced also for this reason in the reimposition of a tariff and the elimination of the domestic excise on textile production. At the same time, rising protectionist sentiment in many other developing countries was no doubt enhanced by the postwar shift in the terms of trade against primary producers, which in any case limited their ability to absorb exports (Farnie, 1979:178–9; Drummond, 1981:294; Alford, 1981:309; Von Tunzelmann, 1981:256; Matthews et al., 1982:466–9).

In these circumstances, the basis for the Lancashire industry's alternative competitive strategy simply evaporated. British textiles were now in head-to-head competition with local or other foreign production that combined extremely low wages with more advanced technology. Both Japan and India had a higher proportion of ring spindles in production than did Britain (Aldcroft, 1968:121–2).

We can retrace the trajectory of the British cotton textile industry in the following way. In its heyday in the early and mid-nineteenth century, superior control over time in production and circulation allowed the industry (and Britain) to exert control over vast territorial markets. This spatial control was achieved through both superior productivity and increasing financial and political control over a significant portion of the globe. In the last third of the nineteenth century, the Lancashire industry lost control over time and, with it, its competitive position in other industrialized regions. But it had a kind of fallback or residual competitive strategy available to it through continued spatial control in the peripheral regions. So long as these territorial markets were uncontested, the British industry remained viable. And, although there was considerable alarm about the prospect of US and German competition in these markets, this threat remained a minor one (Aldcroft, 1968:18–22). It was really the loss of Britain's political capacity to suppress the rise of protected local competition in these markets that rendered this fallback competitive strategy unviable after the war.

Episode 2: Mass Production of the Automobile

In his recent book about Chicago, *Nature's Metropolis*, environmental historian William Cronon provides one of the more eloquent descriptions available of how the product of an individual's labor is abstracted and transformed into a nearly pure flow of value across time and space (Cronon, 1991). The commodity in question is grain. The original distribution system, which carried the grain from the plains to coastal markets, was organized around the transport of grain in sacks, in effect linking individual producers to individual buyers. The key institutional innovation that transformed this system was the creation of the Chicago Board of Trade in 1848, which established standardized grades of corn and wheat.

This accomplished three things. First, it allowed the mixing of the individual farmer's output into homogenized (although stratified) collective output. In this way it abstracted from the identity of the producer, which had originally remained attached to individual lots of grain through the entire distribution process. Second, it permitted the transformation of the technology of distribution. Instead of being stored and moved in piles of sacks, the homogenized output could flow like liquid in and out of grain elevators, railroad cars, and barges, thus vastly reducing the time and labor effort involved in the process. Third, it allowed the development of futures markets, which rationalized the flow of grain across time and space. This enormous innovation secured Chicago's dominance in the North American grain trade against a number of traditional rivals.

Corn, of course, is quite different from cars. Yet Henry Ford's innovation in the mass production of automobiles had as its aim, realized to an extraordinary degree, the transformation of the production of complex mechanical goods into something approximating the liquid flow of grain through Chicago. Ford's actual model may have been the disassembly lines of Chicago meatpackers, but the analogy with grain provides in some ways more useful guidance. One key to this transformation was the standardization and homogenization of output. The subsequent innovation of Alfred Sloan at GM could be thought of as stratifying the homogeneous output into different quality grades for different market segments.

Continuous flow production of mechanical goods: gains and limits

Prior to the innovation of the moving assembly line in 1913, Ford had already taken a number of steps to convert production to a highly systematized operation emphasizing above all continuity and speed. Machine tools, formerly grouped by type, were arrayed according to sequential operations on particular parts, with non-machining tasks (such as heating) integrated into the sequence. Gravity slides were already being used to move parts between machines. This arrangement allowed substantial savings on factory space and forced the smooth flow of work lest parts start to pile up in the aisles.

In 1909, the decision was taken to produce only the Model T (in four versions on the same chassis), which allowed a massive shift to dedicated machine tools. Innovations in machine-tool design permitted consistently accurate work at high volumes, something that would be crucial to true mass production.

The flow of materials from start to finish was further regulated by detailed scheduling and long-term supply relations (with the supplier holding the inventory). Parts were carried to individual workstations as they were needed (Hounshell, 1984:221–36).

The Ford system had already reached such a state of smoothness of flow that Fred Colvin, writing for the *American Machinist* just prior to the development of the moving assembly line, was able to remark: "It is impossible to give an adequate description of the general assembly of the Ford automobiles, as this could only be done with a modern moving-picture machine" (quoted in Hounshell, 1984:236). As a result, Ford already commanded over half of the US market, completing a car every forty seconds of the working day, or roughly 200,000 per year (Hounshell, 1984:228).

Yet the implementation of the moving assembly line thoroughly revolutionized production, allowing unimaginable savings in time. Within a year, assembly time of the flywheel magneto dropped from 20 person-minutes to 5 minutes; of the engine from 594 to 226 minutes; and of the chassis from 12.5 hours to 93 minutes. Not only were the times far faster, they were also consistent and predictable (Hounshell, 1984:248–55).

What I would like to emphasize here is not only the reductions in production time, which were stunning, but the ability to regulate the flow of production. Production time here is both speeded up and *managed* in a way previously unknown. The manufacture and assembly of thousands of individual parts had been made to resemble the unimpeded and undifferentiated flow of grain in a continuous stream through Chicago.

This system worked wonderfully well for over a decade, producing 15 million Model Ts. Or, to put this another way, the system worked well so long as it produced only Model Ts. But the innovations of Alfred Sloan at GM, involving market segmentation and the annual model change, made the Model T obsolete in the very market that it had created. Ford's market share slumped precipitously, and it was forced to introduce the Model A in response. The changeover, hastily done and badly planned, threw Ford's carefully calibrated production system into chaos. The lesson from this experience was that planning for change was as important as production planning. In effect, change needed to be regulated as smoothly as production (Hounshell, 1984:267–301).

One needs to be careful about how much change could be tolerated by the system, even with good planning. It is true that Sloanism implied a very different competitive strategy from Fordism. Ford's strategy had been to maximize output of a basic, standard, and largely unchanging product at the lowest possible price. He rigorously eschewed advertising. Sloan advertised with a vengeance, promoting product change and product differentiation. And he won. As Hounshell notes, Sloanism replaced Fordism even at Ford. Less vertically integrated and less committed to dedicated machinery, there is little doubt that GM was already capable of greater flexibility than Ford in the 1920s (Hounshell, 1984:263–7).

Yet there were still considerable constraints on the amount of change that could be tolerated economically in the industry. Advertising was key to GM's strategy for a reason: it had to sell the *idea* of change in order to induce constant turnover in the market even though the key elements of what constituted a car – the engine, transmission, drive train, and chassis – remained essentially the same for years on end. Much of the announced change was superficial, bearing largely on the external styling, and its impact on production was confined to final assembly (Friedman, 1983; Altshuler et al., 1984).

Thus, the car as product was a much more stable entity over time than the ebb and flow of fins and chrome or the differentiated identities of Buicks and Pontiacs would suggest. Some of this stability was enforced by the technology and economics of production. Deep changes in the product, however well planned, would render too much fixed capital "prematurely" obsolete. These investments still had to be amortized over huge volumes of output, which meant over fairly long periods of time. Gradual obsolescence could be planned and accommodated, but not constant wholesale transformations of the product. Rather than Sloanism replacing Fordism, it may be more accurate to describe the system as Fordism–Sloanism.

There was, in any case, a second factor that rigorously enforced product stability over time. If production of automobiles had been almost magically transformed into a continuous flow process, this was decidedly not the case in product design and development. The development process of new cars or major subsystems was a lengthy and extremely expensive one in its own right. These dollar costs also had to be amortized over large volumes of product. But time in the development process could not be managed as it was in production. The labor processes underpinning the highly specialized tasks of system and component design and engineering could not themselves be engineered and mechanized as was the case in assembly. Nevertheless, development had to be articulated temporally with production; hence, the pace of change in production was regulated by the unmanaged tempo of development.

A third feature should be drawn into the picture. If product stability was enforced by the economics of production and the unmanageability of time in development, it was also *permitted* by the character of competition in the industry. In effect, the stability of the competitive environment and the way competition was managed helped to sustain Fordism–Sloanism.

The key to this was the maintenance of a stable oligopoly. The overtaking of Ford by GM in the 1920s was the last great upset in the industry until the advent of Japanese competition in the 1970s. The hundreds of firms that had vied for market share in the early days of the industry were progressively winnowed down to the Big Three. The surviving firms were in this way protected against both uncontrolled price competition and, crucially, uncontrolled product proliferation, which would have forced them to accelerate the introduction of new or significantly renovated products. It was this protection which allowed them to pursue a strategy of incremental product change and gradual obsolescence of their fixed capital stock (cf. Aglietta, 1979). In this way, too, the turnover time of capital was *managed* and *controlled* – it became a strategic device rather than an abstract compulsion. This is no small achievement, as it goes some way to resolving a deep tension in capitalism between the pressure to constantly revolutionize production and the need to valorize prior investments (Harvey, 1982).

Competition in this environment, then, was channeled away from cut-throat pricing and unmanageable product change. It centered instead on the familiar devices of advertising, brand-name identification, distribution, and financing. This provided an essential buffer to the production system, allowing the smooth flow of throughput to proceed relatively undisturbed. The unmanageability of time in development did not, in this context, pose a serious problem.

Managed time and spatial control

The managed continuity of flow in production in turn allows for an extraordinary degree of spatial freedom. True continuous-flow production, as in chemicals or petroleum production, is normally associated with an extremely high degree of spatial concentration. Chemicals complexes, for example, are typically mammoth because a large number of processes, often implicating several firms, are physically linked together through an intricate array of pipelines. The particular beauty of a near-continuous-flow process in the assembly of complex mechanical goods is that the pipeline can be extraordinarily spatially extensive.

There are two basic prerequisites for this. The first is that the product configuration remain relatively stable over time and the second is that the regularity and consistency of the flow can be more or less guaranteed. As we have seen, Fordism–Sloanism, in the context of a stable competitive environment, allowed both of these prerequisites to be met. These in turn provide the basis for the establishment of a highly internationalized production system. In short, control over time allows an unusual form of control over space.

The automobile industry internationalized very early. Ford began investing in the British market shortly following World War I, for example (Mutlu, 1979; Lewchuk, 1987). The pattern of investment of the two great competitors was different, Ford generally preferring to start up its own facilities while GM often bought existing producers overseas (such as Vauxhall in Britain or Opel in Germany). However, there are some notable general tendencies.

The first is that final assembly was decentralized first and farthest, both within the US and abroad. To this day, components manufacture is much more spatially centralized than assembly (Altshuler et al., 1984).

Second, this spatial expansion had as its principal aim, probably right through the mid-1960s, market access and market control rather than cost reduction. This is true even of much of the investment that went to developing countries during this period. Investments in developing-country markets such as India, Brazil, Argentina, or Mexico were driven mainly by extremely high protectionist barriers associated with import-substitution policies. In general, these markets were not sufficiently large to sustain optimum-volume production, so costs tended to be high in any case. The assembly industry in Canada, for example, was essentially a small, inefficient replica of its southern counterpart (cf. Holmes, 1983; Nofal, 1983). Nor, for the most part, were these developing offshore markets large enough to allow for fully integrated or wholly self-contained production. Thus, the system as a whole functioned on the basis of long-distance – sometimes extremely long-distance – supply lines.

The ability to organize such a spatially extensive production system is directly related to the ability to manage or regulate time in production in the ways described above. Key to this is that the nature of the product changes only slowly and that production flows in a generally undifferentiated stream through the system. No individual part X produced in place A needs to be in place B, perhaps thousands of miles away, at any particular time. What is required is a homogeneous and continuous flow of Xs through the pipeline, which, in this case, takes the form of trucks, railroad cars, boats, and, not insignificantly, buffer inventories. And, as we have seen, what allowed the flow to maintain this particular character was the controlled nature of competition in the industry.

It is useful to recall that this system worked quite well for some fifty years until it was shaken to its core by the challenge from Japanese producers. This challenge posed to the system exactly the two problems it was particular ill equipped to meet: serious price competition and a proliferation of new and significantly differentiated products on the market. The Japanese firms were able to do this for a number of reasons related both to the nature of the Japanese market and to the postwar history of industrial relations there. They had developed different ways of organizing the flow of work and of using labor on the shop floor to enormously compress the time it took to manufacture and assemble a car. Further, they had devised ways of producing a wider array of products on the line without efficiency losses. And they had substantially reduced the time involved in designing and developing new or renovated products (cf. Cusumano, 1985; Altshuler et al., 1984; Abernathy et al., 1984; Womack et al., 1990).

The initial response of the American firms centered on the issue of price competitiveness. What they sought to do was redeploy their already internationalized production infrastructure in a new way in order to reduce costs, particularly labor costs. Thus was born the era of the "world car." This envisaged a hugely complex international flow of parts and assembled cars, connecting up all of the outposts of the production empire (Dicken, 1992). Along the way, production was savagely rationalized in the core automobile manufacturing region around Detroit. Some of it, following the Canada–US Auto Pact in 1965, was pushed northward (Holmes, 1988); the networks in Europe were rearranged, with some southward drift into lower-cost EC countries such as Spain and Portugal; and Latin America, particularly Mexico, was integrated more fully and directly into the flow.

Again, it is worth stressing that the ability of the firms to redeploy their assets in this way hinged on their ability to manage time in production and articulate it with incremental product development. The flow had to be both smoothed and controlled so that the extensive spatial pipeline could function effectively.

The flaw in this scenario is that it didn't respond to the second part of the challenge posed by Japan – the proliferation and rapid renovation of product lines. The competitive environment would no longer sustain the time–space strategy that the American firms had, in many ways remarkably, pioneered. It was a strategy that had enabled the extraordinary dominance of American products in their own and foreign markets for roughly two generations. But this control over space hinged fundamentally on a certain kind of control over time that was no longer valid. What this upheaval in the meaning of control over time and space might mean will be taken up in the next chapter.

Conclusion

In sum, in the first episode, an inability to resolve the problem of time by reorganizing the production system is temporarily compensated by recourse to a competitive strategy whose viability is directly linked to control over space. In the long run, the lack of control over time in production is an insurmountable barrier to the continued growth of the industry. But for several decades at least, control over space allows an obsolete organization of production to thrive. It is only when this control over space is also lost that the project collapses. In this story what is striking is not that the specific character of the relationship among competition, time, and space alters the production system, but rather that it allows the production system to remain unchanged.

In the second episode, by contrast, the resolution of a specific temporal problem in production is dependent on the nature of competition. In other words, the stability of a particular competitive environment sustains the ability of firms to organize production in a particular way. Moreover, the specific temporal strategy involved creates the basis for an historically unprecedented spatial flexibility and extensiveness of the production system. Temporal and spatial mastery, in this case, go hand in hand. In the end, however, a new competitive challenge – based on different principles of production organization and a different vision of the market – disrupts this stable competitive environment and the temporal and spatial strategies that it has sheltered. The effects of this disruption promise to be far-reaching.

3

The New Competition and the Recalibration of Time and Space

Introduction

The consolidation of the system of mass production, US-style, was in many ways a monumental achievement. It provided the foundation for unprecedented economic stability and institutionalized an historically unique set of social practices and understandings across a whole range of issues: how markets work, how firms compete within them, how production is organized, the role of labor and its relationship to management, the role of the state, the relationship between industry and the scientific community, and so on. A profound challenge to this system unavoidably entails a far-reaching overhaul of these deeply entrenched practices and ways of thinking. It is not too much to say that it constitutes a challenge to a whole way of life. Little wonder, then, that the process has been so traumatic.

The result, predictably, has been a round of feverish experimentation as firms try almost anything and everything to re-establish themselves in a new environment. The rapid succession of best-practice mantras – statistical process control, total quality management, intrapreneurship, empowerment, flexibility, benchmarking, lean production, just-in-time, de-layering, downsizing, strategic alliances, and process re-engineering, to name a few – hints at the fluidity of the situation. It seems a safe bet that most large American firms have worked their way through much of this list, possibly even several at a time.

And, indeed, much has changed, although the work is plainly not complete. This chapter analyzes these transformative processes through the optic of time, space, and competition in an effort to understand what they mean and what kind of a world they are likely to produce.

The Crisis of Mass Production

The notion that mass markets are breaking up has become a significant commonplace:[1] significant because standardized mass consumption was the necessary counterpart to standardized mass production; no mass consumer means, unavoidably, no mass producer, and the end of the mass production system. The usual construction – "mass markets are breaking up," sometimes shortened to "the breakup of mass markets" – is, however, oddly agentless. It evokes a kind of natural process, something like the breakup of icebergs in the spring, the difference being that firms, unlike the ocean, have to change how they operate to accommodate this fragmentation.

This style of presentation is itself significant and merits some consideration, since it shapes how the problem of competitiveness is understood and responded to. I would emphasize in particular how well it harmonizes with the ideological orientation and analytical requirements of conventional microeconomics. Though all markets must have both buyers and sellers, it is "consumer sovereignty" (as opposed, say, to producer sovereignty) that constitutes a bedrock tenet of the analysis, while "consumer preferences" remain an untheorizable yet supremely powerful force. The market, understood now as the anonymous mass of sovereign consumers, simply behaves as it will behave and it is the business of companies to respond to its preferences, once these are revealed in the form of effective demand. Consumer preferences are, in a sense, the first mover, the primal force that sets the story in motion.

The thesis of consumer sovereignty, by identifying the individual as the master of his or her own life, is the guarantor of the inherent fairness of the system, despite the fact that it plainly produces unequal outcomes. In this lies its ideological importance. The exogeneity of consumer preferences, meanwhile, provides the essential spark of analytical life that allows the theory to operate.

Mass markets, however, didn't simply break up, like so many icebergs, due to an exogenous shift in sovereign consumer preferences. They were broken up by real social processes and real social agents. It is important to understand why and how this happened.

The stable growth trajectory of the mass production system hinged on three fundamental and intricately connected features: how wealth was produced, how it was distributed socially, and how it was used. For nearly thirty years following World War II these elements worked

---

[1] Important sources for this section include Harvey, 1989, 1982; Lipietz, 1986; Piore and Sabel, 1984; Aglietta, 1979; Boyer, 1990; Coriat, 1990; Kochan et al., 1986.

together in a kind of virtuous circle before falling apart with apparent suddenness – sometime in 1973 by most accountings.

The capacity of the system to continually generate new wealth was based on its capacity to generate steady gains in productivity. These gains in turn were a function of continual improvements in the technology, organization, and scale of production.

In the US, the distribution of the wealth produced was guided by the social accommodations that had been institutionalized during and after the period of the New Deal. Linking wages to productivity growth fostered the emergence of a broadly based middle class that could consume the tremendous output of the production system. The rising flow of tax revenues (and the debt capacity these underwrote) allowed the government to invest heavily in large-scale infrastructure projects (the national highway system, for example) while redistributing income in the form of subsidies to the growing middle class (for example, mortgage deductions) and welfare transfers. Meanwhile, the state became an increasingly important direct purchaser of goods and services produced in the private sector – most notably in the defense arena. The state in this way played a triple role: enhancing the wealth-generating capacity of the system through its infrastructure investments; absorbing some of the tremendous investable surplus generated by the system, which might otherwise have been hard pressed to find profitable employment; and contributing directly and indirectly to the consumption of the output produced.

While all of this was going on, profit rates were high and the earnings retained by firms were reinvested in new technologies, expanded capacity domestically and overseas, and the like. As a consequence, the wealth-generating capacity of the system was further enhanced.

The great originality of the system, taken as a whole, was that it stabilized the relationship between its fabulous and steadily growing capacity to produce and its capacity to consume. It did so in a way that allowed the gradual retirement of existing fixed capital and the steady and profitable reinvestment of the surplus produced.

What, then, went wrong? The answer is a number of things, and it is their particular constellation that defined the timing and character of the crisis and established the new realities to which firms would have to respond.

To begin with, the productivity gains available within the mass production paradigm itself were nearing exhaustion. The potential gains from further mechanization were diminishing while compensatory attempts to increase the intensity of work (by, for instance, increasing line speeds) provoked growing discontent on the part of workers, expressed most famously in the GM Lordstown strike of 1972. The limits to mass production were, in this sense, both technical and social.

In any case, even the wealthiest mass consumer markets were becoming saturated. Everyone already had one of everything and many had two. What was needed was a new wave of geographical expansions of middle-class, mass-consuming markets. Roughly the opposite occurred. Mass production expanded geographically, but mass consumption lagged far behind.

As the European versions of mass production had been put into place after the war, parallel social and political transformations had also ensured the emergence of a broadly based, mass-consuming middle class that could absorb the output produced. This was less true of Japan at the time, and is still not at all the case in other so-called newly industrializing countries. Mass production techniques were steadily taken up in these areas, whether on the basis of indigenous investments or capital flowing in from abroad, but the crucial social transformations did not occur.

Several consequences ensued for the core industrial regions. First, the already threatening problem of sustained overcapacity was made worse. This had serious effects on costs as capacity utilization rates declined, and raised the awkward question of where one could find profitable outlets for investment of accumulated capital. The massive flow of capital into unproductive debt in the Third World and the socialist countries is a sign of how awkward that question was becoming by the late 1970s. Second, linking mass production-style productivity levels with ultra-low wages in the periphery meant that the output had to go someplace else to be consumed: namely, the wealthy core markets. Third, it did so in the form of comparatively cheap goods. Core firms, caught between high wages, declining productivity growth, capacity utilization problems, and low-cost competition, found their costs going steadily up and their profit margins evaporating.

They also found "their" mass markets being broken up by a rapid expansion of the competitive field. There were simply many more producers out there and many more significantly differentiable products. Sovereign mass consumers didn't suddenly become more discriminating in their tastes; they rather suddenly had more real choices along a broader price/performance spectrum.

It got worse. Some of these producers, especially the Japanese, had learned how to produce a more diversified and changeable line of products while still producing at high aggregate volumes. They had the scale, hence cost, benefits of mass production, but had diminished the constraint of standardization. This style of flexible mass production greatly intensified the rate at which product lines could be turned over or renovated.

It was this ability, rather than low costs, which constituted the most far-reaching challenge to the existing system and the firms which were dominant within it. Low costs could, after all, be imitated by moving to cheap places, among other things. But the sudden need to destandardize high-volume production, to compress product life cycles and intensify the rate at which new products could be readied for markets – in short, the sudden need to collaborate in breaking up the very mass markets that mass producers had created and that sustained them – drastically undermined the stability conditions of the system.

Mass markets, then, were broken up because the mass production system was destabilized by processes engendered within its own boundaries and impinging from the outside. These processes together produced a new competitive environment, a new roster of competitors, and a new style of competition. In this third historical episode, transformations in competition and time are seen to drive far-reaching changes in social and spatial processes and relations.

Episode 3: The New Competitive Environment

Competition and time

The great originality of the current period in industrial history lies in the altered relationship between competition and time. Mass production, as we saw in the previous chapter, achieved remarkable gains in managing and compressing time in production. But the system also implied the stretching out of time in product life cycles in order to valorize the tremendous stock of specialized fixed capital and to accommodate the unmanageability of time in product development. The new regime turns this relationship on its head.

Now the central focus is on drastically compressing product development times, from design through scaled-up manufacturing, as well as speeding up the order-to-delivery cycle. Time in production has to be managed to accommodate these new imperatives: the manufacturing base must be capable of rapidly and smoothly adjusting to continually changing product configurations and the specific demands of the moment.

What has happened, in effect, is that time has now become the competitive strategy of the firm. That is to say, firms compete in the market on the basis of their ability to compress time in development and order cycles: the firm that can bring a new product to market faster or turn around an order more quickly and reliably gains a significant advantage – in effect, it is selling speed and reliable service as well as the physical product itself (cf. Stalk and Hout, 1990; P. Smith and Reinertsen, 1991). Such products can command a price premium on the market, enhancing profitability and permitting the high costs of development to be recouped.[2]

Note that, as competition proceeds on this basis, the necessity of continually compressing time is continually reinforced. Everyone has to try to get a little bit faster in order to get the product to market earlier, and they have to do this all the time.

This necessity has led to the proliferation of techniques for speeding up and, if possible, lowering the costs of product development and changing the configuration of products on the line. None of these excludes any of the others, of course. And none of them, as we will see, definitively resolves the problem. What we will also see is that the new relationship between competition and time implies collateral adjustments in the organization of production and social relations in production as well as quite distinctive spatial dynamics.

Time-compression strategies: product development

Simplifying and standardizing components that can be mixed and matched in a variety of configurations is one approach to time compression in product development. It has the particular advantage of reducing some of the stress on the production system: product flexibility is assembled in rather than built in. On the other hand, to the degree that it commits the firm to a more specialized fixed capital base, the risks of serious misjudgments of the market are greatly enhanced. The firm may have a very lean, modular operation that generates a range of goods at low cost, but if it is the wrong range altogether, then the organization will still have a very difficult time adjusting.

Depending on the product, it may be the case that significant functional flexibility can be introduced via software rather than through the hardware. The box will be the same, but what it does will vary. This again is very desirable from a manufacturing/assembly point of view as it stabilizes the production base. But it does so at the rather high price of shifting the time and cost problem into the software development process. Modularizing software development (such as object-oriented programming) seems to offer an alluring way out of this predicament, but it hasn't solved the problem yet and there are many who doubt that it will (cf. Brooks, 1982, 1986). In any case, as with three-dimensional products, the demand to continually compress software development cycles is essentially permanent in this competitive environment.

---

[2] Smith and Reinertsen (1991) provide numerical examples suggesting that, in rapidly changing markets, a delay of just six months in bringing out a new product can reduce its lifetime profit yield by a third.

Strategic alliances and technical collaborations have, of course, become extraordinarily important in recent years. Their most noted virtue is the spreading of the costs and risks of development projects whose resource requirements are so huge that they put even enormous firms at risk. This also frees up the firm's resources to pursue multiple projects simultaneously so it avoids being locked in to a single trajectory. Further, because various pieces of the development project are allocated to specialist partners, significant time economies through task specialization ought to be available.

Perhaps the best evidence of the importance firms place on these alliances is the way in which Honda recommitted itself to its collaboration with Rover even after that firm was abruptly and unexpectedly sold to BMW, provoking undisguised dismay and even anger from Honda. Given that a strategic alliance must be based on trust and open communication or nothing at all, Honda's sense of betrayal was easily understood. Honda's early response indicated that, while it would fulfill existing obligations to Rover, the future of the collaboration was in grave doubt. Only a few weeks later, and with no explanation, Honda reversed field and announced that there were no particular impediments to continued close collaboration with Rover/BMW (*Financial Times*, 1994b). Along with the automobile industry, computers and telecommunications, where the costs of developing complex systems are enormous and the winner stands to gain a commanding position in the market, are hotbeds of alliance activity, with firms often entering into multiple bilateral and multilateral arrangements.[3]

Yet, strategic alliances are by no means problem-free, nor are they exactly cheap. They are very intensive in highly qualified and highly paid labor, including management, scientists, and various technical specialists, who must devote a lot of time to developing and maintaining the relationship as well as to resolving the particular technical problems

[3] Recent examples in semiconductors alone include IBM, Toshiba, and Siemens in DRAMs, Toshiba and Motorola in DRAMs and microprocessors, Kobe Steel and Texas Instruments for high-capacity memories, Intel and VLSI for low-power microprocessors, AMD and Fujitsu for flash memories, IBM and Toshiba in flash memories, NEC and AT&T for 64MB DRAMs, Philips and SGS-Thomson for advanced microchips, Toshiba and Siemens for RISC microprocessors, Texas Instruments and Hitachi for memory chips, IBM and Intel for advanced microprocessors, IBM and Thomson-CSF for advanced chips, Intel and Hewlett Packard for microprocessors, and IBM, Motorola, and Apple for microprocessors. From this casual compilation, one can easily see that firms are engaging themselves in a myriad of relationships, sometimes apparently creating multilateral alliances with numerous shared interests (cf. IBM, Toshiba, Siemens, and Motorola), and sometimes apparently contravening these self-same alliances (cf. IBM and Intel). (See *Financial Times*, 1991a, 1991b, 1991d, 1992d, 1992e, 1992i, 1992k, 1994a, 1994c; *Economist*, 1992a.)

at hand. Multiplying alliances means multiplying the demands on these workers. There are many questions relating to the protection of existing proprietary technologies and ownership of the new technologies developed jointly, or to the precise balance between collaboration and competition between and among partners. At the same time, the evidence of successful alliances is, to date, scarce (cf. *Financial Times*, 1992f).

Meanwhile, technical collaborations along the supply chain have their own peculiar difficulties. In the mass production environment, final output producers treated their suppliers as they treated their workers, which is to say as much like pieces of machinery as possible. Suppliers were highly task-specialized and performed their tasks according to detailed and non-negotiable instructions from the center. They might be quite productive and efficient, but they didn't know very much, as technical and market information was closely held within the gravitational field of the large customer. Now suddenly they are called upon to be actively engaged in designing products and processes while, of course, keeping their costs down. Not only does this require adapting to an entirely new style of engagement with the final producer, which may entail overcoming years or decades of mistrust, but suppliers must also rather dramatically alter who they are. They need to reorient their staffing to create new technical competencies, and in so doing are forced to redefine a whole range of understandings concerning practices, relations, and power within the firm. In sum, they need to transform their identities and commitments. The stakes in doing so are extremely high so there is no shortage of incentives, but the magnitude of the transformation is also great (*New York Times*, 1994a).

Design automation techniques also figure importantly here. They immediately eliminate such time- and labor-intensive tasks as drafting and redrafting to changing specifications, so the one-off gains from automation are potentially great. They expand the ability to experiment without significant time penalties, which is also increasingly important. Yet it cannot be supposed that automation *per se* vastly speeds up the thinking of the designers themselves, so here we must reckon with the limits to speeding up irreducibly human processes.

The other major line of attack has been the commitment to simultaneous or concurrent engineering, which implies a thoroughgoing overhaul of the organization of the development process and internal relations across previously impermeable functional boundaries. Instead of moving through a fixed and unidirectional sequence of design and development phases, each carried out in a separate compartment of the organization, all of the tasks – market research, design, product engineering, prototype development and test, and manufacturing engineering – are accomplished simultaneously and collectively. This eliminates certain obvious kinds of delay, as when a product design turns out to be unmanufacturable and has to be backed up the sequence, and it eliminates a lot of wasted time as those responsible for downstream phases wait for the earlier work to be accomplished (cf. Brooks, 1982; IEEE *Spectrum*, 1991; *Financial Times*, 1992a).[4]

As with strategic alliances, the most daunting aspect of this transformation in development processes involves a significant overhaul in social relations – in this case, internal to the firm. Existing power bases, status markers, and identities have all to be renegotiated, and rather abruptly at that. Long-standing ways of valuing individuals and roles (marketers vs. product engineers vs. process engineers, for example) and understanding who is "us" vs. "them" within the firm are suddenly thrown into question. Loyalties to and identifications with, say, the division, have to be restructured in favor of a temporary inter-divisional product development team. In effect, personal and professional commitments have to be realigned in this encounter with intensified time pressures.

Despite all the gains that have been made, there are two very sobering aspects to this catalogue of time-compression strategies. The first is that they haven't as yet been sufficient. The six years and six billion dollars that went into the development of Ford's Mondeo is only one startling example. Best practice in many if not most US firms still lags behind the Japanese, who grew up in an environment in which this intensified product line flexibility was normal (cf. Fruin, 1992; K. Clark and Fujimoto, 1992; Womack et al., 1990).

The second is that there is no obvious point at which the pressure to continually compress product development times eases. If time is the competitive strategy, then time compression is a permanent goal. Each gain can only be followed by renewed efforts to compress development times still further. Yet, at some point, even with all the flexible automation in the world, the production base will be unable to adapt to the demands placed upon it. If we imagine, at the limit, a regime in which product lines are overhauled on a daily basis, then the potential for

---

[4] An appealing analogy that groups many of these strategies together would be to massively parallel supercomputers, whose whole point is to drastically compress time in processing complex problems. It does so by parcelling out bits of the problem to thousands of relatively simple and cheap processors ("collaborators") which perform calculations simultaneously instead of sequentially, as with complex microprocessor-based supercomputers. But designing the software, which tells the processors what to do, has emerged as a gigantic bottleneck, especially for highly varied commercial applications. Described as "a programming nightmare," this is another illustration of how the problem of controlling time never goes away, it just gets shifted around (*New York Times*, 1994b).

chaos and blockages becomes apparent. The risk of not being able to recover the development costs, however much they have been reduced and spread around, also increases. Further, the demands on human resources must at some point become intolerable. The particular curiosity of this effect is that the problem of speed-up now impinges on the most qualified and highly paid managerial and technical personnel.

The most persuasive evidence that these limits are, in fact, being reached is that Japanese firms, which have been setting the pace up to now, are announcing to anyone who will listen that they are trying to limit the range of products they offer and to slow down the rate at which their product lines are renovated (*Financial Times*, 1992b, 1992c; *New York Times*, 1994c). If one asks under what circumstances Japanese firms seek to publish their strategies in the English-language business press, then the underlying desperation becomes apparent. The trouble is that it is not clear that anyone has the power to follow these rather vigorous signals. As the competitive field becomes more crowded, and as more and more firms commit themselves to a time-based competitive strategy, no one can afford to drop out of the race first. The framework for a collective strategy to modify or limit the trajectory is extremely hard to construct in the present circumstances.

This predicament hints at a rather different meaning to the current enthusiasm for strategic alliances and technical collaborations, not to mention the recent increase in large-scale mergers and acquisitions, many of them internationally based. Besides offering possibilities for cost and risk reduction and for speeding up the development process, it seems likely that strategic alliances also hold out the hope for strategy alignments along a consolidated range of technical trajectories. Mergers and acquisitions accomplish this more directly, albeit more expensively. The desired outcome would be a stabilization of the competitive environment that would allow firms to relax the pace substantially. But this will be difficult to achieve, if only because too many opportunities exist to disrupt these fragile arrangements.

We might recall in this context the great importance of stable, effective oligopoly structures in sustaining the pricing, investment, and income distribution patterns characteristic of old-style mass production. Firms benefit significantly from this kind of controlled competition in a capital-intensive environment, and it would be surprising if they were not trying to reconstruct the conditions for profitable temporal management of their investments in fixed capital and product development. But this is hard to do in an environment which features an unmanageable and growing number of participants, particularly when the competitive strategy is precisely about time compression.

The predicament in which firms find themselves is truly daunting as they are forced continually to disrupt the conditions of their own stable reproduction. I want to stress that this predicament is simultaneously economic, social, and what could be called cultural.

First, it places severe stress on firms' ability to profitably manage their capital resources. Second, it requires a far-reaching yet contradictory transformation of social relations within the firm and between firms. Because of the high premium placed on speed, reliability, and quality of output in the new environment, workers must be encouraged to cooperate and to discipline themselves to the work process. For example, if things go wrong on the line, operators must have the knowledge and, crucially, the commitment to intervene directly and immediately – there is no time to wait for supervisors to be called in to sort out the problem. The operational unpredictability associated with adversarial labor–management relations is unacceptable now as stoppages or slowdowns would imperil a whole, tightly coordinated chain of activities. In this context, workers must be treated rather differently than they were under the old-style mass production regime. Yet they are still workers – variable capital inputs who sell their labor power on the market – and their relations to any given firm are still subject to the pressures of the market and of competition, which may require that they be ejected from the newly collaborative environment. Meanwhile, firms must learn to cooperate with erstwhile competitors or with formerly arm's-length suppliers. The boundaries of firms become more permeable, yet they are still separate capitals and likewise still subject to the pressures of the market and of competition.

As if this weren't enough, firms have to alter their ways of thinking about markets and how they operate, their position with respect to the market and with other economic agents (other firms, workers, stockholders, etc.), appropriate ways of managing economic, technical, and social resources, their relationships with political units, and so on. Taken as a whole, this overhaul of long-standing practices, relations, and ways of thinking amounts to a very considerable cultural upheaval.

The entire transformation expresses itself most acutely in the drive to get new or renovated products to the market as fast as possible. Time has surfaced as a strategic variable to be deployed directly as a competitive weapon, and in this manifestation it directly affects how the production system operates. This works particularly strongly through the spatial character of the system.

Time–space transformations

The redefinition of the meaning of control over time has unavoidably entailed a recalibration of the relationship between time and space.

David Harvey, in *The Condition of Postmodernity*, proposes the term "time–space compression" to capture the inherent jointness and broad scope of this historic change (Harvey, 1989). The phrase draws attention to the complementarity of these twinned mutations. As the time required to circulate goods, information, and capital is shortened through improved technologies of communications and transportation, for example, space becomes in effect smaller, the relative distance between places lessened. Another example of how these work together might be the effect of installing integrated, faster-throughput automated equipment in production. This often leads to dramatic reductions in required factory floor space as a smaller number of faster machines can produce the same volume of output (Schoenberger, 1989a). But there are other ways in which the effect of this altered relationship is less apparently parallel. To emphasize the sometimes contradictory aspects of this movement, I will use the term "time–space transformation" in place of Harvey's "time–space compression."

Under conditions of mass production, as we have seen, the ability to manage time in the production of standardized goods allowed an extraordinary spatial freedom to the system. In significant ways, distance was a solved problem, as undifferentiated goods flowed smoothly and steadily across space. This was a world in which it was plausible for an American firm to develop automobile engines in Detroit, make them in Australia, and ship them to Europe for assembly into the final product.

This world has been irrevocably altered by the transformation of the competitive environment and the dramatic shift in the role and meaning of time in competition. A new round of time–space transformation has had the unusual effect, in my view, of reproposing the problem of space for the system. In other words, the once solved problem of distance has become unsolved again, and this despite the fact that the techniques and costs of communications and transportation have steadily improved. The old time–space strategy has become invalid, and a new one is being worked out in its place. It is, however, fraught with tensions and contradictions.

We can see this new spatial problematic at work in a variety of contexts. Consider, for example, the relationship between R&D and manufacturing within the firm. Right from the start of organized industrial research in the US, firms have seen the value of separating the research function geographically from other operations of the firm. GE, one of the early pioneers of internalized R&D, planned at the outset to locate its new research labs away from its main works in Schenectady, although it eventually compromised by locating the labs in a separate building on site (Reich, 1985). AT&T established Bell Labs in a still reasonably bucolic part of Northern New Jersey. GM's first research labs, headed by Charles Kettering, were located in Ohio (Leslie, 1983). RCA, to cite another example, built its wholly self-contained Sarnoff Labs in Princeton, New Jersey, well away from its manufacturing plants. Even Toyota's first formal research operation was located in Tokyo, although the entire rest of the firm was built up in what became Toyota City (Togo and Wartman, 1993). So pervasive was this pattern that it became a central tenet of theories of the spatial division of labor: industrial research would be concentrated in its own specialized geographical spaces, while manufacturing proper was free to locate virtually anywhere in the world – anywhere, that is, except near the research operations (Hymer, 1972; Massey, 1984).

The benefits of spatial separation of this sort are several. First, it shelters the research and development staff from the day-to-day pressures and demands of the manufacturing operation. Physical proximity risks distracting scientists and engineers from their longer-term work by focusing their attention on an endless series of immediate problems and crises in manufacturing – better to keep them out of temptation's way. As a corollary, unencumbered by the culture and preoccupations of manufacturing, the researchers are freer to explore and create new things. Second, it is widely felt that the spatial clustering of research and development activities across firms creates a vibrant critical mass in which ideas (and often people) circulate easily and productively within the region, à la Silicon Valley. Third, the attractiveness of these specialized locales assures the continual replenishment of the supply of qualified workers, drawn both by the heady intellectual environment and by the absence of a gritty industrial landscape. In short, they are nice places to live and rather exclusive, since entry is gained by having the right qualifications. Since these places tend to be located in places where labor and land costs are high, a fourth benefit is that manufacturing is free to seek out lower-cost locations.

This sort of spatial division of labor both assumed and required that the thinkers didn't need to have intensive and continual interactions with the makers. It also assumed that the makers didn't need to think, particularly. In a mass production environment, these assumptions were plausible, if not necessarily desirable. New product technologies and designs periodically issued forth from the labs and were presented fully formed to the manufacturing people, whose only task was to figure out how to make the thing at an acceptable cost. Contacts between the thinkers and the makers were about transferring information, not collaborating in its creation. The stability of product lines meant that for most of the time, the thinkers and the makers could go their separate ways.

The conditions that permitted this tremendous operational and geographic detachment between product development and manufacturing have, of course, changed. The pressure to continually and ever more rapidly push new or renovated products through the pipeline means at the least that the density of the connections between development and manufacturing increases strongly. The character of these connections also changes. Everyone has to be a thinker now, and the manufacturing people form an integral part of the development team. The new methods of product development require the firm and potentially its partners to assemble shifting groups of people on a continuous basis; these groups unite everyone from market researchers to manufacturing plant managers and sometimes even line workers.

Long-distance computer networks notwithstanding, this kind of intense, continuous exchange and collaboration benefits enormously from constant, face-to-face interaction (Saxenian, 1994; Waxman et al., 1989; P. Smith and Reinertsen, 1991; Stalk and Hout, 1990). According to John Oldfield, vice president of Ford Europe, "Product engineers and manufacturing engineers must be in the same country, and ideally in the same office. You cannot achieve simultaneous engineering by telephone or video-conferencing" (*Financial Times*, 1992a). The erstwhile splendid isolation of the product development process from the production system, and even of the various parts of the development process from one another, is no longer tenable. Where once it was considered a positive gain to separate development organizationally and geographically from the rest of the firm, there is now considerable hand-wringing over the possibility that people on different floors of the same building will be inhibited from interacting sufficiently.

The ideal now is to have everyone together. Naturally, this is not so easy. There are tremendous organizational and geographic sunk costs involved, for one thing. For another, the original impetus behind organizational and spatial separation was in many ways valid. Protecting researchers from the quotidian traumas of manufacturing may indeed be important. Carving out a separate social and cultural space within the firm might well provide a crucial source of renovative impulses which could move a firm off a declining trajectory. Organizing collaborations across multiple partners means that it will often be unrealistic to suppose that everyone might commit themselves to the same place. Further, it is more likely that manufacturing operations will have to reorient themselves spatially to the geographically scarce sources of qualified research and development people rather than the other way round, thus sacrificing at least some of their ability to locate strictly according to their own factor input and cost requirements.

The result of these conflicting pressures is likely to be a certain degree of compromise, turning on the issues of how close is close and the balance between stable and unstable elements of the production process. Is it sufficient to be in the same country? Within an hour's flight time? Which pieces of the organization really do need to be in constant contact and which can be accommodated at a greater distance? What kinds of task require long-term collaboration and which can be handled by sending out a team for a few weeks? The eventual results are impossible to predict, but the important change is in the underlying tendencies. Very powerful centrifugal and, in a sense, chromatographic forces which promoted the geographical dispersion and specialized sorting of production are being overtaken by subtle but nonetheless strong centripetal forces, which promise to significantly restructure the industrial landscape.

Just-in-time

There remains the further issue of compressing order-to-delivery turnaround times. This brings us to the renowned just-in-time (JIT) system, which yields several benefits to the firm, among them reducing inventory costs and space requirements, reducing labor content and time in production, and dramatically compressing order–delivery cycle times. As JIT has been exhaustively discussed elsewhere (cf. especially Cusumano, 1985; Fruin, 1992; also Schonberger, 1982; McMillan, 1984; Monden, 1981), I want to review here just some of its key features. As with time compression in product development, I want to stress that JIT both permits these significant time-compression gains and, once implemented, very definitely requires them. The system overall is made more flexible to demand, but at the price of creating significant new constraints.

The just-in-time system, as it was devised and put into place by Taiichi Ohno at Toyota, combines a kind of ultra-refined Fordism in terms of time compression in the execution of production tasks with a straightforward inversion of Fordism in the temporal management of the flow of goods through the production system. The result is a production apparatus that can rapidly adjust to demand shifts at low cost, especially because the ultra-Fordist aspect of it substantially reduces the labor content of the output. JIT creates the possibility of dramatically reducing order-to-delivery turnaround times, but in doing so transforms this possibility into a fundamental requirement if the system is to operate effectively. It is this transformation from possibility to requirement that produces strong implications for the spatial organization of production.

Taiichi Ohno, by all accounts, had a kind of mania for reducing wasted time in production, and was simply more relentless than the

Fordists in his application of standard Fordist techniques of job analysis and time-and-motion study in compressing task turnaround times. He was determined to eliminate all unnecessary movements and allow no idle time for machines or, especially, workers (Togo and Wartman, 1993; Cusumano, 1985).

Hardly any of this depended on advanced technologies. The most notable and crucial example of this, in terms of product flexibility on the line, was in the time it took to change dies in the stamping department. The time-compression initiatives were as simple as using clamps and fasteners instead of bolts and screws, or figuring out what set-up tasks could be accomplished while the machine was cycling through a previous task. The parts of the die that were at issue in set-ups were standardized so that the die could either be slid in like a cassette or guided by jigs and limit switches. The results of these simple interventions were staggering. Already by 1955, Toyota required only 2–3 hours to change stamping dies, a level not reached by American firms for decades after that. By 1971, dies at Toyota could be changed in as little as three minutes (Cusumano, 1985; Monden, 1981).

Where Ohno departed from standard Fordist practice in this area was in breaking up the rigid task-allocation system linking one worker with one job. By assigning workers to operate several machines, Ohno ensured maximum use of their time. Individual machines might be idle in this system, but workers never were. This entailed a significant rearrangement of the once linear spatial layout of the factory. Different kinds of machines were grouped together in the form of a U so that workers could move fluidly among as many as five to ten operations without losing any time (Cusumano, 1985; McMillan, 1984; Monden, 1981; Fruin, 1992).

Time compression of this magnitude in production tasks was already a significant gain in terms of both output costs and the ability to change product configurations smoothly and rapidly in response to demand. But it also provided a crucial support for the other aspect of Ohno's re-envisioning of the production process: the transformation of the time-management strategy bearing on the flow of material through the system.

JIT is by now universally seen as superior to the just-in-case (JIC) approach characteristic of US-style mass production, which is viewed as something of a historical error, typically American in its undisciplined wastefulness. Yet it is not at all obvious that JIT would be a more effective form of production organization in the context of standardized mass production.

Just-in-case involved producing to forecast demand, with a focus on refining the techniques for pushing parts and materials through the system. The system relied heavily on buffer stocks, which implied high inventory-carrying costs and significant space requirements in ware-houses and on the line. One could imagine a river at flood, pushing everything in its path forward. The only effective intervention is to open sluice gates, channeling the water into reservoirs known as buffer stocks and inventories.

The downside of this system is by now well known. Parts and materials tend to pile up where downstream operators are unable to handle the flow produced at upstream stations. Defective materials are carried forward willy-nilly, impelled by the sheer strength of the flow. A significant amount of capital is immobilized in inventories and the building space to accommodate them. Crucially, the system doesn't handle at all well multiple product configurations on the same line or sudden shifts in demand. One has to be able to dip into the river of parts and materials at any moment and randomly lift out something that is usable. Having to rummage through a heterogeneous pile of product-specific parts to find the one that actually goes with the present work-in-process would be intolerable, hence the premium on standardization.

On the other hand, the system was rather robust. Breakdowns or blockages anywhere along the production chain could simply be by-passed as buffer stocks were brought into play. Carrying high inventories costs a lot, but so, too, does idling an entire production process while a strike is settled at a supplier plant or repairs made on a crucial bit of machinery. At the same time, in a stable and relatively homogeneous mass market, the system doesn't need to accommodate a high degree of variability on the line or rapid demand shifts.

The implementation of just-in-time at Toyota was driven by the small size and fragmented nature of the local market, as well as by the scarcity of capital, in the late 1940s and early 1950s. In 1950, for example, the entire Japanese auto industry produced the equivalent of a day and a half's supply in the US. At the same time, the problem of immobilizing capital in inventory stocks was particularly acute (Cusumano, 1985; Fruin, 1992). Some new method was needed to coordinate the production process while tracking a highly uncertain and variable market in which the margin for error was microscopic. Ford might have misread the market horribly for the Edsel, but it had other products in other substantial market segments with which to absorb the blow. In a market that totalled 30,000 units, a firm that committed itself to a standardized product line would, in the case of an error of that magnitude, simply cease to exist. So the problem of being flexible to qualitatively unstable demand was acutely important in Japan at a time when it was hardly relevant at all in the US. That capability is what JIT provides. JIC clearly doesn't, but then it wasn't necessary in the US at the time.

In JIT, output is calibrated to current demand: final assembly pulls parts and materials through the system, calling them up as needed. In contrast to JIC, nothing is pushed forward. Orders flow backward to the previous station to take only what is needed at the moment an operation must be performed. As far as possible, no one is allowed to make more than the next station can handle immediately and nothing is stockpiled.

Under JIT, the whole supply chain is linked to the final producer on the basis of coordinated time management and time compression. Order–delivery cycles for intermediates and final output drop from weeks or months to days or hours (Fruin, 1992). Indeed, they have to drop to these levels; otherwise, the JIT system cannot function.

The result is a system that can produce a variety of models in small volumes at low cost and change what it is making in rapid response to current demand. At the same time, aggregate volumes (over all product types) may be quite high, so the firm or, increasingly, the system of networked firms gets the benefits of scale economies with something approaching bespoke production (Fruin, 1992).

These gains are very real, and of crucial importance in an unstable and fragmented market environment. For this reason, it is no exaggeration to say that all manufacturing firms (even other Japanese ones) are now trying to become more like Toyota in implementing and refining just-in-time production techniques. If for no other reason, it is important to understand the pressures and constraints associated with these advances.

In order to perform effectively in a just-in-time environment, the firm must be able to guarantee absolute reliability in delivering highly variable output to specification and to schedule. Both timeliness and quality are essential, as the product has to be ready to pass to the next stage of production or to final consumption as called for, with very little margin for substitution in case of defects. The reward for the successful JIT supplier is more flexibility on prices and a more stable hold on the market.[5]

The quality and timeliness guarantees have several implications. The first is that the system as a whole has an inbuilt fragility. Disruption of production anywhere along the line, due to machine breakdowns or

---

[5] Or at least it should be. In the Toyota system, the vast, nested hierarchy of suppliers is under immense pressure to constantly reduce costs and prices, yet Toyota takes care not to appropriate all of the cost savings produced. Strong performers are rewarded not only by better margins, but by long-term supply agreements and the possibility to move up the value-added chain (Fruin, 1992). GM, on the other hand, has not shed its reputation for aggressive-to-the-point-of-rapacious treatment of its suppliers as it has moved to a just-in-time organization of production.

strikes, for example, have a suddenly magnified effect as all processes downstream from the blockage are put at risk. In March, 1996, for example, workers at a GM brake plant in Ohio walked off the job. Within a week, GM was forced to close fourteen (out of twenty-nine) assembly plants and sixteen other parts plants in Canada, the US, and Mexico, costing the company an estimated $30–40 million a day (*New York Times*, 1996). And GM isn't even very good at just-in-time!

As a consequence, the time and quality guarantees produce a number of significant operational requirements that bear very heavily on the character of social relations within the firm and between firms. In a sense, the reliability requirement cascades down through the system until it embraces every supplier, every machine, and every worker.

This means, in the first instance, that workers on the line have to be responsible for the normal functioning of their machines. There is no time, in this environment, for machines to sit idle while repair people are called in from elsewhere in the plant. We may grant that, with computer-controlled machines, normal maintenance and adjustment may be greatly facilitated by menu-driven diagnostic and repair programs, so that the technical skills workers need to have at their command are not so daunting (cf. Schoenberger, 1989a). Still, in an environment that is so unforgiving of quality or temporal deviations, line workers (who, it may be recalled, operate a growing number of different machines) need a range of skills and knowledge about the *system* in order for it to function effectively. The worker has to be able to intervene autonomously and work out a solution to whatever problem presents itself. This marks an acute contrast with old-style mass production, whose temporal management strategies produced no such requirements.

Second, the cascading reliability requirement also produces a very general responsibility requirement for line workers. In a JIT environment, everyone has to work intensely, flexibly (as to task or machine), and alertly all the time. Any slacking on any of these criteria immediately threatens the whole process. The problem of how to supervise each worker all the time to ensure the necessary effort is almost unimaginably immense. Workers in this system need to be self-monitoring and self-disciplining to a rather high degree (although the term "self" might actually refer to the work team). In this context, not only a sense of discipline but the new sense of time have to be internalized by the worker, in a way that is utterly foreign to traditional mass production practice, where time discipline was set by the pace of the line and enforced by supervisors.

The system fragility produced by the new principles of time management is concisely characterized by the head of a British auto parts supplier, who commented: "If we were to have a [labor] dispute, Ford would be shut down in a couple of days and Rover a day after that. That's the legacy of Just-in-Time manufacturing" (quoted in *Financial Times*, 1991e). As the article from which this quotation is taken goes on to point out, this predicament is directly contributing to widespread efforts to develop more cooperative relations on the shop floor. As in the case of product development, we can see how a competitive strategy centered on time compression requires a significant transformation of social relations in production. This transformation, of course, also extends to relations among firms, as suppliers are invested with the same responsibilities as workers on the line.

JIT, taken as a whole, is a way of aligning the production system to the intensified pace of product change and reconfiguration. This kind of production strategy is far less tolerant of distance than standardized mass production in a number of ways. Yet this has almost nothing to do with the dollar costs of transporting goods and information over great distances, costs which are, in any case, generally decreasing as a share of total costs. It is not quite so exaggerated as it sounds to claim that even if transportation were free, distance would still be a problem in a world in which time is the competitive strategy. The real issues, in this sort of world, are time, reliability, and coordination.

By way of a stylized illustration, imagine a standardized mass production system in which an undifferentiated stream of X parts produced in place A is matched up with an undifferentiated stream of Y parts produced in place B. So long as the costs of transportation and, possibly, tariffs constitute an acceptably small share of total costs, distance is not a problem. It is the continuity of the flow over space that counts, and this continuity is guaranteed by the stability and homogeneity of the product.

In a flexible, JIT-style production system, the X and Y parts have, at the limit, specific, differentiated identities. X_1 must be paired up with Y_1, X_2 with Y_2, and so on. Moreover, X_1 has to arrive in place B at exactly the moment that Y_1 has been produced. Now imagine that A and B are thousands of miles apart, with transport by truck, rail, and ship or plane, crossing borders and several time zones. Imagine further that the firm is producing to current demand with a promised delivery date in place C. Add that, in the current market environment, being able to guarantee a specific and early delivery date yields an advantage against your competition. If the firm can't reliably make its delivery dates, it can't sell its product. These constraints apply both to industrial markets, where the firm's output enters into the production process of another firm, and to final consumption goods markets (cf. Taplin, 1994; Gereffi, 1992). Indeed, this is nothing more than a description of the constraints imposed by JIT, which requires guaranteed reliability of supply.

This is why Toyota, which invented JIT, built Toyota City. The system in its most advanced form is extremely sensitive to logistical breakdowns. It is, therefore, far less able to accommodate the spatial extensiveness that is, by contrast, rather well tolerated by standardized mass production.

Does it matter that no firm, not even Toyota, has a perfectly functioning JIT system at present? The answer, I think, is no. What counts is that JIT is increasingly the central organizing principle around which production strategies are structured. Further, as we have seen, production *per se* can no longer be wholly divorced from other activities of the firm. The overwhelming need to compress time in product change, and to smoothly produce a highly differentiated output mix, produces significant geographical constraints: development has to be more closely integrated with manufacturing, and the various pieces of the manufacturing empire have to be more closely integrated and coordinated with one another.

What these tendencies seem to point to is increasing geographic concentration of production as entire networks of firms cluster together to speed up the flow of goods and ideas. The general locational model across sectors would look more and more like that characteristic of continuous flow industries such as petrochemicals, where firms are physically linked together by pipes carrying variegated flows of intermediates from plant site to plant site. But there are contradictory pressures at work since, in the current environment, firms also need to be in closer contact with their key geographical markets. The way these tensions present themselves can be seen most clearly in the context of the investment strategies of multinational firms.

The Multinational Firm, Time–Space Transformations, and Regional Development

The impulse to establish production facilities overseas has a number of sources. But underlying them are two fundamental issues: the limitations of any given national market, even one as large and rich as that of the US; and problems with the availability of appropriate factor supplies, especially labor, which in that case can be summarized as a problem of social relations and class power.

There is a considerable degree of indeterminacy and many contradictory pressures involved in the way these issues may be worked out in practice. Foreign investment isn't the only way of responding to these pressures, and even where it becomes the strategy, the choice of location is subject to additional tensions and trade-offs among conflicting goals and needs. I want to highlight here the particular question of where the investments will go, although in order to do that we need to understand some things about why they are made. What I will argue is that the current competitive environment, with its particular temporal and spatial imperatives, structures the way in which these trade-offs and tensions are resolved, with profound consequences for patterns of regional development.

The market limitations problem has two aspects. The first has to do with the capacity of the domestic economy to absorb the tremendous amount of capital accumulated through prior rounds of activity. This capital has to find profitable investment outlets, yet it is not obvious that it can all be plowed back into wherever it came from in the first place, without creating staggering overcapacity. But there are a number of options, and we have seen them all brought into play in recent decades, with some emerging more prominently at particular conjunctures. They include, for example, shifting capital into different sectors of activity (conglomeratization, finance and debt, property booms), creating new industries (computers and semiconductors), buying up competitors (mergers and acquisitions), and the like.

Investing in new geographical areas, in this context, is simply one more option, but a consistently important one whose significance has grown dramatically in recent years. Naturally, this is not a phenomenon limited to the US. In particular, as the European and Japanese economies expanded following their recovery from World War II, capital also began to flow outward from these areas in increasing volumes. (Dicken, 1992). More recently, firms in many of the so-called newly industrializing countries (NICs) have also begun investing abroad. Paradoxically (although not inexplicably), the US itself has become a major target for foreign direct investors (Glickman and Woodward, 1989; Schoenberger, 1985).[6]

This brings us to the second aspect of the market limitations problem, which revolves around the need to find consumers for all the output produced. Again, there are options: advertising to build on the perception of felt need; trying to expand market share domestically at the expense of competitors; technical or stylistic obsolescence to encourage rapid replacement of existing products; creating new products and, thereby, new markets; and so on. And again, trying to capture foreign markets is of significant and growing importance in this context. Other

---

[6] So-called direct investment is investment in actual operating entities such as manufacturing plants or subsidiaries controlled by the foreign parent. This is in contrast to purely financial flows, or portfolio-style investments in equity and debt instruments – flows which also increased dramatically during the 1980s.

questions come into play here, including the politics of market access (such as protectionism), the choice of which foreign markets to go after, and how they should be approached (whether through exports or through direct investments), but these will be considered below. Suffice it to say at this juncture that larger, richer markets are preferable to smaller, poorer ones.

The problem of appropriate factor supplies raises yet another set of issues. Even something as apparently straightforward as investments in raw materials production is complicated by relative price movements, changing technologies, and questions of political stability. Raw materials have to do something more than exist to count as economically accessible resources. But the key issue from the point of view of manufacturing direct investment turns on labor supplies.

Here we have to ask what, from the standpoint of the firm, makes any given labor supply in a particular place appropriate or inappropriate for investment. The cost of labor is one obvious indicator, although this is surprisingly hard to determine with accuracy. Area wage levels only take on meaning in the context of productivity levels, but aggregate productivity rates may not reveal much about what can be achieved in a particular factory. So, for example, productivity levels in general in Mexico are lower than in the US, but Ford's plant in Hermosillo is generally rated state-of-the-art in terms of productivity and quality of output (Shaiken and Herzenberg, 1987).

A second issue is the availability of specialist skills, where these are needed, or the feasibility and cost of training, and who is likely to bear the costs of that training (the state or the firm). Third are issues related to control and flexibility as well as who bears the costs of adjustment to changing circumstances (cf. G. Clark et al., 1986). What this all boils down to is rather simply stated: can the firm get workers to do what it wants them to do at an acceptable cost?

The great lure of geographically peripheral locations (for example, in developing countries) was supposed to be that workers were cheap, unorganized, and relatively unlikely to contest the wishes of management (cf. Frobel et al., 1980). But the theory of the new international division of labor (NIDL) is far too simple a solution to the problem described above. It skirts the issues of productivity and skill, for one thing, by assuming that the general tendency in manufacturing is progressive deskilling of the labor force. It also fails to notice that even in the heart of advanced industrial areas one can find or construct a labor force that meets many of the desired criteria even for unskilled labor, by hiring newcomers to the labor market (women, minorities) or importing foreign labor – not to mention the option of replacing labor altogether with advanced automation. Nor does this thesis reckon with the disciplining effects of the crisis on high-waged, unionized workers, who have shown themselves increasingly willing to renegotiate long-standing practices and understandings in the employment relation (see chapter 4).[7] And it underestimates the rate at which "traditions" of industrial militancy can be built up even in areas that have only recently industrialized. Motorola, for example, is not unionized in the United States, but it is in Korea.

In sum, we need to be wary about the precise role that labor plays in the industrial location calculus. A whole string of assumptions underlies the NIDL thesis, which sees manufacturing progressively decentralizing to low-cost, third world locations. This string includes the assumption that the problem of competitiveness reduces to costs, that labor costs are the main cost problem of the firm, that finding cheap labor is the only way to resolve a labor cost problem, and that "cheap" labor (taking productivity into account) can only be found in cheap places.

Still, we can't dismiss out of hand the importance of labor costs and labor market rigidities in influencing investment locations. The point is merely that this constitutes a rather complex issue that, moreover, has to be considered in light of the pressures having to do with markets and outlets for accumulated capital.

The ideal location for the multinational manufacturing firm would, arguably, have the following characteristics:

- The market would be large, rich, and growing fast.
- The levels of competition and existing capacity in that market would not be excessive.
- Labor would be readily available, reliable, docile, appropriately skilled, productive, and cheap.
- The political environment would be stable, open, and generally responsive to the needs of business (for instance, receptive to foreign investors, with low taxes, high services to business, and low regulation, and unlikely to change unexpectedly and dramatically).
- The quality of social, economic, technical, and physical infrastructure (such as education, the legal system, capital markets, the supply of highly qualified scientific and technical workers, and transportation and communications networks) would be high, but the cost to business of access to them would be low.

---

[7] By the same token, we should also take into account the effect of the crisis in disciplining the state and/or reducing the power of labor to maintain existing labor market protections. Consider, for example, the current debate in the European Union concerning the problem of labor market rigidities, despite the fact that some of the most onerous restrictions on, for example, hiring and firing have already been relaxed to some degree in such countries as France and Italy.

In the real world, as we know, the largest and richest markets are growing slowly and are burdened with excess capacity in many key industrial sectors. Labor in these areas is skilled and productive but expensive (that's why the markets are so rich) and may be relatively powerful. Similarly, even where the general political environment is business-friendly, the costs and regulations imposed by the state tend to be relatively high. On the other hand, the infrastructure supporting production in rich markets, though frequently in need of expensive maintenance and improvement, is comparatively good.

Clearly, some trade-offs need to be made, but which ones, why, and to what effect? For American manufacturing multinationals, the trade-offs have been made fairly consistently in favor of markets throughout the postwar period. Table 3.1 shows the proportion of US manufacturing investment overseas that was directed to developed industrial nations vs. less developed countries between 1954 and 1994. A number of points are worth highlighting.

Table 3.1   US manufacturing direct investment abroad, 1954–94

	Total ($mil)	Percent distribution	Percent change
1954	5,899	100.0	
DCs	4,567	77.4	
LDCs	1,332	22.6	
1964	16,935	100.0	
DCs	14,045	83.0	
LDCs	2,890	17.0	
1974	51,172	100.0	
DCs	41,973	82.0	
LDCs	9,200	18.0	
1984	93,012	100.0	
DCs	71,898	77.3	
LDCs	21,114	22.7	
1994	220,328	100.0	
DCs	168,992	76.7	
LDCs	51,336	23.3	
1954–64			187
1964–74			202
1974–84			82
1984–94			137

DCs = Developed countries.
LDCs = Less developed countries.
Source: *Survey of Current Business*, various issues

First is that for the period as a whole, the bulk of manufacturing investment – anywhere from three-fourths to four-fifths – went to other developed countries. Second, as the NIDL theory predicts, the share of less developed countries grew in the two decades following 1974, from 18 percent to 23 percent. However, this is by no means a drastic reversal of historical patterns, particularly when one takes into account that the position overall grew by 331 percent in those twenty years. Clearly, there was ample room for a wholesale geographical reallocation of investment that did not occur.

We can also note that the decade 1974–84, when the crisis was most acute, was a period in which the overall growth rate of the position slowed dramatically. This was the time when, it was supposed, manufacturers were racing for the exits, desperate to find cheap labor sources. But we should recall that it was also the period when many manufacturers were preoccupied with reducing and rationalizing existing capacity and had neither the need nor the resources for capacity expansion elsewhere.

Finally, it seems particularly striking that the increasing share of investment going to less developed countries from 1974 to 1994 was roughly enough to restore them to the level they had already attained in 1954. This is not, then, a simple picture of gradual and steady dispersal of investment to cheap-labor areas.

Table 3.2 provides a more detailed breakdown by country of the flow of US foreign manufacturing investment between 1984 and 1994. Here we can see that the biggest "loser" over this decade was Canada, whose share of the total fell from 23 percent to just under 16 percent. Latin America also declined by nearly 3 percent. The gains from this reallocation accrued to the European Union and Japan (each rising by 2.8 percent) and the Asia–Pacific region outside of Japan (up 4.7 percent).

Within these broad regional breakdowns, moreover, much of the investment tended to concentrate in relatively expensive and highly regulated locations. In the European Union, for example, the four largest recipients in 1994 were France, Germany, the Netherlands, and the UK, together accounting for 72 percent of the EU's total. Labor rates in the UK, which received over a fourth of this investment, may be low by Northern European standards, but then so are its aggregate productivity rates. As a consequence, unit labor costs may not be overwhelmingly favorable (although again, one would have to consider what goes on in individual plants). In Germany, which had nearly 22 percent of total EU investment, productivity is high, but so too are wages and social overhead costs, while labor retains what is, by American standards, an extraordinarily (one might think unacceptably) high degree of influence in management decision-making. The lure of the market seems to outweigh these defects.

In the meantime, the share of US manufacturing investment that did flow to the less developed areas was highly concentrated geographically. Just five countries – Brazil, Mexico, Hong Kong, Singapore, and Taiwan – accounted for 66 percent of the total going to the LDCs. Brazil and Mexico began liberalizing their markets in the 1980s; prior to that, market access was heavily dependent on a willingness to invest in local production. The net effect of this historic shift was a slight loss of share in Brazil and a small gain for Mexico.

I am here talking about shares, of course, rather than absolute amounts. In fact, during this time, the position in Mexico increased by 168 percent while Brazil's grew by 109 percent. But these gains did not represent a significant shift in their favor.

On the whole, if cheaper were always better, one would expect to see a different investment pattern: less concentrated geographically, because concentration itself tends to increase costs, and with a more substantial shift from high- to low-cost areas in general. Instead, high incomes, high growth rates, and proximity to suppliers and customers seem to most strongly influence the overall picture.

The US pattern of manufacturing direct investment is generally echoed by total global flows (Dicken, 1992). The principal exception has been Japan, which concentrated its outward investment in neighboring developing regions before turning more seriously to the US and Western Europe, starting in the late 1970s and early 1980s. And, as we have seen, the US itself became a major host for inward investment during the 1980s.

The very consistency of this data is striking. Through good times and bad, although the volume of investment may rise and fall, it goes to the same, expensive places. In the 1960s, when US firms easily dominated the world economy, in the 1970s when they were thrown into crisis, and in the 1980s, as they struggled to transform themselves, they scarcely deviated from their beaten path.

This could all, of course, have simply been a horrible mistake – yet another sign of the obtuseness of American managers, who didn't read or didn't understand the implications of the new theories of international location. Or there could be a valid, although shifting, logic underlying this consistency.

This logic might go something as follows. In the 1950s and 1960s, the dominance of American firms in the international economy was still largely unchallenged. Finding outlets for capital and gaining or securing access to relatively wealthy markets were much more important issues than finding cheap labor. For one thing, price competition was relatively muted in this era, so the motivation for relentlessly compressing wages was small. For another, the main arena for unit cost savings was

Table 3.2 United States foreign direct investment in manufacturing 1984 and 1994 (historical cost basis)

	1984 amount ($mil)	Percent distribution[a]	1994 amount ($mil)	Percent distribution[a]
Total	93,012	100.0	220,328	100.0
Canada	21,467	23.1	35,037	15.9
Europe	**43,661**	**46.9**	**108,855**	**49.4**
EU[b]	39,935	43.0	101,009	45.8
France	4,187	4.5	14,521	6.6
Germany	9,362	10.1	22,131	10.1
Ireland	3,691	4.0	5,766	2.6
Italy	3,264	3.5	8,582	3.9
Netherlands	3,347	3.6	8,908	4.0
Spain	n.a.	–	4,512	2.1
UK	12,654	13.6	27,247	12.4
Other EU	3,430	3.7	9,342	4.2
Other	3,726	4.0	7,846	3.6
Latin America	**15,665**	**16.8**	**30,844**	**14.0**
Brazil	6,544	7.0	13,681	6.2
Mexico	3,988	4.3	10,697	4.9
Other	5,133	5.5	6,466	2.9

Asia and Pacific	10,567	11.4	41,577	18.9
Australia	2,540	2.7	8,002	3.6
China	n.a.	–	765	0.4
Hong Kong	629	0.7	1,902	0.9
Japan	4,120	4.4	15,844	7.2
Malaysia	370	0.4	1,582	0.7
New Zealand	193	0.2	1,274	0.6
Philippines	443	0.5	1,167	0.5
Singapore	1,013	1.1	5,316	2.4
South Korea	211	0.2	1,391	0.6
Taiwan	464	0.5	2,459	1.1
Thailand	n.a.	–	1,341	0.6
Other	584	0.6	534	0.2
Eastern Europe	n.a.	–	1,041	0.5
Other	1,652	1.8	2,974	1.4

[a]Totals may not add due to rounding.
[b]European Union, 1994 members.
Source: Survey of Current Business, various issues

derived from scale economies rather than labor rates. This latter factor also tends to produce a preference for large markets rather than inexpensive factor supplies.

Not by coincidence, the late 1960s and early 1970s was the period in which the influential theory of oligopolistic or ownership advantages as the driving factor behind multinational investments was elaborated (Hymer, 1976; Caves, 1971, 1974; Dunning, 1981).[8] The theory proposed that multinationals could, essentially, outcompete local firms in foreign markets due to certain superior capabilities related to proprietary technology, access to capital, management skills, and the like. If anything, the main competitive threat came from other multinationals that might get there first (cf. Knickerbocker, 1973). Firms moved production abroad in order to capitalize on these advantages and secure a larger share of the target market than could, presumably, be guaranteed by exports.

In this kind of a world, the general spatial tendency should be progressive expansion – widening the net of geographical emplacements to capture more and more of the growing world market. This was especially advisable given the political sensitivities involved. Even in advanced industrial countries, considerable anxiety was provoked by the specter of national markets being flooded by American goods. Producing and employing locally offered some degree of political cover. Good corporate citizenship implied trying to look as much like a local firm as possible.

In the decade or so following 1973, this rosy picture changed dramatically. Markets stagnated, competition from technically competent and capital-rich foreign firms increased, and costs became a more pressing issue. The influential theory of the new international division of labor emerged amid successive waves of capacity cutbacks in the old industrial cores of the US and Western Europe (Frobel et al., 1980; cf. also Lipietz, 1982; Vernon, 1966). The NIDL would, it was thought, mark a wholesale shift of manufacturing investment and employment to peripheral regions of the global economy, with output exported back to the center. The logic behind the theory seemed impeccable. Firms had the capacity to do this, they could economize enormously on wages and social overhead costs, and they could escape the rigidities of labor

---

[8] One might also include here the product cycle theory, which supposed that the first round of outward investment would flow to key export markets before drifting progressively toward cheaper factor supply regions (Vernon, 1966). Theories that highlight the multinational's ability to internalize transactions in the face of market imperfections also suggest a strong incentive to locate in major foreign markets (cf. Teece, 1981; Buckley and Casson, 1979).

markets and labor practices that had been built up in the core regions over decades of industrial experience; in short, why not?

The answer is complicated, because, of course, firms did pursue this strategy to some degree and in different ways including, for example, subcontracting to offshore firms rather than direct investment. The $1.2 billion average annual outflow of manufacturing investment from the US to developing countries from 1974 to 1984 is not a trivial sum – and certainly not insignificant to those places in which it tended to concentrate. There is, moreover, evidence that the investments which were made in low-labor-cost areas tended to be more labor-intensive than investments in the industrial core.[9] On the other hand, many of them were also driven by the problem of gaining access to markets protected under import-substitution regimes – especially in key Latin American markets such as Mexico, Argentina, and Brazil. We might recall also here that the threat of moving to low-cost export platform areas was used as a negotiating weapon in concession bargaining in the industrial core, increasingly as the decade of the 1970s wore on (cf. Kochan et al., 1986; Bluestone and Harrison, 1982; G. Clark, 1989). So in practice, the importance of the kind of spatial flexibility implied in the NIDL view of the world was quite real.

It remains the case, however, that the share of total manufacturing investments going to low-labor-cost countries was relatively small and remained so, even as the apparent need for cheap labor was weighing more heavily on the firms involved. In retrospect, this is not so hard to understand. In a world of stagnating markets, overcapacity, and increasing competition, the fight for market share becomes all-important. There are powerful incentives, including psychological ones, to sit in the market and defend it rather than abandoning the field and, perhaps, missing out on important information. As uncertainty increases, the need to be close to the action grows. Ironically, where foreign investment once seemed an exercise of undisputed strength, it becomes a response to an increasingly contested competitive environment.

At the same time, investments in this environment are made more with a view toward increasing efficiency and reducing labor content (capital deepening) rather than expanding capacity (capital widening). So the impulse to gradually spread out over the globe receives a further check.

[9] This probably derives from two rather different sources: investments in sectors where, given the technological possibilities at the time, labor costs tended to be an important share of total costs (such as semiconductor assembly and textiles), or where the investments were actually too small to yield maximally available economies of scale. But this latter factor would suggest that many of these investments were made with a view to market access in these areas.

In this way, between two strong but contradictory incentives – toward the market and toward low-cost locations – the market proved, on the whole, stronger. Even as their cost profiles and profit margins deteriorated, firms remained committed to high-cost regions.

As we move into the 1980s and the era of full-fledged time-based competition, the ties to markets, whether industrial or consumer, are reinforced. The cement is the implied guarantee involved in entering into time-based relationships with buyers. The guarantee bears on rapid response in the first instance, but it must also increasingly promise consistency of response over the long run as relationships between buyers and suppliers become more complex and technically sophisticated. The guarantee is signaled by the commitment of resources to production in the market. In my conversations with people who run multinational firms, the word "presence" was repeatedly (indeed, almost invariably) invoked to characterize this market pull. What is meant is a kind of public display of one's commitment to the market over the long run, a commitment that is made more credible in proportion to the magnitude and technical sophistication of the investment (Schoenberger, 1990).

Presence can be bought in various ways that fall short of actual production: having one's own sales and service operation instead of relying on independent distributors, for example, or establishing a technical center that may even do some R&D for local applications. These kinds of activity gain in importance to the degree that service and training packages are an essential part of any hardware purchase. They can also serve as listening posts, relaying current information about the market back to headquarters.

The strongest guarantee, however, is offered by the presence of manufacturing at the market, backed up by the kind of technical competence and depth that ensures the firm is able to respond to changing local demands. As firms downstream in the production chain come under increasing pressure to diversify and increase the pace at which they turn over their product lines, these requirements percolate through the hierarchy of suppliers, tying everyone to the same frantic schedule and to the same places.

What has changed since the 1960s and even the 1970s is that firms can no longer proliferate investments to a steadily growing assortment of individual country markets, expanding their presence and buying important political cover along the way. Conditions then allowed – indeed promoted – spreading out as much as possible, locating discrete pieces of the manufacturing chain in different places, the whole knit together by the continual movement of standardized parts across the landscape. Under the new conditions of time-based competition, the incentives to cluster spatially become more pronounced, across and within firms. This tendency is reinforced by persistent overcapacity problems, which are forcing cutbacks and reconcentration onto a smaller physical base in a variety of sectors (such as steel, autos, computers, and commodity chemicals). To this may be added the impact of more sophisticated automation techniques, which greatly reduce waste and increase the rate of throughput, allowing more output to be produced from any given physical plant.

A further source of spatial consolidation of production derives from the rapid pace of technological change in products, qualified by the uncertainty inherently involved in predicting the precise rate at which new products will be brought on line to replace older generations. Under these circumstances, the logic behind a product cycle-type strategy of shifting older products to peripheral production locations while retaining newer ones in the core is progressively attenuated. With more flexible process technologies, older products can be coproduced with newer ones, thus ensuring better capacity utilization rates in the face of expected volatility in demand for newer or niche products (see Schoenberger, 1989a, 1990).[10]

What these tendencies imply is a kind of shrinking back onto a more consolidated production base which must, nevertheless, remain international. Firms have to juggle deeply conflicting issues of market size, market growth rates, the politics of market access, the logistic and relational commitments of time-based competition, and cost control, while making long-lived investments in a world whose short-run dynamics are increasingly turbulent. How might these often-competing factors be negotiated?

The answer, I think, is a kind of concentrated deconcentration organized around geographically coherent, multinational market regions. I want to sketch here a stylized version of the scenario to get a clearer fix on its characteristics, before offering some necessary qualifications.

Industrial location and regional change

From the point of view of the multinational firm, the goal would be to create, together with its most important suppliers, one rather tightly integrated production complex in each of its primary target market

---

[10] It is worth stressing that while much attention in the academic literature has shifted to economies of scope (cf. Piore and Sabel, 1984; A. Scott, 1988), the people who run businesses continue, in my experience, to be heavily preoccupied with economies of scale. Flexible technologies may be used to produce a range of products, but the aggregate volume across product configurations must be high enough to justify the very high cost of the equipment. Coproducing older and newer products on the same line is a vital way of stabilizing output volumes at the necessary levels.

regions. The complex would include a broad array of manufacturing activities, but also some degree of technical and strategic responsibility given the necessity of responding to the particularities of the market. The market regions would include, for example, North America (Canada, the US, and Mexico), the European Union together with its eastern and Mediterranean fringes, the Southern Cone of South America, East Asia, Southeast Asia, and, depending on how things turn out, South Asia, the former Soviet Union, and, at the limit, Southern Africa. Not every firm, of course, would necessarily target all regions.

If every lead firm and its suppliers settled in an independent location, this would still allow for considerable spatial spread over all such complexes. But because final output producers, within and across sectors, often share key suppliers, the tendency toward spatial concentration may embrace a fairly broad array of firms and activities. In this way, one can foresee the reconstitution of something resembling the dense industrial arcs, occupying a consolidated swathe of territory, that characterized the traditional mass production industrial heartlands centered on the Great Lakes in the US and the Midlands through the Ruhr in Northwestern Europe. There is no guarantee, however, that these new industrial heartlands will be reconstituted precisely on the sites of the old.

From the point of view of regions, this scenario implies a rather particular sorting out of the industrial landscape.[11] The new industrial heartlands, not surprisingly, are in the most enviable position. They host an assortment of interlinked firms, diversified as to sector, size, and occupational requirements. The prospects for continued growth are good, as any given investment entrains complementary commitments by related firms. The prospects for stability of the investment base over time are excellent, since the increasingly dense web of cross-commitments reduces the footlooseness of any given firm. In effect, industrial complexes must move as a whole if they are to move at all, which seems, at a guess, unlikely.

On the downside, if something does go wrong, the negative effects may also reverberate rapidly, perhaps catastrophically, through the complex. One can foresee, for example, intense place-based competition within a broad industrial region as various pieces of the whole, centered on competing lead firms, vie for supremacy or, at least, the right to

---

[11] Regional economies, of course, are not constituted solely by multinational firms. Implicit in the argument to follow, however, is that they do stand in a dominant position in individual sectors (in terms of output, assets and employment), and that their influence over the behavior and prospects of other firms is strengthened by the increasing complexity and depth of the new style of inter-firm relations.

exist. Places more closely tied to GM, for example, may be at risk compared to places dominated by Toyota, and so on.

Further, to the degree that lead firms and their key suppliers move together, replicating their relationships in the various cores, already existing firms in a region may find themselves marginalized. Given the intensity of effort needed to construct and sustain more collaborative buyer–supplier relations, there are probably limits to the extent to which these can be proliferated with new sets of local firms. The latter may be incorporated into the complex as subordinate suppliers, but are less likely to enjoy the benefits of membership in the operational core, although they are located in the geographic core.

Finally, it is important to understand that membership in the new industrial heartland does not solve all social and economic problems. One of the reasons that production can cluster in high-labor-cost areas is that so little labor is involved, given current automation technology.[12] Direct labor costs as a proportion of total manufacturing costs, and even more as a proportion of total sell costs, are becoming progressively smaller. In interviews with many corporate executives, words such as "minuscule" and "irrelevant" were repeatedly used (see Schoenberger, 1989a, 1990). This means that there continue to be strong processes of exclusion at work that will affect large numbers of people no matter where they live. As Emily Martin argues in her book *Flexible Bodies*, the criteria defining who is an acceptable (that is, sufficiently flexible) worker and who is not are becoming more rigorous and selective in the new competitive environment (E. Martin, 1994).

A second type of region may constitute what could be called the new semi-periphery. What distinguishes the new from the old in this case is that the semi-periphery will now have a particular geographical identity: it must be located adjacent to the new industrial heartland. This requirement is driven by the pressures of time-based competition and, more specifically, just-in-time production. The new semi-periphery will host the less qualified, more standardized, and more input-cost-sensitive segments of the production chain. But the output of these operations must be able to flow smoothly and uninterruptedly to their respective industrial cores.

What sort of development trajectory does the status of semi-periphery imply? It seems likely that the dominant linkage structure (bearing on the flow of goods, services, information, and profits) will be

---

[12] For an interesting analysis of the relative roles of trade and automation as the source of unemployment in core industrial nations, see A. Wood, 1991, who shows that job loss associated with automation vastly outweighs that which can be attributed to imports from low-cost countries.

externalized, tying individual plants to operations in the new industrial heartland rather than densely to one another within the region. It also seems probable that the kinds of occupational and income structure produced will be relatively truncated, except where (as in parts of the former Eastern Bloc) low-cost (but well-paid by local standards) supplies of technical and scientific labor can be mobilized. And, since available locations in the semi-periphery are numerous, there is certain to be considerable competition between places for investment, reinforcing the pressures to keep costs low and regulatory regimes accommodating (witness the fears of countries on the periphery of the EU with respect to Eastern Europe).

The eligibility requirements for membership in the semi-periphery are actually rather stringent and in certain respects contradictory. Besides being in the right location, these places must be, in effect, hybrids of developed and developing economies. They will need to offer low wages and relatively unfettered labor markets, but literate, reliable, and trainable labor forces, as workers may be operating quite advanced machinery to close tolerances and an unforgiving schedule. They will need well-functioning and reliable physical infrastructures (transport and communications) and clarity and stability of the institutional and political environment (no questions, for example, about the status of private property in general or foreign-owned property in particular). It will be a further advantage if they can be viewed as potentially important growth markets in their own right, although this requirement coexists uneasily with the preference for low wages.

Thus Mexico, for example, or parts of Southern Europe, may be formally in the core by virtue of their trade status (in NAFTA and the EU), but functionally semi-peripheral. And then there is Eastern Europe. Here we find a relatively cheap yet educated and skilled labor force, but one which needs to be rather suddenly adapted to new styles of work and work discipline and a new labor-market regime (cf. Dunn, forthcoming). At the same time, the infrastructure is inadequate while the institutional and political environment is, for the most part, still shaky. Further, the market potential, despite early enthusiasm, is still in doubt. The kinds of change that would make Eastern Europe "safe" for really large-scale investment – opening core markets to its exports, massive support for infrastructure development, and employment and incomes stabilization, etc. – have yet to materialize solidly.

The case of Eastern Europe strikingly illustrates the tension between maintaining a low-cost labor reserve and expanding markets for output that bedevils capitalist development processes. But it is not unique in this respect. The whole category of semi-periphery is produced through this tension.

However large the territory embraced by the new industrial heartland and the new semi-periphery, there is still much more left over which unavoidably remains peripheral to these development processes. The difference between the old periphery and the new one is simply this: that the processes by which these territories are excluded from the general sweep of development are stronger and more rigorous.

In a NIDL kind of world, the presumption was that manufacturing investment would gradually (or even rapidly) trickle ever outward, tying these regions more closely to the core. This was by no means the gateway to a glorious future, as the kinds of occupation and income produced through this investment were acknowledged to be severely limited. But it was better than nothing. Now even this unenviable and unstable future seems even further out of reach. Neither markets in their own right, nor close enough to the action to be reliable production sites, peripheral regions have little to sell in the new competitive environment. Only the most desperate investors, who can devise no better strategy than squeezing labor costs to the vanishing point in the hopes of hanging on to small fragments of the market, will look to these most desperate places.

This is the scenario in broad outline. It is a logical construct that is driven by the dynamics that seem to be most powerfully entrained by the new competitive environment and the new round of time–space transformation. The symptoms, as it were, of these changes can be detected in a wildly diverse range of industrial activities: steel (most notably mini-mills), chemicals (witness the strong shift since the early 1980s out of commodity chemicals to specialty chemicals of various descriptions), textiles and apparel, semiconductors, computers, automobiles, consumer electronics, lighting fixtures, white goods, and machine tools, to name a few. But of course these tendencies, powerful as they are, cannot simply be inscribed on the industrial landscape as though on a blank slate.

There is, first of all, the legacy of existing fixed capital and its geographical character. While firms have given every indication that they can write off plant and equipment wholesale when necessary, the kinds of adjustment required to achieve this scenario in its pure form would be monumental. So the scenario must be qualified by compromise, both on the target configuration, and on how fast even that is attained.[13]

We need also to reckon with the possibility that a reconsolidation of industrial structures in certain industries will attenuate the pressures for these kinds of change (cf. Harrison, 1994). Some combination of mergers, failures, and strong collaborations might yet allow the competitive

[13] For a thoughtful treatment of these issues, see Mair, 1991.

environment to be restabilized under the leadership of a few dominant firms. There is probably no going back to the conditions of standardized mass production, but one could imagine a significant relaxation of the intense temporal pressures produced by the current competitive regime.

The main thing one can't foresee, of course, is how people will react to these processes and dynamics and whether the strength of their reaction will be sufficient to force development paths onto different trajectories. Perhaps a vigorous entrepreneurial class will emerge in unexpected places to challenge the dominance of core firms. Perhaps political shifts will allow states to intervene in more effective ways to protect those who are disadvantaged by these processes and to alter the terms on which investment can take place. Perhaps broadly based social movements will emerge to challenge the practices and understandings associated with the tendencies described here. It is safe to say that these transformations will be played out through an engagement with complex and powerful socio-cultural forces that must unavoidably leave their mark on the outcome.

Conclusion

The upheaval in the competitive environment and the associated round of time–space transformation has had profound implications for the organization of production systems, the chances for survival of individual firms, and the life prospects of different regions in the global economy. The kinds of change described here do not produce a unique and determinate outcome, but they do shift the balance of constraints and possibilities within which firms operate, creating pressures which guide the choice of options that firms are likely to adopt, and shifting the whole system onto a new trajectory. If the outlines of that trajectory remain fuzzy, it is nevertheless distinct from that characteristic of mass production.

One thing that is clear, though, is that the new trajectory, like the old, will produce highly uneven social and spatial outcomes. Some places and groups of people will thrive under the new regime, while others will be excluded.

This is a very old story under capitalism, and it might not seem worth retelling except that the processes of inclusion and exclusion implied by the new trajectory are historically specific. The way these processes work now and the kinds of outcome they will produce are different from the way they worked in the past. For this reason, it is important to get a fix on their underlying dynamics. What I have tried to show in this chapter is that understanding how the categories of competition, time, and space have been transformed provides a crucial vantage point from which to assess the emerging reconstitution of the social and industrial landscape.

These categories of competition, time, and space are generally viewed as natural and stable: we all know what they are, and their meaning is unchanging. Here I have tried to show instead that they have very specific meanings in different historical periods and that this historical content produces very powerful dynamics influencing how the industrial system as a whole operates. They are intimately and profoundly bound up with a whole range of material practices, social relations, and understandings. In short, they are very deeply a part of what we can call corporate and industrial cultures.

As the specific historical content and meaning of these categories changes, so too does this ensemble of practices, relations, and understandings – this culture. We have seen examples of this in the new practices related to product development and just-in-time production, in the pressures favoring the development of more knowledgeable and autonomous workers, and in new understandings about how markets work and the firm's position in them.

It is precisely the all-embracing nature of these transformations, involving not only how we do things, but how we understand what we do, that makes them so monumentally challenging. Two decades into these transformative processes, many firms are still struggling to adapt successfully. We need to understand better the real dynamics of this struggle.

4

The Sources of Industrial Rigidity

Introduction

One of the legacies of product cycle theory that was more difficult to shake was the notion that we could afford to let go of entire industrial sectors as they matured and, more or less "naturally," migrated to other areas of the globe. The compensation for this loss, it was supposed, would be the continual generation of new products and industries in the wealthiest and most technically advanced countries or regions (cf. Vernon, 1966). On this calculation, it was acceptable to lose, say, the textile industry if it was replaced by household electrical goods, and their loss could be tolerated if you could be sure of moving into microchips and computers. The enthusiasts of post-industrial society could even contemplate with equanimity the loss of manufacturing as a whole, confidently anticipating a clean, white-collar future organized around the production and exchange of services (Lawrence, 1984).

There are a number of strong objections to this view (see, in particular, Storper, 1985). We know, for example, that much of what passes for services employment grows out of manufacturing and is about servicing manufacturing activities. If manufacturing collapsed, services would not be far behind (Walker, 1985; Cohen and Zysman, 1987). When individual industries are viewed in the context of their manifold linkages to other sectors, the prospect of any one of them disappearing is less comfortably tolerated, as the loss of one sector turns out to put many others at risk. Thus, steel, machine tools, or automobiles may attain the status of protected "strategic" sectors and are effectively exempted from the rules of this particular game, although the criteria for exemption tend rapidly to become fuzzy.

More immediately pressing was the discovery that the new industries that did grow up did not compensate for the employment losses of the old. Steel and automobiles were losing jobs at a faster rate than computers and semiconductors were generating them, and the workers rationalized out of the old sectors were rarely absorbed into the new, which tended to rely on different categories of worker (scientists and technicians, women and immigrants). Further, the new jobs tended not to be created in the same places that were experiencing sizable employment loss, so on a local level, the presumption of regeneration was frequently short-circuited. The consequence of the loss of a whole stratum of well-paid, reasonably secure blue-collar employment in these mature industries was social polarization and the overt blocking of the promise of upward mobility through the ranks of industrial labor (Harrison and Bluestone, 1988; Mishel and Bernstein, 1994).

A further threat to the integrity of this virtuous scenario was the fact that there began to be many more competitors for the leading edge of the product cycle. If, in the 1950s and 1960s, the US could confidently expect to be the site for the generation of entire new industries, by the 1980s its vanguard status was increasingly called into question. This perception usually took the form of the exasperated complaint that the technologies the US invented were commercialized by the Japanese, so the focus was on the apparent bottlenecks that derailed the progress from invention to innovation. The paradigmatic example was the VCR, although upon closer examination it seems clear that what the US invented (and successfully commercialized) was expensive and complex video technology for the broadcast market, while the Japanese focused their attention concertedly (and successfully) on developing the technology for home use (Rosenbloom and Cusumano, 1988).

At the same time, production costs in the US were too high to securely hold any other place in the product cycle. If the US could be neither the (unchallenged) vanguard nor the lagger, where was it? Increasingly, the answer seemed to be, "nowhere."

To add theoretical confusion to practical gloom, it also eventually became apparent that the category of mature industry in the product cycle was unstable. A car might still be a car, but the way the industry worked entered a period of drastic upheaval and turmoil, prompting some to speak of its "de-maturity" (Abernathy et al., 1984). If an old product couldn't be relied upon to stay old, then the ways industries change needed to be rethought.

For all these reasons, then, and despite the fact that much popular and scholarly attention has focused on the issue of new product technologies and new industries, the more pressing question arguably concerns the circumstances under which old firms in old industries can renovate themselves. Since most regions cannot expect to give birth to wholly new sectors based on emerging technologies, their fates necessarily hinge on the capacity for transformation of existing firms and industries.

What would this transformation entail? Certainly it involves altering the technology and organization of production processes and thus the use of labor on the shop floor. This has been the subject of considerable research seeking to evaluate the degree to which new technologies (CNC machine tools, robots and other forms of programmable automation) are being integrated into production across a wide range of sectors, and with what effects on the labor process, skills mix, and labor relations in the firm (cf. Rees et al., 1985; Thwaites and Oakey, 1985; Kelley, 1990; Kelley and Brooks, 1991; S. Wood, 1989; Gertler, 1993). But if the previous analysis has been at all persuasive, it should be clear that the adoption of "best-practice" manufacturing techniques (such as "lean production") is not, by itself, sufficient.

To put this another way, it should be clear that the categories of productivity and competitiveness are not identical, although they have long been treated as though they were. In that reading, the firms or regions with the highest productivity levels and the lowest costs would prevail in the market – end of story. If that was ever true, it is no longer. In the case of the United States, it is not hard to show that the country still enjoys a productivity advantage in the mass production of many standardized goods (*Financial Times*, 1993; McKinsey Global Institute, 1993). The problem is that it is not easy to sell them to anyone. Real competitiveness in international markets requires something more than good productivity statistics.

In fact, the profound rationalization and restructuring of major industries that occurred in the 1970s and 1980s achieved many of its desired effects. Excess capacity was shed, the labor content of goods progressively diminished, and the breakeven point in production lowered. Following on the shrinkage of direct labor requirements, the next target for drastic cutbacks became the vast ranks of white-collar indirect labor, especially middle management as organizational structures within the firm were overhauled. Allied with exchange-rate shifts, these changes contributed significantly to shoring up the competitive position of many firms and industries, in the US market and abroad. Still, one can hardly conclude from this that the problem of industrial competitiveness in the US has been solved. The transformation is incomplete.

I want to propose in what follows that this transformation requires new ways of thinking as well as new ways of working. This puts me in an awkward position, since work practices can be observed and measured while thinking is inherently difficult to assess. Moreover, the thinking in which I am interested is not what could be called instrumental – thinking about what to do – but reflective – thinking about what to be. What I hope to show is that examining corporate strategic behavior through the lens of this reflective thinking (which I will want to link with the idea of corporate culture, although in a somewhat different sense from the way it is usually employed) will help us to understand some of the deeper and more intractable problems of corporate and industrial transformation.

First, however, it will be helpful to consider some of the available explanations of industrial rigidity. These tend to focus on what could be called structural causes of rigidity – that is to say, those causes that are produced more or less automatically by the workings of the economy, of complex organizations, or of society as a whole, rather than by the (miscalculated) discretionary choices of actual historical individuals. There are two reasons for reviewing them here. The first is that they are good explanations. They do in fact advance our understanding considerably. But I also want to show that, even if they are taken together, there is still, in effect, an unexplained residual that requires investigation. This residual, I will argue, has much to do with a particular notion of corporate culture and identity that will be elaborated in subsequent chapters.

Any review of a complex debate such as this one is bound to insist on distinguishing with excessive precision among categories that, in practice, overlap a good deal. With this caveat in mind, the effort here will be to isolate the fundamental assumptions motivating each type of analysis to better understand what they are able to explain and what they cannot account for. Rather than attempting a detailed literature review that acknowledges all possible permutations of the discussion, the focus will be on broad problem areas.

Bureaucratic Impediments to Change

The rise of the modern corporation was characterized by a previously unknown scale and diversity of operations and by the need to work out new managerial forms to guide and coordinate this increasingly complex entity (Chandler, 1962, 1977). Management itself became a specialized activity, subject to an increasingly refined division of labor involving strategic decision-making, planning, coordinating, and monitoring the activities of others – including other managers. In short, firms became bureaucratized, exhibiting all the strengths and weaknesses of the type.

Organizational sociologists are widely agreed that bureaucracies are very efficient in handling routine tasks in a stable environment. Routine and stability are the necessary underpinnings for a well-defined and enduring division of labor that, in turn, allows the bureaucratic machine to operate more or less automatically, according to known rules (cf. Perrow, 1986; DiMiaggio and Powell, 1991).

Bureaucracies are thought to handle change badly in two senses. First, they are inefficient in the face of a turbulent environment, being unable to accommodate the need for rapid and continual change by virtue of their structure. The division of labor that is so effective in carrying out a known and stable set of tasks is thrown into disarray if the tasks are constantly changing. The extreme compartmentalization of information characteristic of an advanced division of labor undermines the organization's ability to recognize and respond to significant disruptions that do not present themselves in the established categories. Often the left hand truly does not know what the right hand is doing, so the organization can end up working at cross-purposes with itself.

Second, bureaucracies are inevitably political arenas in which the occupants of each box on the organization chart will struggle against all the others to preserve and, if possible, to expand their own turf. Changes that threaten the box's existence or the career path of its occupant will be fiercely resisted. In this sense, the incentives to the people inhabiting the organization may eventually run counter to the organization's interests, often by blocking much-needed, even necessary change. This is most obvious in the case of a complete political stalemate in which the organization as a whole is held hostage to its parts. But even if one part of the organization manages to mobilize enough power to break the stalemate, we cannot be sure what interests are advanced thereby.

If we ask what allowed the bureaucratic corporation to flourish for so long in the United States, the answer, *contra* Chandler, must include market power, since it was this that stabilized the competitive environment. In the current, turbulent environment, all the pathologies of bureaucracies come to the fore (cf. Kanter, 1983). Firms are inhibited from adapting since they cannot take sufficiently radical (non-routine) decisions, or cannot implement these, once made, in the spirit of the decision (that is, against the resistance of the bureaucratic structure itself). In this way, an organizational form that was once itself an impressive innovation becomes the chief obstacle to further innovation.

It would be foolish to ignore the rigidities that can easily become entrenched in real organizational life. But this argument translates so easily into a view of large firms as dinosaurs that some reconsideration seems necessary. Large Japanese firms, to cite one obvious example, do not seem in imminent danger of extinction. This could be a function of their own market power (which stabilizes their environment, although no one else's), but this then begs the question of how they attained their position. Since the answer seems to have much to do with their rapid response to changing markets, the issue remains open (cf. McMillan, 1984; Dore, 1985; Fruin, 1992).

There are a number of ways of re-examining the assumptions underlying this general argument. One could ask, for example, whether bureaucracies must inevitably be confounded by the need for change, given their structure. The answer is yes only if the demarcations that define the specialized division of labor are both absolutely impermeable and inherently unchangeable. If these two conditions hold, then the various pieces of information held by different parts of the organization can never be recombined in new ways, and the organization cannot take account of new kinds of information that do not fit the predetermined categories. The informational stalemate, in this context, is what generates the organization's inability to handle non-routine tasks well.

This sort of stalemate may be tendentially characteristic of bureaucracies, but there are, at the least, some interesting counter-tendencies available. One is the possibility of developing routines for handling the non-routine that specifically hinge on recombining pieces of the structure as the need arises. "Skunkworks" – where a multidisciplinary crash project group is isolated from the rest of the firm while it focuses on its task – are an example, as are the new methods for rapid product development described earlier (concurrent engineering and the like). As the pieces are recombined, information flows across task boundaries in new ways, thus breaking the first element of the stalemate.

But how, short of the sort of imminent catastrophe which even the most fossilized bureaucracy would be hard pressed to overlook, would the organization know the need had arisen to mobilize its routines for non-routine work? Here one needs to look for evidence that the organization can develop mechanisms for gathering and processing this sort of information in a timely way. The mechanisms can include developing new parts of the organization whose task this is. As Stinchcombe notes, if the organization waits for the information to arrive in the form of price signals in the market, it is probably already too late (Stinchcombe, 1990).

Perhaps the best way of exemplifying this argument is by rearranging Stinchcombe's analysis of different kinds of management information system (at the Norwegian State Oil Company and elsewhere) as a virtual longitudinal process, encompassing project design through long-term operations (see Stinchcombe, 1990:ch. 3). The starting point is that the people involved in these various activities need very different kinds of information in different forms in order to do their jobs at all.

The initial authorization to undertake the project, for example, will depend on comparative cost information that clarifies the firm's potential status vis-à-vis competitors. This information, by necessity, will be gathered in the form and units standard in the industry rather than according to the firm's normal internal cost accounting practices. Plans and specifications for plant and equipment will embody information and knowledge that are peculiar to construction and procurement rather than operations and maintenance.

Once the project is in place, though, information needs change. Operating cost analysis will be done according to the norms of the firm, not of the industry. It will be used, not to justify the capital outlay, but to identify strategically important arenas for cost reduction. Operations and maintenance will be less interested in procurement costs to build or the vendor's statistics on machine performance than on failure intervals for parts in use *in that plant* in order to decide maintenance schedules and organize spare parts supplies.

In the meanwhile, the early versions of software developed to run machines or generate reports will target the broadest and highest-payoff categories of function and information. With experience, however, users will start to identify more specialized or appropriate kinds of output, for which the programmers will be able to develop new subroutines, and so on.

The point here, in this linear example, is that each activity generates the preconditions for its successor, which will find it necessary to organize new information in new ways in order to carry out its own task. But one can also imagine a more synchronic analysis that would focus, for example, on how the normal activities of external actors, or even of one part of an organization, tend to generate the need to respond in some way on the part of other areas of the organization. In so doing, they generate the need to develop new kinds of information.

In short, people are continually confronted by the need to adapt in small and large ways in order to do their jobs. If established bureaucratic norms and practices really did override *all* other impulses, the result wouldn't be merely slow response but paralysis and breakdown, as no one could actually perform her or his tasks at all. In this sense, we should expect organizations to grow in the direction of new sources and types of information.

What this line of argument suggests is that the pathologies associated with bureaucracy are not necessarily intractable, which is not to say that they don't pose serious problems. Still, if the problems remain unresolved, it is not certain that they can be reduced wholly to the existence of the bureaucracy itself.

In any case, another, in some ways deeper question is whether the management of large, complex organizations must inevitably take the form of a large and complex bureaucracy with a stable and well-defined division of labor, or whether such a bureaucracy, once established, must remain in place for the life of the organization. Here there is considerable evidence that firms are, at the least, strenuously trying to "debureaucratize" themselves, and some evidence that they can do so successfully while still remaining impressively large (Sabel, 1989). One type of evidence is the increasing depredation of the ranks of white-collar middle management in the US. Eliminating the place-holders means eliminating the places in the bureaucracy. The bureaucracy becomes both smaller and simpler in structure, hence less susceptible to the kinds of impasse described above. This is concomitant with the effort to reduce the layers of management separating the top of the organizational hierarchy from the shop floor, stimulated greatly by the example of large Japanese firms. The aim is explicitly to improve the flow of information and response times to new problems and opportunities, but this inevitably involves considerable resynthesis of bureaucratically divided tasks and, in some cases, their reallocation to non-management personnel (Aoki, 1984, 1994).

A particularly aggressive and apparently quite successful firm in this context has been Asea Brown Boveri (ABB). In 1991, with revenues greater than $25 billion and 240,000 employees worldwide, the Zurich headquarters staff numbered 100. ABB has grown largely through mergers and acquisition, so it has been faced with the problem of reproducing its lean management style in a variety of established contexts. This it has done with a vengeance. Headquarters staff at US-based Combustion Engineering was reduced from 600 to 100 following its 1989 acquisition. The Finnish company Stromberg went from 800 to 25. ABB's German headquarters, in Mannheim, shrank from 1600 to 100. Overall, out of its 240,000 employees, only 15,000 (or roughly 6 percent) are described by Chairman Percy Barnevik as middle managers (Taylor, 1992).

General Electric, under the leadership of Jack Welch, has also emphasized organizational simplicity as a key part of its turnaround strategy. The company did this by eliminating management layers wholesale and drastically reducing the size of the headquarters' staff. As Welch describes it:

> Cutting the groups and sectors eliminated communications filters. Today there is direct communication between the CEO and the leaders of the 14 businesses. We have very short cycle times for decisions and little interference by corporate staff. A major investment decision that used to take a year can now be made in a matter of days. (quoted in Tichy and Charan, 1992:20)

These examples by no means prove either that it is easy to escape the real rigidities of large organizational structures or that this process is in any way automatically produced by changing circumstances. Indeed, it is almost certain that such a transformation is extremely difficult, even traumatic. But the fact that it can be done breaks the assumed inherent links between large organizations and unadaptable bureaucratic structures.[1] These links, in effect, can only be maintained if one assumes further that people are the absolute prisoners of the institutional structures that they create. It does not require a naive voluntarism to suppose that there is considerable room for maneuver remaining within these social constructs. This then requires us to look beyond the existence and the form of the bureaucracy itself to understand the causes of corporate or industrial rigidity.

Information, Uncertainty, and Sunk Costs

One of the most salient characteristics of large, mass production firms is that they have a tremendous amount of fixed capital in place that has been built up over time. This historical stock reflects past technological and organizational strategies in production as well as a high proportion of existing assets of such firms. The need to change significantly and rapidly what the firm is and what it does runs head on into this legacy of fixed capital stock.

Further, in times of retrenchment, the problem of sunk costs becomes particularly thorny. These are costs that cannot be recovered (for example, by selling off surplus assets) or closed out in the short run (as with the case of pension liabilities) even when an operation is terminated.

In periods of robust growth, sunk costs are not a serious threat to the firm, as assets can be gradually reconfigured rather than written off. Indeed, one of the peculiar strengths of mass production firms in their heyday was that they were, in effect, organized systems for the gradual

---

[1] One could expand this statement to argue against the proposition that complexity can only be managed by bureaucracy *or* by the automatic mechanisms of the market. If the latter, then we are back to the conclusion that large firms are dinosaurs. This way of formulating the issue may seem a hard-to-avoid invitation to engage in the debate over markets and hierarchies (cf. Williamson, 1985; Pratt and Zeckhauser, 1985). I will resist the invitation, however, on the grounds that the real problem with hierarchies stressed in this debate is based on the assumption that principals are the hapless victims of their agents, which seems to me a rather one-sided view of power relations within the firm. At the same time, the argument here should also suffice to show that complexity can be handled outside of pure market mechanisms without immediately running into the presumed impasse of hierarchies. For thoughtful critiques of the debate, see Perrow, 1986; Sabel, 1992.

obsolescence of fixed capital (cf. Aglietta, 1979). This was a signal achievement, as it went some way to ameliorating one of the deepest contradictions of capitalism: the constant pressure for technological change on the one hand, and the need to fully amortize previous investments on the other (Harvey, 1982).

But this ability to incrementally retire fixed capital rested on a stable competitive environment which was ensured by reasonably stable oligopolies in the relevant industries. The stability of the environment provided, crucially, a considerable degree of certainty about product and market configurations beyond the immediate short run, allowing fixed capital to be retired and replaced in a planned and orderly way.

Quite typical, in this context, was the controlled timing of new product introductions to avoid making obsolete prior product generations (and the specialized plant and equipment that produced them) before the investments in them could be fully recovered. Thus, even as large firms were first organizing formal R&D laboratories to promote new product technologies, they could withhold new devices from the market until profits from older technologies had been fully mined. Bell Telephone, for example, delayed the introduction of the integrated telephone handset for years after its development with precisely this end in view (Reich, 1985). Histories of industrial innovation are replete with similar stories (Jewkes et al., 1959).

The weight of past investments, both in plant and equipment and in product development costs that need also to be recovered, constitutes, then, a serious drag on the rapid reconfiguration of many key firms and industries.[2] At the same time, the disruption of stable market structures has proposed vehemently the prospect of sudden, frequent, and unplannable revisions to the fixed capital stock. Similarly, the problem of sunk costs becomes extraordinarily acute in periods of persistent overcapacity, which also exactly characterizes the present environment in many sectors. In the face of these conflicting pressures, it is easy to detect the outlines of an impasse.

Gordon Clark, for example, argues persuasively that what appears in retrospect to have been a suicidal (in other words, irrational and inexplicable) inability to respond to new forms of competition on the part of American firms in the 1970s and 1980s can in fact be explained once this predicament of sunk costs is adequately taken into account (G. Clark, 1994). The point of departure for Clark is uncertainty about

---

[2] Also implicated are certain nominally variable costs which have taken on some of the aspects of fixed costs via contractual relations. Thus, traditional rules, relations, and expectations imbedded over decades in collective bargaining agreements with production labor may also impede the ability of the firm to react appropriately to changes in the competitive environment. This particular issue, however, will be taken up below.

the long-run implications of observed changes in the economic environment, including price shocks and the intrusion into relatively stable
market configurations of new sources and forms of competition. Under
these circumstances, although the firms' short-run vulnerability may be
recognized, it is not immediately clear whether these disruptions will be
sufficiently durable and far-reaching to require a thoroughgoing restructuring of their own operations in response. In this context, the high
costs of restructuring, involving the writing off of considerable amounts
of fixed capital and incurring high sunk costs, provide a plausible
underpinning for the adoption of a "wait and see" attitude.

Instead of directly challenging the new competitors, as Clark shows,
firms accommodated their entry by withdrawing from more peripheral
product and geographical markets that were the particular targets of
foreign firms, consolidating in those markets that could be defended,
and gradually investing in greenfield sites that afforded lower long-run
costs of production. This gradual and partial process of rationalization
was significant enough to cause severe economic dislocation in many
regions, but neither deep nor fast enough to effectively respond to the
competitive challenge, which did, in the end, prove to be permanent.[3] In
this sense, a strategy which was eminently rational at the time, given the
balance of uncertainties and high costs of restructuring in the short run,
in the longer run puts at risk the very survival of the firms involved.

This is a powerful argument, as it links the very real problems of
decision-making under uncertainty and the potentially enormous costs
of "premature" and unplanned obsolescence of existing operations.
Mair, for example, shows how difficult it is for Toyota's competitors
(including other Japanese producers) to institute "true" just-in-time
production given the existing geographical allocation of their facilities.
These geographically sunk costs enforce a certain amount of gradualism
in the approach to current "best practice" in the industry (Mair, 1991).
If one considers that this type of story is normally associated with conditions that only make the problem worse – for example, diminished
revenue flows, which impair the ability of firms either to finance new

---

[3] Foster (1988) makes a similar argument concerning the way established technology
leaders in an industry frequently respond to new technological initiatives on the part of
new entrants to the field. He also describes a strategy of accommodation to early loss
of market share rather than aggressive attempts to confront the challenge. His point,
however, is that a misreading of the importance of this encroachment delays a response
until it is too late for the erstwhile leader to hope to catch up with the new technology.
The consequence is a sudden collapse of sales and profits and a change in leadership in
the industry. But in his recounting of how this process worked out in the transition
from bias-ply to radial tires or from vacuum tubes to solid-state electronics, his argument centers not on uncertainty *per se*, but on wrong interpretations of the available
evidence.

investments internally or to gain access to external capital markets on favorable terms – the terrain for maneuver available to firms in this predicament appears heavily constrained. Still, if we can plausibly show that there was some room for maneuver, along with strong incentives to act in some ways rather than others, then we can perhaps entertain the idea that the actual outcome was neither the necessary nor the inevitable product of these circumstances. In short, while the twin problems of uncertainty and sunk costs actually do constitute very serious constraints, they may not entirely explain the outcome.

I want to consider the general problem of uncertainty as a separate topic below. At this point, I wish only to treat it as an historical question which could take this form: what did they (management) know and when did they know it? There are really two kinds of knowledge that managers would have to possess with some certainty in order to act effectively in the face of a new competitive challenge, all other things being equal. The first, as Clark suggests, is the knowledge that the challenge is both a large and a durable one. In the absence of some degree of certainty on this point, it would be irresponsible to write off billions of dollars' worth of assets that were, in fact, economically viable, and invest billions more unnecessarily.

Here I would suggest that US managers in key industries such as automobiles and steel already knew with considerable certainty and accuracy that the new competition was serious and durable by the mid- to late 1970s. This, for example, is the period in which protectionist measures were successfully sought from the federal government in steel and already on the table for automobiles and machine tools. These kinds of initiative, given that they involve mobilizing considerable political and legal resources, would hardly be made if the disruption in the firms' markets were considered small enough to be manageable and/or temporary.[4] Further, although the problem of inflation arguably dominated public debate in this period, this was also the time in which discussions of industrial policy briefly flourished in government hearings, academic writings, and the business press (cf. US Congress, 1977, 1981, 1982; US Dept of Labor, 1980). In short, it seems possible to argue that, already during the Carter administration and gathering force in the early years of the Reagan administration, there was relatively little

---

[4] One estimate of the current costs of bringing a trade complaint before the US International Trade Commission, which adjudicates charges of dumping, ranges from $500,000 to $1 million (*Financial Times*, 1992g). If, in the past, this sort of investment, when successful, has been recouped through higher prices, it suggests that one needs to be reasonably certain of success before undertaking it. Note that this sum does not include the costs of lobbying Congress or the executive branch and other costs associated with mobilizing political support for protection.

uncertainty remaining about the fact of the problem in terms of its importance and its probable longevity.

The second kind of knowledge that managers need in this situation concerns the nature of the competitive threat (that is, what exactly makes it so threatening); or, to put it another way, they need to know with some certainty what an appropriate response would look like. This is a bit trickier, since what managers may be thought to know in this regard depends on how they interpret the information available to them. What we can show, however, is that the general outlines of an appropriate response were not unknowable by the early to mid-1980s. A growing technical and business literature on the Japanese production system was already available at this point, for example (cf. Drucker, 1971; Sugimori et al., 1977; Monden, 1981; Hatvany and Pucik, 1988; Schonberger, 1982; Abernathy et al., 1984; Friedman, 1983; Dore, 1985; Ohno, 1984; McMillan, 1984; Cusumano, 1985). This is apart from whatever efforts the firms were undertaking themselves to figure out their competition. It remains possible, of course, that managers systematically drew the wrong conclusions from the information available to them. This is not, however, a problem of uncertainty.

One doesn't need to posit a world of perfect information in order to suggest that important things were known with considerable certainty and accuracy about the magnitude and the nature of the problem some fifteen to twenty years ago. This still leaves the weight of sunk and fixed costs as a serious obstacle to an effective and sufficiently rapid response.

The question, then, is whether the existence of high sunk costs unavoidably imposes a possibly fatal gradualism on the response of large, capital-intensive firms to new market conditions. This amounts to saying that firms under these circumstances cannot afford to be competitive. But one may equally ask under what circumstances firms can afford *not* to be competitive. Capitalism is, after all, a very high-stakes game, and competition can be an effective enforcer of the rules.

In general, one may expect to find the most rapid and profound restructuring of the existing capital base during periods of crisis when firms confront combined problems of excess capacity, stagnating markets, and "excess" competition. Much of this, of course, is accomplished through the failure of entire firms and the devalorization in whole or in large part of their assets. This process, although deeply traumatic, helps clear away the overhang of accumulated capital, eventually allowing the resumption of investment and growth in its wake (cf. Harvey, 1982; N. Smith, 1984). But if we accept the proposition that firms do not commit suicide, then the more interesting case concerns firms that must strategize about the magnitude and the pace of retirement of existing fixed capital, the incurring of sunk costs, and investment in new plant and equipment, given the competitive environment on the one hand, and the risk of "excessive" or overly rapid write-downs of existing assets on the other.

Biting the bullet: Ford vs. GM

A particularly illuminating example concerns the divergent strategies of Ford and GM during the 1980s. Ford is universally praised by industry observers for having committed itself to a process of significant change in the early 1980s. That it did so is perhaps because the firm's situation was so dire. As one Ford executive described the perception at the time: "We *really* believed Ford could die" (quoted in Pascale, 1990:122).

The firm moved rapidly to significantly reduce capacity and employment. This meant abandoning the traditional model of maintaining capacity for market peaks and, crucially, acknowledging that the Japanese producers were in the market to stay. The number of production workers was reduced 45 percent from 191,000 in 1978 to 105,000 in 1986. Between 1980 and 1988, the company reduced its white-collar employment by 47 percent. Capacity reductions were accompanied by vertical disintegration as Ford increased external sourcing from 20 percent to 50 percent of the value of its cars (Pascale, 1990; Womack et al., 1990). This shrinkage, in combination with altered production and labor-management practices, meant that the overall efficiency of Ford assembly plants in the US rose 40 percent from 1979 through 1988. By way of comparison, GM achieved a productivity gain of only 5 percent for the same period (MIT Commission on Industrial Productivity, 1989; Pascale, 1990; *New York Times*, 1990a). While Ford still lags behind the Japanese in terms of ability to rapidly design and redesign products and to coproduce them on the same flexible production lines with state-of-the-art efficiencies, it has nevertheless come closest to the standards set by the Japanese producers (Womack et al., 1990).

At the outset of the 1980s, then, Ford considered its market situation, the lessons to be learned from Japan, and those from its relatively successful operations in Europe, and concluded that it had to become a different kind of company. GM looked at essentially the same set of factors and apparently concluded that it had to become more like GM.

This meant above all pursuing an extremely expensive technological solution to the problem of Japanese competition. GM's total capital spending in the 1980s amounted to some $75 billion to $80 billion worldwide, of which $40 billion went into new plants and automation. Another $8 billion went for the purchase of Electronic Data Systems and Hughes Aircraft, both of which, it was hoped, would feed new technologies into the parent firm (*New York Times*, 1992c; *Economist*, 1991; Pascale, 1990).

This strategy is widely considered to have been a disastrous failure. Some of the advanced technologies that the firm imported into its factories could not be made to work. While the company was pouring billions into flexible, programmable automation technologies, it was simultaneously focusing its factories on a small number of standardized body styles so that the advantages of the flexible equipment were not exploited (MIT Commission on Industrial Productivity, 1989). As indicated, the productivity gains yielded by this tremendous investment program were astonishingly meagre. At the end of the decade, GM still needed an estimated 4.55 workers to assemble one vehicle compared with 3.01 at Ford (*Financial Times*, 1992h).

GM also remained loyal to its strategy of vertical integration, sourcing some 70 percent of its parts internally. The company further remained committed to maintaining peak levels of capacity even as its market share plummeted (MIT Commission on Industrial Productivity, 1989; McAlinden and Smith, 1993). It was only toward the end of the decade that it began a serious program of plant closures.

In sum, the firm essentially applied a layer of flexible automation onto its traditional scale and organization of production and work. Among other things, this meant that it retained its enormous superstructure of supervisory, engineering, and managerial personnel. At the end of 1991, its salaried, white-collar workforce in North America numbered 113,000. By contrast, Toyota's entire worldwide labor force, including production workers, amounted to only 104,000 in that year (*Economist*, 1992b).

The dogged pursuit of this costly technological strategy is all the more surprising given that GM had ample evidence internal to the company concerning the viability of alternative models of production. The most pertinent example for our purposes is the NUMMI joint venture with Toyota.

In the early 1980s, GM entered into an agreement with Toyota to produce automobiles at a reopened GM assembly plant in northern California. The plant would be run by Japanese managers using unionized, former GM workers. In operation since 1984, it is, by GM's current standards, a remarkably "low-tech" facility. GM knows, further, that the plant ranks highest in quality and productivity within the firm (cf. MIT Commission on Industrial Productivity, 1989; Brown and Reich, 1989; *Economist*, 1993; Womack et al., 1990). The company placed a number of its own managers on site, who reported in detail on Toyota's "low-tech/high-motivation" approach. Yet the lessons from NUMMI have not, evidently, diffused back to the rest of the firm to any great degree (*Economist*, 1991). Indeed, by some accounts, they have been strenuously resisted. Visits to the facility, even by GM personnel, are reportedly tightly controlled, and the original on-site GM management team has been broken up and scattered within the corporation, reducing its ability to make an impact elsewhere (Pascale, 1990).

GM, quite belatedly, acknowledged that it had to significantly cut its domestic capacity. In a series of announcements dating from 1990, the firm made public plans to close 23 plants employing some 75,000–80,000 workers in order to cut capacity by 25 percent (to 5.4 million vehicles) by the mid-1990s. The salaried workforce was slated to decline to 71,000, and the production labor force to 250,000 – in both cases, just half the 1985 level. As part of this strategy, GM has exited from certain kinds of components production, including, for example, bearings, axles, forge operations, and some kinds of motor (*Financial Times*, 1992l; *New York Times*, 1990b, 1991a, 1992b, 1992d; *Wall Street Journal*, 1992).

Several lessons emerge from these parallel stories. The first is that, faced with similar problems and uncertainties in the competitive environment and presumably similar constraints in terms of fixed and sunk costs, the two firms adopted completely different strategies. Ford moved immediately to downsize and overhaul its operations, incurring the sizable costs of adjustment along the way. GM instead committed itself to an incredibly expensive and misguided project of technological supremacy. Nearly a decade after Ford, GM finally embarked on what had by then to be a crash program of capacity reductions, which, at a guess, made the adjustment costs even higher than they might otherwise have been.

There are two ironies here. First, at the beginning of the 1980s, GM was a far richer company than Ford and so, one presumes, could have more easily afforded to absorb even quite high sunk costs. In any case, it is hard to imagine that the sunk costs it risked were anything like the magnitude of the investments it actually made. Second, the firm had excellent inside information that the Japanese challenge was not, in the first instance, a technological one and that a purely technological strategy was probably not the solution to its competitive problems. In this context, we can acknowledge that the problems of uncertainty and sunk costs are real, but it seems clear that they are not determinate. Firms can still make highly divergent strategic judgments within these general constraints.

A second lesson seems to be that the impact of sunk costs must be considered in light of other kinds of cost. GM, for example, has lost billions of dollars as a result of its slowness to adapt. It has spent tens of billions more on a faulty strategy. The firm, arguably, made the wrong choice about which kinds of cost to incur.

The third lesson has to do with the links between uncertainty and adjustment costs. Did the firm make bad choices about which costs to incur because its judgment was unavoidably impaired by uncertainty, or did it misread the available information? One does not need to argue that the right choice was obvious *a priori* to suppose that the divergent example of Ford or GM's strenuous resistance to the example of NUMMI provide some indication that uncertainty was not the only problem. At the very least, one could posit that the links between uncertainty and sunk costs are mediated by other factors.

In sum, neither uncertainty nor sunk costs, separately or together, entirely explain the inability to adapt. It is possible to show that firms can have reasonably certain and accurate information about both the magnitude and the nature of the problem confronting them and still fail to react appropriately. We also know that firms do write off significant amounts of fixed capital rather suddenly when conditions are sufficiently severe. Yet it is quite clear that firms such as GM have not yet successfully reorganized themselves to adequately confront this competitive challenge that has been deepening for some fifteen years, despite considerable asset retirements and new investments. There is something else wrong with this picture.

Problems of information and knowledge

This leads us back to the general problem of uncertainty and imperfect information in real economic life. The acknowledgement that markets do not convey perfect information (or the same information to all participants) was an important moment in economic theory and behavioral analysis. We do not need here to rehearse the various lines of argument that have grown out of this recognition (but see Simon, 1961; Cyert and March, 1963; Akerlof, 1984; Stinchcombe, 1990; Perrow, 1986; Williamson, 1985). But if we accept the proposition that the people who run firms cannot know everything, this surely doesn't entitle us to suppose that they don't know anything. In trying to understand what inhibits rapid corporate or industrial adjustment to major changes, it is important to consider (adopting the language of the behavioralists) where the practical boundaries of bounded rationality actually lie.

The question, in other words, is whether the imperfectibility and cost of information and its related uncertainty are what hamper firm adjustment to changed circumstances. In the previous section, I tried to suggest that there are circumstances in which we can plausibly show that firms have access to reasonably good and accurate information – that is to say, they actually do know quite a lot about what their problems are and what they need to do about them – and yet they still fail to react appropriately. While the issue of what managers know at any given moment is an elusive one, I would like to amplify on the proposition that managers can normally be expected to know quite a bit about such crucial variables as the strategies and capacities of their competitors, the state of relevant product and process technologies, and changes in the market. If this is true, then the adjustment problem is less about lack of information (or its cost) and uncertainty, and more about what prevents firms from translating accurate knowledge into appropriate actions.

There are several reasons to suppose that the cost or an actual lack of information and related uncertainty are not wholly satisfying explanations for the inability to react appropriately to significant change. Stinchcombe, for example, shows how organizations act as evolving information-processing systems that grow new parts of themselves to gain access to important news about the relevant uncertainties in their environment. As information is accrued in this way, uncertainty is progressively reduced (Stinchcombe, 1990). This kind of analysis, which he illustrates through a number of case studies, helps us to think of information acquisition and uncertainty reduction as continuous and self-revising processes, which in turn alters our notion of what information costs, uncertainty and risk really look like. As Stinchcombe describes it:

> Uncertainty is reduced through news; and finally the residual uncertainty is transformed into risk, and people make their bets. Or perhaps better, people make small investments and build a small structure to collect relevant news; if the news is good, they make bigger investments and develop a larger structure to collect relevant news; and so on. Uncertainty is transformed piecewise into risk. (Stinchcombe, 1990:5)

In my own interpretation, this analysis detaches much of the cost of information gathering from specific transactions (cf. Williamson, 1985), since much of this function is a necessary and normal part of general overheads, and even transaction-specific information will often have, in effect, multiple uses. Another way of thinking about this might be that strategic planning and decision-making, which are what we are concerned about, are quite different from operational transactions (consider, for instance, the difference between strategizing about the nature of supplier relations and entering into a specific purchasing contract). Further, an information base that is built up over time helps reduce the costs of new information, since the organization learns with experience where to look for news and how to process it. Similarly, retrospective judgments on past information and the decisions made from it are also information that is, essentially, costless.

Finally, the progressive narrowing down of the terrain of uncertainty as information is accumulated, as Stinchcombe describes it, gets us away from a kind of high-hurdle effect in which large quanta of information have to be expensively organized and applied to any given decision. In short, the fact that the firm has a history constitutes an important qualification on the burden of information costs and uncertainty in adjustment. Only in the case where radical changes in the environment burst on the scene literally overnight will this prior history be invalidated.

The corollary to this point, of course, is that people also have histories. The people who run firms, in particular, embody a great deal of knowledge. Indeed, that knowledge, and their skill in using it, is what they are paid for. In a country such as the US, with a high degree of job mobility, this knowledge often extends to detailed understandings of competitors' strategies, operations, and ways of thinking. This body of knowledge can be mobilized repeatedly (at no additional cost) and is itself revisable with new experiences and new information. The stock of revisable prior knowledge is also likely to reduce the cost and difficulty of obtaining and processing new information. Further, it may be expected to set boundaries on the scope of uncertainty, or at least clarify what is really uncertain.

The point here is not to deny that information and uncertainty represent real problems for the firm and may hamper adjustment. But it does not seem useful, either, to suppose that the inability of firms to adjust to changed circumstances is fundamentally a problem of the cost and availability of information.

This, of course, leaves open the possibility that bad judgments are made from the information obtained; that some types of information are systematically privileged in decision-making, with unfortunate consequences; or that people embodying the wrong kinds of knowledge are in charge. What could be taken as a product of uncertainty and imperfect information, in these circumstances, is actually a misreading of the available information and, therefore, of the actual risks involved in different decisions. The critique of the rise of financial accounting methods and practitioners in business management, for example, centers on just these issues (Hayes and Abernathy, 1980; Johnson, 1991). But this is another question, one that will be returned to in later chapters.

Class Stalemate

In the United States, the particular form of labor–management relations institutionalized in the decades prior to 1960 sharply constrained firms' flexibility with respect to wage rates, work rules, and job assignments.

This system of "job control unionism," worked out under the protection of the state during and after the New Deal, also exerted a strong influence on the regulation of wages and work practices in non-unionized sectors. However, under conditions of strong economic growth, continued productivity increases, and relatively controlled competition (consequent on a high level of concentration and market power in key unionized sectors and the general absence of foreign competition), this system was perfectly compatible with high profits. In the unionized sectors, which tended to be the most capital-intensive, stability in labor relations in order to avoid the risk of idling, expensive, fixed-capital stock was arguably a more important goal for firms than driving wages down to the lowest possible level. In exchange for labor peace, firms accepted the institutionalization of continued real wage increases and the contractual delineation of tasks and job assignments. They retained, however, control over broader strategic decisions related to the level and nature of investment (Aglietta, 1979; G. Clark, 1989; Armstrong et al., 1984; Kochan et al., 1986; Lipietz, 1986).

In the 1960s, then, the position of labor in the United States was unusually strong, further bolstered by low rates of unemployment. The decade was characterized by increasing shop-floor militance (Kochan et al., 1986:38–40). Even as economic conditions began to change in the 1970s (rising rates of unemployment, increasing foreign competition, stagnating productivity, and pressure on corporate profits), this model of labor relations appeared immutable. If anything, the strength of labor appeared to be growing, as the state (even under a Republican administration) extended its protections through such means as the establishment of the Occupational Safety and Health Administration.

The widely perceived result was a class stalemate in which labor had the power (through contractual relationships and a favorable political environment) to inhibit the ability of firms to adjust effectively to changed circumstances, either through cutting costs or through transforming work processes. This was particularly true in unionized sectors, where labor costs continued to rise as productivity growth slackened. By the late 1970s, the gap between union and non-union wages had risen to 30 percent, up from 19 percent a decade earlier (Kochan et al., 1986:41). This was easily translated into the charge that the defense of high wages in unionized sectors was pricing US firms out of the market. Perhaps even more damaging in the long run was the possibility that adherence to outmoded work rules would prevent the timely uptake of new technologies and new ways of organizing the work process.

The issue, then, is whether rigidities built into US labor–management relations account for the inability of firms to adapt to new competitive circumstances. An alternative way of posing the question is whether labor – particularly organized labor – had the power during this period to obstruct the kinds of change that would have reversed this competitive decline.

In retrospect it is possible to show that the power of labor in the US was already being severely eroded in the decade of the 1970s (cf. Kochan et al., 1986; G. Clark, 1989). With the advent of the Reagan administration in 1980, this erosion became an overt attack, carried out in the general political arena and pursued through important institutional channels. In the face of mounting economic dislocation (unemployment and instability in labor markets), the strategies of firms to circumvent the influence of unions, and a shift in the political climate, labor's effective ability to block adaptation was substantially undermined. While it may have sought to resist or delay change (and may even have succeeded in doing so in scattered instances), the balance of power had shifted decisively by the early 1980s. Yet the competitive problems of American industry continued to worsen. Under these circumstances, it is difficult to sustain the thesis that recalcitrant labor has been the source of firms' inability to react appropriately to new competitive conditions. Rather, it seems more plausible to argue that the mounting crisis, which ravaged unionized industrial sectors in particular, had the effect of exerting considerable discipline on labor, reducing its capacity to resist the changes proposed by management. If this is correct, responsibility for continued industrial decline lies elsewhere.

The economic conditions sustaining the power of labor had already begun to unravel in the late 1960s, although the evidence of this was not, perhaps, driven home until the sharp recessions of the early and mid-1970s (Bowles et al., 1983; Bluestone and Harrison, 1982). Still, it is possible to suppose that labor was not forced to reckon seriously with its changed circumstances until late in the decade with the recession engineered by Federal Reserve Chairman Paul Volker (Greider, 1987). Subsequent job loss in manufacturing was severe, and disproportionately so among union members. Of the roughly 2 million manufacturing jobs lost in the four years from 1980 to 1984, a little over half were unionized. Not coincidentally, this was a period in which concessionary contracts were widespread. In collective bargaining contracts covering a thousand or more workers in these four years, about 50 percent of covered employees accepted a wage freeze or wage cut for at least a year. Concessions on work rules were also common. Indeed, so widespread were wage and work-rule concessions that they have been described as "unprecedented in the post-Great Depression period" (Kochan et al., 1986:115–18). At the same time, strike activity declined markedly (ibid:134–5).

Of course, no imaginable concessions are likely to bring US manufacturing wages down to the level of a Mexico or a Thailand. But that was never supposed to be the point, as high productivity and technical innovation ought to allow for high wages and high profits. On the issue of work rules, Kochan, Katz, and McKersie argue that what they characterize as old-style union plants are still markedly less flexible than either new-style union plants or, in particular, non-union plants (Kochan et al., 1986:104–8). But since most manufacturing plants in the US are, in fact, non-union, there appears to be considerable room for both task and numerical flexibility.

The point here is a traditional one: that increasing economic insecurity weakens the capacity of labor to resist the demands of management. Even if we allow that it takes a while for the lesson to sink in, by the early 1980s, there could have been very little doubt in anyone's mind about the general direction of events. Unions in particular were on the defensive, as unionization rates in the non-agricultural workforce had slipped below 20 percent by 1984. Although this decline is often attributed entirely to structural and demographic changes in the economy, the contrast with Canada and Western Europe, where the same sorts of change were occurring without a similar decline in unionization, is instructive (cf. Kochan et al., 1986:47–51).

Kochan, Katz, and McKersie, in their analysis of American industrial relations, provide considerable evidence of an increasingly broadly based movement on the part of US industry to combat unionization. Efforts in this regard date back to the 1950s, but diffused widely thereafter (even in generally unionized sectors), especially in the 1970s and 1980s. In their view, management's strategy to construct an alternative, non-union industrial relations system was, by and large, successful. This was especially true in sectors and firms that had never been organized, and for new entrants to traditionally unionized sectors. But the influence of the new model has also extended to unionized firms (Kochan et al., 1986:47–80). While for some firms, this was simply a way of cutting labor costs, the real importance of the alternative system centered on the flexible use of labor on the shop floor, individual motivation, teamwork, and greater employee involvement (ibid:93–100). In short, the new model of industrial organization, already widely diffused by the beginning of the 1980s, incorporated the kind of flexibility and worker responsibility currently thought to be an integral part of an adequate response to new competitive pressures. By the early 1980s as well, increasingly beleaguered unions were accepting many of these new practices and conditions (ibid:144–5).

In this context, it is worthwhile considering the evolution of labor relations at GM, which has historically taken a relatively hard line against the UAW, culminating in the famous strike at the Lordstown assembly plant in 1972. GM's first idea, it should be noted, was to escape the UAW by relocating production to non-union plants in the south. This "southern strategy" was successfully resisted by the union, by no means a common outcome. Subsequently, in GM's two major domestic experiments in transforming the production process and labor relations – the NUMMI joint venture with Toyota in California and Saturn in Tennessee – the union agreed to dramatically revised and quite flexible work organization and compensation deals (Brown and Reich, 1989; Kochan et al., 1986; *Economist*, 1985; *New York Times*, 1985; O'Toole and Lewandowski, 1990). Thus, even bolstered by its success in countering GM's most explicitly anti-union efforts in the early 1970s, the union proved willing to engage in far-reaching revisions to the seemingly entrenched traditions of collective bargaining.

Finally, the collapse of the New Deal coalition in the political arena both provides evidence of the diminishing power of labor in the US, and further undermined it in practice. The Reagan administration effectively redefined the terrain, most pointedly in the breaking of the air traffic controllers' strike in 1981, and perhaps most enduringly in the reorientation of the National Labor Relations Board, which proceeded to dismantle decades of precedents favorable to labor (G. Clark, 1989; Edsall, 1984). The political discourse of the time succeeded in portraying organized labor as a particularly grasping "special interest group" intent on preserving and expanding its sphere of privilege against the public interest. This anti-union stance was an important component of what the conservative analyst Kevin Phillips has characterized as a new class war of the rich against the poor (Phillips, 1984). Thus, labor's ability to regain in the political arena what it had lost in the economic sphere and on the shop floor was effectively foreclosed.

In sum, it is hard to make the case that labor, even organized labor, had the power during this period to systematically, and on a large scale, block the transformations in technology and work organization that were generally held to be necessary. Moreover, as the case of GM suggests, the unions also got the point and engaged actively, if not necessarily enthusiastically, in this process. Whatever resistance was offered seems unlikely to account in a general way for the difficulties of corporate transformation. If the problem of corporate adjustment hinged on the inability to revise work practices and labor relations, it is difficult to show that the source of this inability lay in successful worker resistance.

There is, of course, the question of whether the problem of competitiveness hinged on high US wages or the defense of outdated work practices to begin with. For this to be the case, we would need to show that direct labor rates and the work practices successfully defended by labor against management constituted the main source of cost problems. We would also need to show that unit costs and prices, as opposed to, say, product performance, design, and quality, were the central competitive problem. On both issues, there are grounds for doubt.

As a first cut, there is considerable evidence that direct and indirect labor content rather than wage rates *per se* constitute the major production-cost problem for US firms in comparison with their Japanese competitors. In automobiles, for example, Womack, Jones, and Roos compared a GM assembly plant in Framingham, Massachusetts, with a Toyota assembly facility in Takaoka, controlling for size and options packages of the output and the nature of the tasks performed on site. In 1986, GM required 31 labor hours per assembled vehicle as opposed to 16 for Toyota. Although the Toyota plant relied more heavily on robots for painting and welding, it was not, in the authors' estimation, significantly more "high-tech" or capital-intensive than GM's. Nor can it be argued either that Toyota knew something GM didn't know, or that GM was paralyzed by worker opposition, since the comparable assembly line at GM's unionized joint venture with Toyota in California (NUMMI) was 19 hours. The authors further single out the weight of indirect labor (line supervisors, etc.) as a significant burden on US mass producers (Womack et al., 1990:78–83). In this and other industries, other sources of cost problems that conceivably dwarf wage rates in their impact include overcapacity, high design and development costs, and product designs that do not lend themselves to efficient manufacturing.[5]

Still, if the competitiveness problem did hinge on costs, it might be argued that labor-cost reductions were the only feasible short-run target compared with capacity reductions, reorganization of production processes, or redesign of products. Yet, as indicated, the level of layoffs in the key mass production industries during the 1980s was extraordinarily high, even leaving aside the effects of wage concessions. In short, substantial labor-cost reductions (and productivity improvements) were achieved in this period, and the competitiveness problem remained. This could mean that, while costs were the problem, labor cost reductions were not a sufficient solution. Alternatively, it could mean that costs were not the only or the largest problem, and cost reductions in general were not a sufficient solution. Either way, a hypothetical class stalemate does not seem to account for the lack of success in adjustment.

[5] Womack, Jones, and Roos also provide comparisons for labor content and time involved in new product development in the auto industry. American producers required on average 3.1 million engineering hours per new car compared with 1.7 million in Japan. Average development times were 60.4 months and 46.2 months, respectively (Womack et al., 1990:118).

In any event, it remains the case that the lowest-cost, most efficient imaginable production of the wrong product will not solve a competitiveness problem. Had workers in the US simply agreed to accept Japanese wages and work practices while producing "more of the same," it seems safe to conclude that the problem would not have gone away. Something more is at issue.

Regional Obsolescence

A prominent argument in the geographical literature suggests that the rise of new industries in an old industrial area – and, presumably, the renewal of existing industries in that place – is blocked by the inherited legacy of the region's social, economic, institutional, and physical infrastructure. This, in effect, ties together many of the previous themes and roots them historically and geographically. The rigidities produced over time in, say, wages and work practices, organizational forms, inter-firm relationships, political commitments, and the like, combined with a physical infrastructure that was built up to suit the requirements of the old production organization but is ill adapted to the needs of the new, prevent an existing industrial region from transforming itself in the light of new circumstances. The expected outcome is that new industries are likely to grow up in previously unindustrialized areas or "new industrial spaces." Meanwhile, existing firms and industries, in their efforts to restructure, are also likely to abandon the old region and colonize new areas in the erstwhile industrial periphery (such as the "sunbelt" or the third world) in order to obtain, as it were, a fresh start. The new regions offer the chance of constructing a social and physical landscape precisely suited to the new or renewed industries (A. Scott, 1988; Storper and Walker, 1989; Bluestone and Harrison, 1982; R. Martin and Rowthorn, 1986; Massey, 1984; Carney et al., 1980; Tabb and Sawer, 1984; Gordon, 1977; Frobel et al., 1980; G. Clark et al., 1986; Chinitz, 1962; Markusen, 1985; Markusen et al., 1992; Peet, 1983, 1987).

As this argument has been constructed, different features have been emphasized by different writers. Chinitz, for example, provides strong grounds for linking the inadaptability of the Pittsburgh region to the overwhelming historical dominance of large firms in the steel sector (Chinitz, 1962). The big steel "mindset" of the region shaped people's career aspirations and expectations, making it less likely that they would, for example, turn to sectorally diverse, small-scale entrepreneurial activities. At the same time, the close connections between big steel and regional financial institutions meant that small entrepreneurs in other sectors were, in any case, unlikely to have access to capital. Although Chinitz was writing before the steel industry went into crisis, in these circumstances, when it eventually went down, the entire regional economy would be unavoidably dragged down with it (cf. also Markusen, 1985). In this piece, Chinitz was trying to understand the origins and persistence of a regional economic "monoculture" in contrast with the more diversified economic base of New York. What he can't tell us, then, is what prevents big steel from transforming itself *in situ* to ward off the crisis despite such apparent advantages as the great concentration of sector-specific expertise and close integration with local financial institutions.

The various lines of analysis that go under the names of deindustrialization, the new international division of labor and global Fordism, on the other hand, argue in effect that firms *did* react to new circumstances by shifting capital out of older industrial regions altogether (Bluestone and Harrison, 1982; Frobel et al., 1980; R. Martin and Rowthorn, 1986; Lipietz, 1986; Peet, 1983, 1987; Massey, 1984). The objective here was to escape the high wages and rigid labor practices of older areas by relocating to newly constituted, unorganized labor markets in the periphery, lacking in the traditions of industrial struggle. If this strategy could not be implemented domestically (witness GM's failure to prevent unionization of its greenfield plants in the south), the third world provided many inviting opportunities. The underlying supposition is that it is the history and social characteristics of places that eventually block new investment and, by extension, industrial renovation.

Despite the great plausibility of these accounts, as an empirical matter it is not obvious that escape to the periphery constituted the principal reaction of firms in the US to new competitive pressures – although the efficacy of the threat to do so played a significant role in extracting concessions from existing labor forces. As described in chapter 3, most foreign investments by US manufacturing firms during the 1970s and 1980s went to other high-labor-cost regions – especially Western Europe – with, in many ways, stricter regulatory environments for labor relations. During the same period, the US itself became a major location for foreign manufacturing investment, much of it concentrated in the traditional industrial heartland (Schoenberger, 1985, 1989a, 1991; Glickman and Woodward, 1989). This latter movement in particular suggests that the foreign competition, anyway, found it entirely possible to construct acceptable labor relations and practices in these regions despite their historical legacies. Granted, they may have done so by hiring different kinds of person (non-union, new entrants to the labor market, women, etc.), but this would mean the wage and work-organization rigidities that domestic companies were fleeing were not so much place-specific as firm-specific. Here again there is some question about the real source of the inability to revise labor–management relations in view of the relative weakness of labor in this period.

The most broadly articulated accounts of the "new industries, new places" theme provide important guidance for understanding why and how this re-sorting of the industrial landscape may occur despite some strong counter-pressures (A. Scott, 1988; Storper and Walker, 1989). In particular, while the lure of a fresh start may seem quite compelling, there are significant costs and risks attached to it. Creating a new place to support a new or renewed industry requires assembling or creating *de novo* an appropriately skilled labor force and supplier network. Possibly substantial efforts must be devoted to mobilizing the political resources to develop the necessary social and physical infrastructure – education, transportation and communications, water and sewage, and the like. Firms in this geographical outpost run the risk of excessive isolation from important geographic markets or key early users of the new product, and thus from strategically valuable feedback on performance requirements or the behavior of competitors. By any reckoning, creating a new industrial agglomeration is a large undertaking.

For firms in new industries (such as automobiles in the early twentieth century or semiconductors following World War II), the costs and risks of abandoning an already developed industrial terrain in favor of a bespoke locale are thought to be acceptable for several reasons. The skilled labor force and dense supplier network of the established region may be entirely irrelevant to the new sector, for example, so that the costs of creating a sector-specific labor supply and supplier base would have to be borne in any case. Certain diseconomies of agglomeration may be avoided: high land costs, congested or aging infrastructure, etc. As pioneer firms cluster together in the new locale, their early market success provides the revenue stream that, collectively, can support the high costs of developing the needed economic, social, and physical infrastructure. If the product is sufficiently distinctive, the market will come to the firms no matter where they are, or will accept whatever they offer. In a general but non-trivial way, the culture of the new community will be closely aligned with the culture of the new sector. Social practices, norms, and understandings will not need to be (perhaps painfully) revised, but will have an inbuilt appropriateness.

Even in the case of new industries, the newness of the new industrial spaces they inhabit can be overdrawn. As Storper and Walker acknowledge, emerging industrial regions tend to be located in or near second- or third-ranked metropolitan agglomerations rather than in entirely undeveloped peripheries (Storper and Walker, 1989:15). Not only did Silicon Valley, for example, grow up within easy reach of the diversified industrial, commercial, and (crucially) financial base of San Francisco, but the shift to solid state which gave the Valley its name occurred after a reasonably lively history of electrical and tube-based electronics activities (Leslie, 1993b; Saxenian, 1994). Still, the argument that an entirely new industry will benefit from locating in a place constructed after its own image has considerable plausibility.

When the issue concerns the renovation of existing industries, however, the "fight or flight" calculus may need redoing. In this case, the firm does risk losing access to highly appropriate specialist skills (unless, as in the case of Saturn, it can persuade workers and suppliers to relocate with it). The relative power of workers and management to defend divergent visions of the revitalized industry is, of course, much at issue. As suggested above, however, it can be plausibly argued that management had the power in recent decades to successfully impose its preferred course of action. Further, the leading corporate citizens of the established agglomeration may be supposed to have some power to shape local political commitments concerning social and physical infrastructure investments. Certainly, there is ample evidence that newly entrepreneurial older cities are eager to please the people who run firms (Harvey, 1988; Goodman, 1982). High land costs in dense agglomerations may not be a significant deterrent to downsizing older firms that have long since paid off acquisition costs on their current sites. For these reasons, it is not completely obvious that firms are fatally impeded by the inherited social and industrial landscape from reorganizing themselves *in situ*. Or, to put this another way, recognizing the costs and difficulties of this endeavor does not allow us to assume *a priori* that they are either vastly greater than those associated with creating a new industrial space or, in principle, insurmountable. If they have not been surmounted in practice, there are grounds to question whether this is due to the irreparable obsolescence of the place or to problems more properly specific to the firms that inhabit it.

Conclusion

This overview, necessarily abbreviated and partial, has sought not to demonstrate that these various arguments are invalid but rather to create a sense of uneasiness, a sense that something important and hard to define is yet missing. A part of this desired uneasiness is related to the choice of units of analysis. In the effort to understand how corporations deal with a world that is and is not of their own making, we have tended to treat the firm as the irreducible social unit. This unit can, to be sure, exhibit differing forms of organization, internal social relations, economic predicaments, and the like, and it can be subject to a range of pathologies. But the firm is the key actor. Its inability to adapt to change is then a function of these organizational and social attributes and pathologies.

This angle of approach is not an unwarranted one. But as the burgeoning literature on the topic of corporate culture suggests, it is important to press beyond the boundaries of the firm itself to understand the origins of these attributes and maladies. In what follows, I want to consider how the firm is constituted as a society, how it constructs its identity, and the relationship between culture, identity, knowledge, and action. The view of corporate culture I want to elaborate here departs in significant ways from that encountered in academic writings on business. In doing so, I hope to make more distinct some of the deeper causes of corporate rigidity.

Part II

Corporate Culture, Strategy, and Change

5

Corporate Culture and Strategy

Introduction

The Mamelukes were slave warriors, found in many parts of the Islamic world up through the eighteenth century. Largely of Turkish origin, they were renowned for their extraordinary ability in fighting wars on horseback. They were particularly important in Egypt after the fall of Baghdad to the Mongols in 1258. So crucial was their victory over these same Mongols at Ain Jalut in 1260 that the Mamelukes of Egypt achieved political power under their own sultans.

As described by military historian John Keegan, Mameluke recruits were intensively schooled in the *furusiyya*, the skills of mounted warfare emphasizing unity of horse and rider, close coordination, and the handling of weapons while mounted, especially the bow, the lance, and the sabre. Significantly, the Mameluke system was specifically non-hereditary: each generation of warriors was recruited from the outside. But the system nevertheless remained resistant to new ideas. Fresh recruits were, through the process of the *furusiyya*, transformed into "traditional" Mameluke fighters. In this way, and fatally, they failed to respond to the emerging techniques of infantry warfare based on the use of gunpowder (Keegan, 1993).

That the Mamelukes were aware of gunpowder seems clear. In the early sixteenth century, threatened by both the Portuguese and the Ottoman Turks, they implemented a crash program to produce cannon and form units of gunners and musketeers. But, as Keegan notes, these units were composed of non-Mameluke fighters and were kept quite separate from (and ancillary to) the main, cavalry-based core of the Mameluke forces. Nor did they adapt their tactics to the imperatives of the new technology. Instead, they threw traditionally equipped cavalry into battle against Ottoman musketeers and were disastrously defeated. In 1516, Egypt became a province of the Ottoman empire.

Surprisingly, this wasn't the end of the story, as a slave-based fighting force continued to be useful to the Ottomans. The Mamelukes even managed to regain positions of political power in the empire. Yet they clung as strongly as ever to their traditional methods of fighting wars. In 1798, they were easily routed by Napoleon in the Battle of the Pyramids. As late as 1811, when they were finally massacred by Muhammad Ali, the Mamelukes deployed sword- and bow-armed cavalry against cannon and muskets.

In brief, then, despite three hundred years of terrible evidence, the Mamelukes resisted the lesson that warfare had been irrevocably transformed. Yet there is no reason to suppose that they were particularly stupid or inept. Nor, clearly, was there any problem about access to information. The information was literally at their feet, in the bodies of their dead comrades. How, then, to account for the Mamelukes' suicidal adherence to their military traditions?

Keegan argues that warfare is a cultural activity, both expressive and productive of a culture's values, traditions, and ways of thinking. To the degree that success reinforces or validates these traditions and modes of thought, the culture becomes more difficult to change. Though the Mameluke culture was at the outset extremely successful from a war-making point of view, its success fostered a narrow cultivation of the military traditions that first brought them to power. Keegan maintains that it is "a besetting fault of triumphant warrior systems that fail to fund economic and social diversification from the fruits of victory, that they become fossilised in their moment of glory" (Keegan, 1993:31).

This could be nothing more than a restatement of the cliché that armies are always preparing to fight the last war, but for two things. First, the Mamelukes persisted in fighting the same last war for three hundred years, which seems to be stretching a point. Second is the attention drawn to social and economic diversification as the antidote to fossilization. But what kind of antidote is it, and who is able to use it?

In the case of the Egyptian Mamelukes, what seems clear is that their social and political power was inextricably linked to their mastery of the rigorous and arcane practices of the *furusiyya*. As Keegan writes, the Mamelukes "owed their dominance to their monopoly of elaborate skills of horsemanship and archery, which to abandon for the commoner practices of musketry or fighting on foot might have toppled them from their position" (Keegan, 1993:32). The Mamelukes' particular style of warfare required years of intensive training to master, and this skills monopoly guaranteed their social position. By contrast, almost anyone can learn to stand and fire a gun in a relatively short time.

In a world of gun-based infantry warfare, the Mamelukes might be perfectly effective soldiers, but they couldn't be a ruling elite. In this sense, the antidote of social and economic diversification, although it might have saved them on the battlefield, could not protect their social and political position and identity. The Mamelukes faced either social or military annihilation. In the event, they "chose" a military end. But it seems fair to say that only the threat of another kind of death altogether constitutes a strong enough motive to account for three hundred years of Mameluke persistence in fielding mounted archers against guns.

Keegan is quite right to link social and economic change with cultural transformations. But the story of the Mamelukes draws our attention to how fraught with contradictions and dilemmas this connection may be, especially for those in positions of power.

The fate of the Mamelukes may seem quite remote from the situation of the large post-war corporation. But I see it as a particularly striking instance of a more general problem that is highly relevant to the experience of once-dominant firms over the last twenty-five years. During this time we have watched any number of major firms, whose practices and products once defined their industries, struggle to save themselves in the face of new competitive challenges. The list of such firms is a familiar one: GM, Ford, Chrysler, IBM, Xerox, RCA, US Steel (USX), TWA, Pan Am, and so on. Some of these firms have successfully fought their way back from the brink of destruction while others have vanished. The fate of the rest is still in doubt.

Why did this happen? Or, more precisely, why did this happen to such a large group of firms in a particular time and place? And again, why did this happen despite the availability of reasonably good information about the nature of the competitive challenge and the kinds of strategy that would constitute an appropriate response?

Change and resistance

This chapter takes on the question of why corporations don't act in their own best interests, even when they have access to good information about what to do. It proposes that the answer lies somewhere in the realm of corporate culture, which, in turn, is intimately involved in the production of corporate strategy.

At the outset, we can observe that firms change all the time. They buy new equipment, hire new people and move the old ones around, enter new markets, reorganize departments and functions, change suppliers, develop new products, and so on, and they are constantly engaged in these activities. So the question is not so much why firms don't change, as why they embrace particular kinds of change while resisting others.

We saw, for example, in the case of GM that the firm committed itself wholesale to a hugely expensive strategy of advanced automation while rejecting the strong lessons about production processes, labor relations, and product quality that were widely available at the time, both internal and external to the firm. The firm's strategy entailed change on a large scale, but the wrong kind of change (see above, chapter 4).

RCA provides another kind of example. The company became a household name on the basis of its pioneering innovations in radio and television. In the early 1940s, it established one of the most advanced corporate research laboratories in the world, adjacent to Princeton University. The Sarnoff Laboratories' mission was to ensure RCA's continued technological dominance in its various military and consumer markets. Instead, a costly commitment to the flawed Selectavision video-disc system brought the company to its knees.

As Margaret Graham shows in her detailed analysis, the commitment to Selectavision was built up and solidified over fifteen years, despite considerable internal dissent and the availability of alternative technologies for both disc and tape. Along the way, RCA passed up an opportunity to deepen a long-standing collaborative relationship with Matsushita by developing a standard format that would have broadened the product's potential market. It also suppressed internal efforts to develop tape-based systems, as well as a simpler and cheaper recording and playback technology (Graham, 1986).

We can acknowledge that the alternative technologies had problems of their own, so the decision on where to place the company's bets was by no means obvious. But Graham makes clear that the factors driving the decision in favor of Selectavision had as much to do with the labs' culture and RCA's sense of its own identity as with technical or economic issues. The labs' scientific staff, for example, was much more intrigued by the technical and scientific problems associated with Selectavision than with its more pedestrian alternatives. RCA, meanwhile, prided itself on its history of technical leadership and was loath to give up its claims to proprietary technology. Now, RCA had made a fortune from licensing its radio and television technology, so a general preference for relying on its own resources is understandable. In this case, however, it led the company repeatedly to dismiss possible collaborations that might have drastically reduced development and production costs and created a viable product. The result was a tremendous delay in bringing to market a version of Selectavision that offered limited performance capability compared with alternatives already available, and that suffered from a shortage of programming (Graham, 1986).

Perhaps RCA was doomed in any case. But this kind of story alerts us to the need to understand how commitments – to technologies, markets, operational styles, and the like – are generated and how they acquire the force to shape the overall trajectory of such a large and complex organization as the modern corporation.

The issue, then, is how and why certain kinds of change are selectively embraced or resisted, especially when this occurs in the face of evidence that rather clearly suggests an alternative course. It may be objected, though, that during the 1970s and 1980s, messages about what to do came from so many sources and in so many voices that there was no reasonably clear and consistent lesson to be drawn from them. If this were true, firms may have been listening hard, but all they could hear was a cacophony, not useful information, and so they can't really be faulted for pursuing inappropriate strategies. My own view is that, despite the babble of voices each claiming a unique insight, a rather concise set of basic themes actually did emerge during this period. These themes centered on quality, flexibility, collaborative labor relations, responsiveness to the market, and speed of response.

On the other hand, we must acknowledge that the boundary between misreading the evidence and taking plausible risks that don't prove out is, at the margin, blurry. There are areas in which reasonable people may differ for good reason, and even sound judgments may be thwarted by the unexpected. But there are also areas in which good evidence is misread or ignored. If we imagine a matrix relating the quality of the evidence to the "goodness" of the strategy, it seems likely that there is a large enough area of good evidence and bad strategy to merit attention.

Culture and the corporation

Culture is a notoriously elusive topic and connecting it up to patterns of change and resistance in the firm will take some work. We need to understand some things about what culture is and what it does, how it is produced, and how it changes. Anthropologists, whose domain this is, have been debating these questions for roughly a century, from various theoretical perspectives and with quite divergent objects of analysis (cf. Ortner, 1984; Applebaum, 1987). So at the outset, the terrain is difficult.

The problem is made all the more difficult by the peculiarities of corporations as social agents. The corporation is both a collection of individuals and a self-reproducing institution whose identity is linked with, but not the same as, those of the people who work in it. Specific individuals come and go, but the corporation remains. As these individuals enter into the life of the corporation, they are shaped by its culture, but they also produce its culture through their activities and their relations.

At the same time, individuals come into the firm as adults, already formed by the broader culture of which they are a part. By the same token, the firm exists in a diffusely determined cultural context: postwar, American, techno-industrial, Western, individualist, and so on.

There are great difficulties, then, in sorting out the relationship of the part to the whole. The analysis, in my view, must remain sensitive to these difficulties without trying to impose misleadingly clear boundaries between the categories of person, culture, and firm.

This chapter explores ways of thinking about corporate culture and how it structures change. In chapter 6, these ideas will be applied to detailed case studies. Here, though, I want first to review the emerging conventional wisdom about corporate culture and then to offer an alternative understanding of what it is and how it works. A closer look at the specific issues of values and tradition follows. The focus then switches to the dominant cultural producers in the firm – top management – and explores the kinds of change they are likely to promote and to resist. A final section explores the relationship between corporate culture and strategy.

Approaches to Corporate Culture

As the management literature has taken up the idea of culture, it has emphasized a fairly consistent set of themes and problems. Corporate culture is generally viewed as a set of social conventions embracing behavioral norms, standards, customs, and the "rules of the game" underlying social interactions within the firm. These conventions are linked to an underlying set of values (also called philosophies or ideologies) that provide more general guidance in shaping behavioral patterns. Yet again, culture is identified with shared meanings and assumptions, often reinforced or expressed through symbols, rituals, myths, and ceremonies (cf. Schein, 1992; Kotter and Heskett, 1992; Hampden-Turner, 1990; Trice and Beyer, 1993; Ouchi, 1981; Deal and Kennedy, 1982).[1]

---

[1] It can be noted that where the problem of culture has featured in cognate disciplines such as economics and sociology, it has also tended to be viewed as a problem of rules, norms, and traditions (cf. Nelson and Winter, 1982; DiMaggio and Powell, 1991).

These categories are hardly ever seen as exclusive. Instead, they may be associated with different layers of social practice and consciousness, some visible and accessible, while others are hidden and, for that reason, thought to be much harder to change. Thus, behavioral patterns and norms (the surface) may reflect underlying values, which may in turn reflect shared assumptions that are so deeply held and taken for granted that they cannot be directly confronted or debated (Schein, 1992; Kotter and Heskett, 1992; Trice and Beyer, 1993; Ouchi, 1981).

For the most part, cultures are seen as coherent and unifying *systems* that are necessary for the stability and smooth functioning of the corporation. What these systems do is create shared understandings concerning appropriate behaviors, attitudes, and ways of thinking. Although the existence of potentially conflicting subcultures within the firm may be acknowledged, only rarely are dissent and fragmentation brought to the fore as an inherent aspect of cultural processes (J. Martin, 1992). Also unusual is a view of corporate culture as a form of social control (Kunda, 1992; Van Maanen, 1991).

Corporate cultures are usually thought to be produced largely by top management, especially the firm's founders. As described by Schein, the leaders' values produce what may be thought of as initial hypotheses about the way the world works. To the degree that these hypotheses produce successful decisions, the values are validated and reinforced. Over time, they are transformed into deeply held, implicit, shared assumptions. The culture, then, represents and embodies the cumulative shared learning experiences of the group (Schein, 1992; see also Kotter and Heskett, 1992). Schein, who writes from the viewpoint of cognitive psychology, is a particularly strong exponent of the view that cultures are necessarily integrative and act to produce stability and consistency in the firm. To the degree that we encounter cultural contradictions, this is a result of incongruities between the espoused values and the "real" underlying assumptions (Schein, 1992; cf. also Argyris and Schon, 1978).

In this context, the relationship between culture and strategy is largely instrumental. A change in strategy may require a change in values and behaviors. Thus, a strategy focusing on responsiveness to the market may require a set of values in which product quality is very important, as opposed to values which may have, in the past, emphasized quantity of output (cf. Kotter and Heskett, 1992).

The connection between corporate culture and competitiveness or performance emerges most strongly in two somewhat overlapping ways. On the one hand, it is closely linked to organizational form: whether centralized or decentralized, formal or informal, segmented or integrated, hierarchical or flat. In contrast to the traditional organization of large American firms, current opinion favors decentralization, informality, integration, and flatness (cf. Kanter, 1983; Dertouzos et al., 1989; Piore and Sabel, 1984).[2] These institutional characteristics are thought to be associated with a culture high in individual commitment (as everyone feels a sense of ownership in the enterprise and a sense of responsibility to colleagues) and collective innovativeness (the scope for generating new ideas is maximized, as everyone is encouraged to contribute).

A second focus is specifically on the social norms and values that shape behavior and attitudes. These have mainly to do with the nature of social relations internal to the firm – whether across functional specializations or between management and labor – and external to the firm (with suppliers and customers). We have learned to speak of cooperation, teamwork, empowerment, high-trust environments, respect for the individual, and participation. These norms and values are often liked with certain kinds of solidaristic and/or motivational strategy: cultures of pride, of creativity, of innovation, of change. They may also be associated with operational commitments (often referred to as values) such as quality, responsiveness, or caring for all the stakeholders of the firm (Kanter, 1983; Dertouzos et al., 1989; Kochan et al., 1986; Maidique and Hayes, 1988; Sabel, 1982; Piore and Sabel, 1984; Kotter and Heskett, 1992; Kunda, 1992).[3]

A very distilled version of the argument would be that values produce behaviors and commitments, which in turn (if all goes well) produce a competitive firm. In this sense, the values strategy works in the same way as that centering on organizational form, by mobilizing a greater sense of commitment to and responsibility for the fate of the firm, eliciting more creative inputs and intensive efforts, and so on.

In this view of the world, then, culture operates through learned behaviors and attitudes. Cultural change is about adopting new values (and/or organizational forms) and learning the new behaviors appropriate to them. But the values and assumptions run very deep and are, in

---

[2] Kanter, indeed, is somewhat unusual in seeing culture as a direct product of organizational morphologies. As she writes: "Out of the design and structure of the organization arises a set of patterns of behavior and cultural expectations that guide what people in the system consider appropriate modes of operating. . . . The highest proportion of entrepreneurial accomplishments is found in the companies that are least segmented and segmentalist, companies that instead have integrative structures and cultures emphasizing pride, commitment, collaboration, and teamwork" (Kanter, 1983:178).

[3] I should perhaps note that not everyone who writes about corporate competitiveness specifically dwells on the issue of corporate culture, but the general resemblance of the ideas and categories at issue is sufficiently strong to make the connection.

many cases, tacit. They are reflected in entrenched traditions, customs and habits of practice and of thought. In this light, cultures are seen to be inherently resistant to change. Ouchi puts it succinctly: "The only way to influence behavior is to change the culture. A culture changes slowly because its values reach deeply and integrate into a consistent network of beliefs that tend to maintain the status quo" (Ouchi, 1981:75). Schein offers a more psychologized version of the model: "Once we have developed an integrated set of such [shared] assumptions, which might be called a thought world or mental map, we will be maximally comfortable with others who share the same set of assumptions and very uncomfortable and vulnerable in situations where different assumptions operate" (Schein, 1992:22–3). For Schein, in fact, what is required to change a culture is a leader who can recognize when the old culture has become counterproductive, and can envision and impose a new culture. The essence of leadership, in this context, is the ability to step outside one's cultural assumptions in order to effect the change.

Alternatively, the impediments to change could be cast as individuals or groups defending their vested interests in the old structures and norms, as, for example, in the case of unions defending obsolete work rules that protect the status or the jobs of their members (cf. Trice and Beyer, 1993). But this is usually viewed as irrational, even foolish behavior (insofar as it threatens the existence of the firm and so the jobs themselves) and thus closely resembles the problem of blindly clinging to no longer functional traditions.

Finally, it should be noted that, apart from the connection with organizational form, culture tends to be seen as occupying a distinct realm within the firm, one that can be worked on separately from, say, technology, market orientation, or strategy. Kotter and Heskett are most explicit about this. Figure 5.1 reproduces their chart illustrating the four factors that shape managerial behavior (Kotter and Heskett, 1992:6). Here, corporate culture appears separately, along with formal structure, leadership, and the competitive and regulatory environment. We might ask why structure and leadership styles are not also part of the culture, or whether the culture of the firm has not been influenced by its competitive and regulatory environment.

The Culture of the Firm: A Reconsideration

The view of corporate culture that I wish to propose is both broader and considerably messier than the characterizations reviewed above. These are not so much wrong (it is meaningful to speak about assumptions and values) as narrow and incomplete. As a consequence the

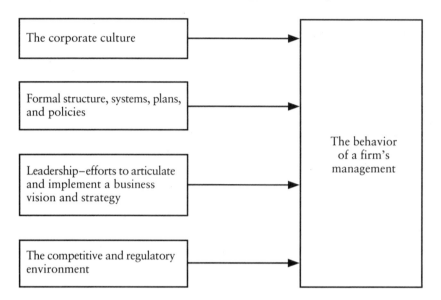

Figure 5.1 Four factors that shape managerial behavior
Source: Kotter and Heskett, 1992:6

processes of cultural change within the firm are, I think, misspecified. Further, we can derive very little guidance as to why resistance to change, where it occurs, is so selective.

In this alternative view, culture is inherently and deeply implicated in what we do and under what social and historical circumstances, in how we think about or understand what we do, and how we think about ourselves in that context. It embraces material practices, social relations, and ways of thinking. Culture both produces these things and is a product of them in a complicated and highly contested historical process.[4]

Material practices include the technology and organization of production, the division of labor, work tasks, and processes (including the work processes involved in management, research, sales, etc.), and the actual products produced. Work is simultaneously a material and social activity. Through it we develop practical skills and derive meanings and values about what we do. We also develop understandings and expectations about the social practices involved in this activity. This is the sense in which culture is about what we do and how we do it.

[4] This definition is influenced by a range of anthropologists and social theorists, including Mintz, 1985; Fox, 1985; Godelier, 1986; Geertz, 1973; Williams, 1977; Bourdieu, 1984; and Roseberry, 1982.

Social relations include the behavioral norms and standards that are emphasized in the management literature and that provide the tacit framework for everyday social interactions. But they also centrally include the basis on which power, rights, and obligations are produced and allocated within the community, how they are legitimated or enforced, how they are contested, and how they are stabilized.

Ways of thinking, finally, imply not only ideas and meanings, but the processes of interpretation and the construction of knowledge. Raymond Williams uses the term "practical consciousness" to express his view that ideas or ways of thinking are a part of material social processes, both produced by our activities and the necessary condition for undertaking them at all (Williams, 1977). We have to think in order to do, but what we do shapes how we think. More broadly, what we can imagine is shaped by the pressures and limits characteristic of a particular social order and by our position in it. But we can also create new explanations or interpretations, perhaps in the encounter with new conditions, that allow us to revise our understanding of or attitude towards existing practices and relations.

What culture does, in this sense, is to create a way of life. One could also say that this is a world in which humans, through their actions and their social relations, produce culture at the same time that culture produces them. This allows us to keep an eye on the practical, historically specific constraints to action and innovation at any particular juncture without eliminating the possibility that changes may, indeed, occur.

It is, in a way, misleading to speak of a single culture, for even within the firm there are many sites of cultural production. We should expect that any number of "subcultures" will coexist in varying degrees of tension with one another (cf. J. Martin, 1992). Engineers tend to see the world differently from accountants, salespeople, and machine operators, for example. The very rich literature on working-class culture, both inside and outside the firm, describes one important arena of what might be thought of as countercultural production (cf. Brody, 1980; Montgomery, 1979; Hareven, 1982; Lazonick, 1990; Braverman, 1974; Aitken, 1985; Williams, 1977). But we must still recognize the existence of a dominant culture which is produced by the dominant – in this case, top management – and which establishes the social reality in which subcultures and countercultures emerge and against which they contend (cf. Williams, 1977; Gramsci, 1971). Culture is very much about power.

Is culture inherently resistant to change? I think the answer must be no. Culture is never static or achieved; it is always in the process of becoming. Cultural change, then, is normal. It is always being produced by virtue of the fact that our practices, relations, and ideas are always being confronted with new problems and conditions, some of them created by the culture itself, some produced in the firm's environment.

Culture, in this view, changes through the continual production of new problems, tensions, and contradictions (cf. Pascale, 1990). But the process is power-laden and conflictual and the kinds of change that are selected depend on how conflicts are resolved in practice. In this way, the process of cultural change (and, therefore, the possibility of corporate transformation) is structured yet indeterminate: both path-dependent and potentially path-breaking.

The relationship between corporate culture and strategy is also more intimate than is normally conceived. Strategy embodies knowledge and interpretations about the world and the firm's position in it. It is an exercise in imagining how the world could be or how it ought to be. In this light, strategy is produced by culture. At the same time, since the past strategic trajectory of the firm embodies specific configurations of practices, relations, and ideas, culture is also produced by strategy. The two are mutually constitutive categories.

It follows from all of this that the problem of cultural change cannot be separated from other problems of the firm such as organization, strategy, technology, market orientation, and the like. Corporate culture is not a kind of behavioral overlay on an existing organizational and technological substrate (the firm) that can vary independently of the base. It follows also that the problem of cultural change and corporate transformation runs much deeper than habit or tradition. What is at stake is the power to define a very particular social order – the firm – and its relationship to its environment.

So cultural change inevitably involves a struggle over power. By this I don't mean the rather circumscribed one envisioned in, say, organizational sociology over who runs this or that bit of the world, but a struggle over who has the power to construct and defend a specific social order and the practices, behaviors, knowledge, and understandings appropriate to it. At the same time, cultural change involves a struggle over identity – over who and what the firm is. When these struggles are sufficiently acute, they amount to a kind of cultural crisis in which competing models of the social order, and the material and human resources and identities tied to them, are threatened with devaluation and oblivion. The outcome of these struggles will determine which kinds of change will be welcomed and which resisted.

We can summarize the differences involved in these alternative views of culture through some dichotomies. The management literature view of culture is generally idealist. It describes a world in which cultural meanings determine actions and behaviors. While experience and learning may be essential to the validation and institutionalization of the culture, the process is really put into motion by ideas, values, and assumptions. The alternative presented here is a materialist view of culture, in which practices, relations, and ideas are mutually constitutive.

The idealism of the first view helps to account for the absence of power and social position from the discussion. Though culture itself is seen to be quite powerful, and even though the ideas and values which underlie corporate cultures are those of managers and leaders (in short, the powerful), there is no notion that culture is also *about* power. In the second view, by contrast, culture embodies a social process through which power relations are worked out and made effective.

We can also contrast an understanding of culture as an achieved system with an approach that emphasizes process and open-endedness; and, similarly, culture as emergent with culture as both produced and producing. These factors are in turn tied up in contrasting views of culture as a unifying system that is inherently resistant to change as opposed to a dialectical process which produces specific kinds of change. Finally, there is an important difference in a view of culture as the subject of strategy compared with culture as constitutive of strategy.

Dichotomies are always too clear about their own boundaries. Nevertheless, I believe these contrasts frame a terrain in which the problem of corporate culture and transformation takes on a very different light.

Corporate culture, power, and selective change

If culture is in part about power, we need to explore what that power is about and how it may be threatened. This can provide some guidance in understanding what kinds of change will be accepted and which resisted.

The largest American firms (say the Fortune 500) rose to positions of considerable power during the course of the twentieth century. I want to suggest that what this power implied goes beyond our conventional notions of market power, understood as the ability to set prices and quantities of output and to consistently enjoy (in effect, "own") a significant share of domestic and international markets in a particular industry.

Some caveats are in order, although they boil down to the idea that power does not need to be unchallenged or unconstrained to count still as power. Thus, except for regulated monopolies such as AT&T before the breakup, any firm, no matter how large or dominant in its industry, still faced competition from other firms. Any firm, no matter how large or dominant, still faced potentially important constraints imposed by organized labor or by increasing state regulation of labor practices, environmental effects, and so on. Indeed, as the firms' size and scope grew, these constraints tended to become more significant (cf. Galambos, 1995; Galbraith, 1956). By the same token, even the most dominant firms couldn't utterly control markets; consumers could, in the end, refuse to buy the products they offered.

Still, they were and are extraordinarily powerful social agents. This power is rooted in their command over vast social, material, and human resources and defended (indeed, promoted) by the power of the state – in this case, the most powerful nation in the world. So we can recognize the real constraints while supposing that these firms had more power than most social agents to define a very particular reality.

They had, for example, more organized power than most of us to define markets, to create social needs, and to shape tastes. The old adage, "find a need and fill it," was always misleading. What the most powerful and innovative firms did was to create a need and fill it. And the needs were created in tandem with the cultivation of specific tastes or the desire for particular product attributes: sweetness, size, speed, form, color, loudness, etc. Even where these tastes were arguably rooted in innate human preferences (such as for sweetness) or fundamental needs (such as for geographic mobility), the producer could still play a very strong role in elaborating and directing their expression and the social practices of which they became a part (Mintz, 1985). Thus, a preference for sweet tastes doesn't necessarily imply that Americans should become a nation of soda-pop drinkers, let alone a Pepsi Generation, or should all be raised on pre-sweetened breakfast cereals. Similarly, the need for geographic mobility doesn't necessarily mean that Americans should all become owners of large, rear-wheel-drive automobiles.

A second crucial arena for firms is that they had collectively the power to institutionalize (again, within constraints but quite effectively nonetheless) particular models of competition and production. Competition in the mass production model was channeled away from pure (also known as "cut-throat") price competition or constant product innovation/renovation, and channeled into controlled product differentiation, advertising, brand loyalty, distribution, finance, and the like. While this didn't eliminate the possibility of, for example, price wars or dumping, these were anomalies, for the most part entered into for tactical reasons (to deter unwanted competition or to discipline existing competitors) or due to conjunctural circumstances (temporary over-capacity and gluts). In general, competition presented itself in a known and accepted array of forms (and from known and accepted quarters).

This model of competition, as suggested earlier, was closely articulated with the model of standardized mass production (see chapter 2).

This model embraces a characteristic organization and technology of production, and a particular approach to social relations within the firm. One of the crucial advantages of this ensemble of practices for the dominant firms within the model was that it did much to stabilize their environments, allowing for the rational management and reproduction of their social and material assets over time. This is another very important kind of power.

The elaboration and institutionalization of these models of competition and production constitute a very particular and far-reaching kind of social and cultural reality. They helped define, for example, a historically and culturally specific meaning for the categories of space and time (see Harvey, 1989, and above, chapters 2 and 3).

They were also part of the process of constructing particular processes of valuation. That is to say, firms had the power to define how different categories of person and activity would be valued within the firm, and these definitions were shaped by the specificities of the models. For example, these implied that labor would be treated as an undifferentiated cost that should be eliminated wherever possible rather than, say, as individual participants who should be cultivated. The models helped create a world in which quantity would be valued more than quality, and in which figuring out a way to save a dollar in the manufacture of a component would be valued more than the product's operating efficiency or its responsiveness to the customer's actual needs.

By the same token, these models of competition and production implied certain processes of inclusion and exclusion. This could mean not only who was included in the corporate "us," but also, for example, who was included in the set of eligible competitors and, thus, who would be taken seriously. It doesn't, for example, seem far-fetched to propose that part of the reason that American firms failed for so long to respond to the threat of Japanese competition was that the Japanese firms didn't "qualify" as accepted competitors whose actions required a response. In this sense, the Japanese were not so much inscrutable (hard to read) as ineligible (not on the reading list in the first place).

Taken together, what these various powers amount to is the power to define a social order and the conventions and understandings appropriate to it. The social order that is in this way produced also shapes the firm's sense of identity and its way of understanding the world. Understanding what corporate power is about in turn draws our attention to specific kinds of vulnerability and likely areas of resistance.

One kind of vulnerability derives from the fact that corporate knowledge is also situated knowledge. Powerful as they are, the way firms interpret the world is structured by their position in it. This situatedness may produce what could be thought of as a predisposition to systematically read evidence about the state of the world in certain ways – or, alternatively, to systematically misread certain kinds of evidence. Yet again, it may imply systematically ignoring certain kinds of evidence altogether so that information, though available, becomes uninformative.

In other words, what we might call the practical consciousness of firms is both structuring and structured. Even the most powerful social agents – those that are dominant within an existing social order – are constrained in their ways of thinking by the very processes and practices they were so instrumental in creating. In this sense, the problem with information is not so much that it is hard to come by as that it must be interpreted in order to constitute knowledge (hence, strategy). But the process of interpretation is unavoidably culturally inflected, and this structures the knowledge that can be produced. This is also, then, one of the ways in which culture produces strategy.

The second area of vulnerability concerns the nature of a competitive challenge and the kinds of change implied by it. We normally think of competition as being about products and prices, and, indeed, this is the form in which it is expressed and most certainly the form in which it is noticed. But some kinds of competitive challenge take place on a much deeper and broader terrain, and unless that is understood, the meaning and importance of product and price initiatives will be misconstrued and responded to inappropriately.

We need to distinguish two kinds of competitive challenge: that which takes place *within* a common social order established by long-dominant firms, and that which occurs *between* different social orders. The first kind, which might be thought of as normal competition, takes place on the terrain defined by the existing ensemble of material practices, social relations, and ways of thinking. In short, it takes place within the culture. It may still imply significant changes, but these will be adjustments or intensifications along an existing cultural/strategic trajectory: for example, more automation, faster line speeds, different product features, reorganized reporting relationships, entrance to new geographical markets, or altered price structures.

Competition between social orders, on the other hand, is more far-reaching. The competing social order embodies very different conceptions of the market and the firm's relationship to it, and different models of competition and production, along with their specific understandings of time and space and processes of valuation and inclusion. Responding to this kind of competition with the adjustments and intensifications characteristic of normal competition is inadequate – something like fielding more and better-trained archers and swordsmen against gunners.

The potential sources of this kind of competition are many. The challenge posed by Japanese firms is one important example – not simply because Japanese culture is different from American culture, but because the material practices, social relations, and ways of thinking that developed in (and helped to produce) Japanese firms were different. These differences reflect the circumstances in which Japanese firms grew up: the specificities of the market, the history of labor relations, the strategy of the state, and so forth.

But the challenge can also emerge from within a country, an industry, or even a firm as the practices and understandings of groups within it begin to diverge from the dominant culture. The competition between the East Coast and West Coast electronics and computer industries is one example (Leslie, 1993b; Saxenian, 1994). The relationship of NUMMI and Saturn to the rest of GM can also be characterized as produced by divergent models of the social order.

I should note that the appropriate response to this second type of competition isn't necessarily becoming exactly like the competing social order. This may not even be possible. Japanese firms will always be better versions of themselves than any American firm can hope to be, and anyway, even they have their problems. But insofar as the old social order cannot compete with the new, then far-reaching changes are necessary.

The threat to the Digital Equipment Corporation (DEC) posed by computer workstations provides one example. DEC, it may be recalled, made its fortune by challenging IBM and the dominance of large, expensive mainframe computers by developing its line of smaller, cheaper, yet powerful PDP and VAX minicomputers. Yet it was almost completely undone by an apparently wholly analogous assault on the market it had created by still smaller, cheaper, and powerful computer workstations. While we might have expected DEC to continue to push its advantage down the size and price curves, it instead had the greatest difficulty responding when other firms jumped into the lead. By 1992, the firm was closing in on $3 billion in quarterly losses. Ken Olsen, its legendary founder, was forced out.

I want to stress that the competition DEC faced was not only about size, function, and price. DEC's new rivals had staked themselves on open architectures and operating systems, and a different way of thinking about how the power of a computer can be distributed to users. They also embraced a style of highly collaborative relations with specialist suppliers rather than trying to keep everything in-house. In short, they had a very different conception of what a firm in this business ought to do, how it should understand its market, and how it should relate to both customers and suppliers. The market, needless to say, overwhelmingly endorsed this new approach.

AnnaLee Saxenian, in her book *Regional Advantage*, provides an explanation of DEC's downfall that centers on the company's inward-oriented culture and enduring commitment to vertical integration and proprietary systems (Saxenian, 1994). As a result, DEC, much like the Mamelukes, refused for years to acknowledge the validity of this alternative set of practices and understandings even as its profits evaporated. This was not because change in general was anathema to DEC – it was a very technically progressive firm. But the kinds of change necessary to respond to the new competition threatened DEC's identity and its way of life, both of which were bound up in its commitments to integrated operations and proprietary technology. It was that kind of change that was unacceptable to the dominant culture – that is, the culture of the dominant: Ken Olsen and DEC's powerful and highly centralized Operations Committee (ibid; cf. also Ferguson and Morris, 1993).

In sum, the response required by this sort of competitive challenge is a thoroughgoing reconfiguration of corporate identity and culture. But, as we can see from the DEC example, this is problematic because it throws into question the entire ensemble of material practices, social relations, and ways of thinking of the firm. And it particularly throws into question the nature of power relations. In the competing social order, the traditionally dominant are, almost by definition, no longer dominant. The powers that they possess and the forms, processes, and understandings that they have created are effectively devalued.

Responding to this sort of competition is peculiarly difficult. First of all, it is hard to see what is at stake, since this doesn't appear in the product or the price lists. More importantly, however, an appropriate response may require significant devaluations of the resources tied to the old social order.

It may be helpful to think about this as a rather unusual problem of sunk costs.[5] Here it is not just specialized material assets (such as plant and equipment) that only have value in the specific context in which they were put into place but are quite valueless outside of that context (G. Clark, 1994; Collis, 1991). We have also to reckon with specialized social and cultural assets that have value only in the context which produced them (and which they produced). The defense of these assets may foreclose otherwise appropriate responses to this second type of competition, since the appropriate responses also imply the devaluation of those assets. In this way, there are very powerful forces influencing the selective pattern of change and resistance.

In this context, we can better understand, for example, the not uncommon circumstance in which firms contain within themselves

---

[5] My thanks to Gordon Clark for suggesting this to me.

thriving exemplars of an alternative culture while the rest of the firm adheres to the practices and understandings of the dominant culture. The alternative cultures often come into being on the periphery of the firm, both organizationally and geographically. Saturn and NUMMI within GM are one example. Xerox PARC in California and IBM's personal computer operation in Florida are others. As I will argue in the next chapter, organizational and geographical distance may be important (perhaps necessary) conditions for the emergence of the alternative culture within the firm. But this distance also allows the rest of the firm to remain uncontaminated by the new practices and understandings being produced within it. The dominant culture can contain a counterculture, but if the alternative constitutes a threat to the dominant social order, it will not easily be embraced.

Values and processes of valuation

We can get some idea of the complexity of the problem and the stakes involved if we revisit the question of values as they are normally treated in the business literature. What can we really deduce about values and how they work in the context of corporate culture and competitiveness?

At the outset we can suppose that not only do the "right" values need to be selected (that is, those contributing to competitiveness), but they have to be plausible (that is to say, credibly articulated), consistent with one another and over time, widely shared, and made to seem a natural feature of the environment. In principle, one cannot extol a culture of pride while creating trivial jobs, proclaim respect for the individual while monitoring that individual's every move, or ask some stakeholders (workers, suppliers) to care for a firm that is visibly sacrificing their interests in favor of others (management, stockholders). Now in fact, as we know, these things happen all the time, and so part of the cultural work of the firm is to make actual practices appear to be consistent with the announced values. This might include, for example, finding ways of telling people that their work is valuable even if they know it to be boring and inconsequential. Such common practices as special awards for individual performance or group ceremonies for meeting "the target" (whatever it might be) are about engineering a congruence between values and practice (Rosen, 1991). There is no guarantee that they succeed, but the effort is an important part of validating the dominant culture.

The values also need to be internalized and made taken-for-granted from top management on down, so that people have a sense of the rightness of things and also of their rights in the context of the culture, but without needing to appeal explicitly to that culture for validation.

Thus, in a collaborative culture, workers simply know that they can voice suggestions or even criticisms to supervisors or, for that matter, to the president, and everyone accepts this as legitimate. The values, in short, need to appear to be "natural," incontestable, and inherent rather than constructed socially and through a historical process of conflict and negotiation.

The degree to which this relationship between values, culture, and competitiveness is accepted in current debates is reflected in the willingness to suppose that the Japanese competitive advantage is in significant measure "cultural." The culture, in turn, is seen to rest on an underlying value structure that emphasizes the group, rather than the individual, and harmony at all costs, producing a culture of cooperativeness that unites all members of society (or the firm), no matter what their social position, in sacrificing personal or class interests for the benefit of the whole. Remarkably, subscribing to this view requires one to overlook a quite recent history of overt, sometimes violent labor conflict and to detach the notion of culture from the real social practices that sustain (and are themselves reproduced by) the prevailing social order (cf. Cusumano, 1985). We may ask, in this context, whether lifetime employment *reflects* a culture of harmony and cooperativeness or actually produces it. A simple appeal to values produces no particular enlightenment on that score.

Further, a "culture as values" approach is implicitly reflexive in that it also requires a specific (cultural) understanding of how people are to be valued. Thus, a culture of participation presumably assumes that everyone is capable of contributing valuable ideas if given the chance, so it is worthwhile taking the time to listen to them and to think about what they say. This seems pretty straightforward, but if we play the idea out even a little bit, we immediately encounter potentially profound complications.

Note, for example, that in theory and practice, labor is normally viewed as an abstract category. In mainstream economic theory it is analyzed as a homogeneous unit of input with a given price that is perfectly substitutable with others of its type or with capital. In the context of actual corporate practice, labor has long been viewed simply as a cost. But a corporate strategy based on a shared, mobilizing culture must at least act as though workers are also *persons* with specific identities, and that they are valued *per se*.

This constitutes a significant, though largely unacknowledged, contradiction in the discussion on corporate culture, since the realities of corporate life under capitalism imply strong limits to the degree to which this way of valuing people in themselves can be deployed. The recent travails of GM provide a succinct illustration. The firm has strenuously been announcing its commitment to participatory and collaborative relations within the firm, yet, facing massive overcapacity in the industry, it was still forced to shut down a large number of facilities. In doing so, it incurred the plausible charge that it was playing individual plants (groups of participants) off against others with the goal of extracting concessions. But even without this suggestion of manipulation, what is clear is that GM was forced summarily to devalue the very people whose inherent value it had just explicitly claimed to recognize.[6]

Yet that is not the end of the story, since under conditions of overcapacity, the question of competitiveness turns precisely on whose capital and labor will be devalued and whose will be spared. If certain kinds of culture enable firms to be more competitive, then firms must commit themselves both to the values and to the underlying processes of valuation as though they believed there were no possibility of failure. There *is*, however, a possibility of failure, in which case the firm is forced to renege on its commitments to at least some members of the community, thus throwing the credibility of its commitments more generally in doubt – that is, undermining the culture or, at least, producing a different one than intended. Indeed, under conditions of persistent overcapacity, there is a guarantee of failure for someone, even if all firms in the industry adopt the "right" (that is, competitive) values and culture.

As a first cut, then, if we can think of cultures as being not only about values but about processes of valuation – how things, people, or relationships are to be valued – then the complexity of the problem of cultural change in the firm becomes more apparent; or at least more firmly rooted in material conditions and processes as well as in the world of ideas. The closest analogy is perhaps to the former Soviet states as they seek to become capitalist. There, an immediate problem is to understand what private property is and how it will be valued. Here, the problem is how to understand the relationship of different categories of person (workers, suppliers, customers, stockholders, managers) to the firm and how these individuals will be valued.

A further complication is this. If people are to be valued as real persons with real (biographical) identities, then it must be recognized that they have real histories and specific interpretations of those histories. Changing the culture may mean changing the sense of identity and revising these historical interpretations. This can be no small task.

Consider, for example, the process of transition from adversarial to collaborative labor relations. A long history of possibly bitter struggle,

---

[6] Kanter somewhat obliquely acknowledges this problem when she notes that "Growth is helpful, of course, in encouraging people to see change as an opportunity rather than a threat" (Kanter, 1983:134).

which, while it was being lived, was based on divergent but genuinely held views of justice and rights, must somehow be recast (reinterpreted) as a tragic mistake. Identities which were built on different processes of valuing "us" vs. "them" must now be overhauled so that everyone becomes "us." The bitterness and anger (and the reasons for them) must in some sense be "forgotten."[7] Note further that this is all quite likely to be taking place in the context of downsizing, so that large numbers of "us" are being ejected from the corporate community even as the idea of the community is being reaffirmed – or perhaps more accurately, put into place. Small wonder, perhaps, that it often seems to require the threat of imminent annihilation ("we really believed Ford could die") to trigger the process – revising processes of valuation and historical interpretations so that a catastrophic devaluation of human and material resources can be avoided.

Traditions, paradigms, and commitments

If culture were indeed essentially a package of norms, values, and customary behavioral patterns, then the obstacles to cultural change might plausibly be sought in the immobilizing weight of custom, habit, and tradition. Note, however, that there is a strong essentialism at work here: we are simply loath to give up the ways of a lifetime, even when a changing environment has made these customs so dysfunctional as to threaten our (corporate) existence. Traditions, in this sense, provide a comforting – if false – sense of continuity and stability in the face of uncertainty and external turmoil. They may be highly efficient in the sense that meanings and roles in daily life do not have to be continuously renegotiated. But by their very efficacy, they tend to blind people to the need for change.

Further underpinning the supposed power of tradition to block change is that it is viewed as agentless and non-strategic. Traditions simply emerge or coalesce out of an anonymous history of practices and understandings. Although they may have a function, they have no particular goal or point: they simply are.

There is a peculiar sleight-of-hand involved here. Traditions are seen as the product of a long, historical evolution, yet, at some point, they apparently become fixed and everything within their orbit congeals.

---

[7] Ernest Renan offers an interesting gloss on the problem when he writes: "Or l'essence d'une nation est que tous les individus aient beaucoup de choses en commun, et aussi que tous aient oublié bien des choses." A rough translation would be "Now, the essence of a nation is that all the individuals have many things in common, and also that they have forgotten many things" (cited in B. Anderson, 1991:6).

History, in effect, stops in this realm of social practice and consciousness. To the degree that culture is equated with tradition, the difficulty of cultural change is both inherent and self-evident.

Even as an empirical proposition, however, this explanation of cultural rigidity seems hollow, as it is all too easy to point to instances of rapid social adjustment to quite extraordinary changes. When automobiles were made broadly affordable through mass production, after all, the masses started driving everywhere. Pretty soon, it turned out, we were all part of the "culture of the automobile."

There is, moreover, considerable historical evidence that numerous deeply revered traditions have been invented out of whole cloth – quite literally in the case of the Scottish kilt – and rapidly propagated so that they take on an air of timeless naturalness (cf. Hobsbawm and Ranger, 1983). This suggests that they can also be uninvented and replaced by new ones if the need is sufficiently acute. The shifting pattern of "traditional" political enmities and alliances (consider present-day France and Germany) is a case in point. Moreover, not everyone needs to subscribe wholesale to the new traditions in order for them to be effective. Any number of French citizens may privately harbor suspicions about Germans, but the political and economic alliance with Germany remains intact.

A particularly telling example in this context concerns the nineteenth-century European nationalist movement, whose leadership was significantly composed of the local (national) bourgeoisie. Members of this national elite were commonly raised in the imperial languages (German, Swedish, English, etc.), yet as part of this political struggle they adopted the local vernacular languages – Czech, Hungarian, Welsh, Finnish, etc. (B. Anderson, 1981). It is hard to imagine a tradition to which one would cling more devoutly than the use of one's customary language, since this is so caught up with one's sense of identity and capacities of self-expression. Yet the move makes a lot of sense, since the point was precisely about claiming and validating a new social and political identity.

The issues at stake are illuminated by the case of Norway following its independence from Denmark in 1814 and its separation from Sweden in 1905. The problem of defining and validating a "true" Norwegian language, distinct from Danish and Swedish, occupied the political and social agenda for well over a century. The debate was not over whether an "authentic" Norwegian language should be institutionalized in the society, but rather over which version of Norwegian it would be. Riksmål, more closely identified with Danish, was the "traditional" language of culture, officialdom, and the bourgeoisie; it was concentrated geographically in the cities and, more generally, the eastern part of the country. Landsmål was a hybrid Norwegian, synthesized in the late nineteenth century from various rural dialects, mostly from the western part of the country. Its claim to authenticity was based on its ties to Old Norwegian and to its folk origins, but its political strength was also linked to its urban, working-class constituency.

The protracted struggle over linguistic reform had little to do with the weight of tradition in the sense of people generally resisting new forms of expression. Indeed, some partial, compromise reforms were institutionalized without great difficulty. The real sticking points were political and social, and their resolution depended on the degree to which either side had the power to validate its own vision of the social order (Haugen, 1966).

While it no doubt takes some work to realign long-standing practices and understandings, it seems clear that the specter of tradition, as it is commonly invoked, is an insufficient explanation for rigidity. Rather than abandoning the notion altogether, though, it seems useful to propose that traditions are at once more plastic, more dynamic, and more selective than the traditional notion of tradition allows. They represent a highly particular version of the past which, as Raymond Williams argues, "is intended to connect with and ratify the present" (Williams, 1977:116). We need, then, to understand which (or whose) traditions are selected, and why. If we see tradition as an actively produced social dynamic rather than an inherited social artifact, then we have, I think, a better chance of understanding why and how it can play a contradictory role within the firm.

It might be possible, on the other hand, to sidestep the issue of tradition by recasting it as a problem of entrenched mindsets or paradigms.[8] Early elaborations of this approach can be found in Veblen, with his notion of "trained incapacity," or in Dewey's idea of "occupational psychosis," in which psychosis means something more akin to mindset than madness (see Burke, 1954 [1933]). For both, specialized training and a history of experiences and material practices produce in the individual a way of thinking or an interpretive framework that, while quite successful in the circumstances which produced it, may lead to serious misjudgments when the circumstances change.

In short, this interpretive system, because it is so well grounded and so broad in scope, may block its own revision. The Mamelukes' adherence to the practices of the *furusiyya* might be one example (although, again, three hundred years seems hard to account for in this way). Critiques that trace the decline of manufacturing firms in the US to the

---

[8] These might be akin to what Schein has in mind when he speaks of "thought words" (Schein, 1992:22–3).

fact that they were increasingly run by people trained in finance and accounting, who were, consequently, blind to problems of manufacturing or product technology, also fit within this general frame (cf. Hayes and Abernathy, 1980; Johnson, 1991).

Historian of science Ludwik Fleck, in a similar vein, speaks of "thought styles" as the directed perception and appropriate assimilation of what has been perceived given existing knowledge and epistemological orientations. Only those observations which are appropriate to the thought style can attain the status of fact or truth. Thought styles are produced and consolidated within "thought collectives" that establish a historically and culturally dependent way of understanding the world (Fleck, 1979 [1935]). The thought collective structures what is thinkable and unthinkable within its frame of reference and manages anomalies so that they either come to conform with the precepts of the thought style or are hidden from view. In this way, the thought collective is stabilized for greater or lesser periods of time. Change, in this schema, is essentially a dialectical process, produced through the encounter with other thought styles or with ideas on the margin of the present thought collective. The result is a reconfiguration of the thought collective and a shift onto a new trajectory for the thought style.

Kuhn's version of this idea captures the dilemma as the normal effect of a paradigm shift in which some adherents of the old paradigm are simply unable to accept the new ideas, however good the evidence in their favor (Kuhn, 1970). The paradigm establishes the rules for selecting or recognizing problems, and indeed so frames the terrain of research that whole classes of questions simply cannot be asked within its boundaries. In this way, a range of commitments, from the methodological to the ontological, is built up in those practicing within the paradigm.

These increasingly rigid commitments, much like trained incapacity or occupational psychosis, prevent the individual from seeing the world in a different way, even in the face of strong evidence in support of the new paradigm. Thus, Joseph Priestley, who has a plausible claim to the discovery of oxygen, was never able to see it as anything other than dephlogistated air (Kuhn, 1970). Galambos makes an effective case for the power of commitments in his analysis of AT&T's inability to understand and respond to the threat posed by MCI (Galambos, 1933).

For Kuhn, crisis and the availability of an alternative paradigm are the necessary preconditions for a paradigm shift. This seems to be an accurate description of the situation of American firms. The onset of the crisis of mass production can be dated to the late 1960s and early 1970s (cf. Galambos, 1995). The alternative paradigm has centrally to do with flexibility (Piore and Sabel, 1984; Harvey, 1989).

Note, however, that the crisis has been with us for some two decades, and the broad outlines of the alternative paradigm have been in circulation since at least the late 1970s and early 1980s, with the first of the spate of academic and business literature on Japan and other national models of production (see above, chapter 4). Indeed, the *language* of the new paradigm has been widely accepted in business circles, as everyone now speaks fluently of empowerment, decentralization, and total quality. But the practical import of this conversion is hard to assess. IBM, to cite one example, has been announcing thoroughgoing decentralization programs for some years now (Pascale, 1990), yet it never escapes condemnation for being drastically overcentralized (cf. *Economist*, 1992c; *Financial Times*, 1992j; *New York Times*, 1992a). At the very least, then, publicly signing on to the new paradigm is not conclusive evidence that the paradigm shift has occurred. And it is hard to avoid wondering why it has taken everyone so long.

These arguments all, in one way or another, stress the serious disjunctures that can occur between our real, material circumstances and how we understand or interpret those circumstances – in short, how we represent the world to ourselves and how we perceive the conditions for action in that context. They allow for the sorts of story in which overwhelming evidence in favor of one interpretation of the world can be repeatedly ignored, even though this puts the assets of the firm and the position of the decision-makers at extraordinary risk.

The sheer magnitude of the stakes involved provide good reason to probe further in this line of analysis. We need to understand why the power of the commitments invoked by Kuhn, Galambos, and others is so strong that it can actually threaten the social existence of those who hold them. That is to say, not only are the assets of the firm at risk of annihilation, but the social position of the top manager is similarly put into question. What, we may ask, is so beguiling about the old paradigm, so compelling about the old commitments, that one risks being read out of history. This is a form of what used to be known as false consciousness – with a vengeance.

A second aspect of this kind of explanation that requires more attention is that not all changes are equally resisted. The very same people who apparently simply cannot get the point about quality or cooperation can fill their factories with state-of-the-art automated equipment and never blink. On the side, they may be embroiled in fantastically arcane financial maneuvers so new in conception that no one actually understands them, while every second or third year finding it possible to cope with a major organizational overhaul. Those who become top managers usually do so by proving themselves able and willing to operate in any corner of the organization and in any corner of the globe, and to change both every few years.

What this suggests is that newness, *per se*, is not the problem and that we need an explanation that can account for why some changes are readily accepted, while others are resisted despite overwhelming evidence in their favor and drastic sanctions for inaction. As with traditions, paradigms and commitments are highly *selective*. And again, we need to understand which (or whose) paradigms and commitments are selected, and why. In order to do this, we need to analyze the producers of the dominant culture of the firm – the highest-level managers who are involved in strategic decision-making.

Corporate Strategists: Identity and Commitments

What this means, in effect, is that we need to theorize the corporate strategist. We do this, of course, in a sort of truncated way when we assume that the people who run firms are maximizers or satisficers, but this single dimension doesn't give us much to go on. In particular, it doesn't explain why these satisficers or maximizers may systematically make bad decisions under certain conditions. Alternatively, we could suppose that the answers could only be found in the psychologies and biographies of the individuals involved. In that case, though, it would simply be an unlucky coincidence that whole groups of once highly successful firms should go astray at roughly the same time.

In what follows I focus on managerial identities as a way of understanding the power of their commitments to certain trajectories of change and the strength of their resistance to others. I also want to use the concept of identity to negotiate the difficulty posed by the fact that corporations both are and are not the people who work in them and, more specifically, the people who run them.

Managerial identities: power and the sense of power

John Sculley, in his autobiography *Odyssey*, offers an intriguing description of the headquarters of Pepsi, where he started his career under the leadership of Don Kendall:

> In 1970, Kendall moved the company's world headquarters ... to a 140-acre site in Purchase, New York, where he personally selected and supervised the installation of an elaborate sculpture garden. He brought to the campus the symbols of power that PepsiCo would come to represent. On its approach to Westchester Airport, the corporate jet would routinely circle over Pepsi headquarters, providing a glimpse of the P-shaped, man-made lake on the lavish corporate campus. A limousine would greet you,

ready to sweep you back to headquarters. It made me feel that I belonged
to an elite fraternity. . . .

The ultimate perk was a button beside Kendall's desk that controlled
the Pepsi fountains which shot a powerful stream of water more than 40
feet into the air above the lake. (Sculley with Byrne, 1987:8–9)

Three things are particularly worthy of note in this quotation. One is
the sense of power expressed through an apparently absolute domina-
tion of nature: the P-shaped lake and the "ultimate perk" of the button
controlling the flow of water. The people who run Pepsi are really masters of all that they see, not just of the people who work for them, but
of the environment as well.

Second is the way in which this power is repeatedly revisited and
reaffirmed. Executives whose time is no doubt worth several hundred
dollars per minute – who are, indeed, chieftains of society in which
"time is money" – nevertheless "routinely" take time to circle over the
headquarters in order to remind themselves of who they are and what
they have wrought.

Third is Sculley's own sense of belonging to the elite fraternity.
Whatever the internal struggles among that elite and however diverse
the personalities involved (and Sculley describes both vividly), it does
form a distinctive community, membership in which shaped Sculley's
own sense of himself, his ideas about what was important (processes of
valuation), and his goals and aspirations. This is a community that
knows itself by its power.

I wish to propose that the identities of top managers are intimately
caught up in the fact and the sense of power. In other words, managers
as social agents are powerful people and the experience and sense of
this power shapes their perceptions about themselves and about the
world. In this view, identity is a social and historical product, not
merely a biographical and psychological one.

The term "identity" risks a certain fuzziness, but I think it can be
helpful nevertheless. Linking the decisions of corporate strategists to the
defense of their sense of self offers a way of understanding an apparently suicidal resistance to unambiguous evidence that, in a way, measures up to the magnitude of the stakes involved. It thus provides a
window on the nature and the power of the managerial commitments
that shape corporate strategy. Further, it casts some light on why resistance to change is so selective – that is, why some quite radical transformations are embraced wholeheartedly while others are rigorously
shunned. This allows us to avoid recourse to the idea that people who
are, in many cases, paid millions of dollars a year for their business acu-
men are the helpless prisoners of tradition and habit.

In parallel, I will want eventually to link this way of thinking about how social identities are produced with arguments about positioned or situated knowledge which propose that what we can know or how we interpret available information depends on who we are (our social identities) and where we are located historically, culturally, and geographically (cf. Haraway, 1991; Rosaldo, 1989; Williams, 1977). While this literature is often concerned with putting into evidence and validating the situated knowledge of the powerless, I think it is useful to explore too how the situatedness of the knowledge of the powerful affects their understanding and ability to act. I should note that this is an argument not that there is no "reality out there," but rather that what we make of it and how we act with reference to it depends on our social being and our socially shaped *sense* of reality.

In this section, I will try to relate the "objective" sources of managers' power with some propositions about what the sense of power entails and how it shapes identity. This part of the argument draws on Bourdieu's analysis of the divergent sources of social capital, how and to what ends they are mobilized, and how they are defended (Bourdieu, 1977, 1984). I want, as a heuristic device, to represent managers as having to manage two kinds of assets: the real material assets of their firms, and the assets represented in their own social capital. Insofar as this social capital is internalized and reconfigured as identity (what we are is translated into who we think we are), the stakes involved in the process of managing these separate but related asset structures become more sharply defined and the contradictions inherent in this process more apparent.

One of the interesting things about the social power of high-level managers is that it derives from a variety of seemingly disconnected material, historical, geographical, and cultural sources. This very diversity creates a kind of tacit coherence and self-reinforcement, as the manager's experience in different spheres of his life tend to yield the same message. Further, it tends to naturalize the experience and the sense of power: the manager knows that he has it and feels that this is right without having to explain it, to himself or anyone else ("it comes with the territory").[9]

The material sources of a manager's power include class and position, income and wealth. Technically, what makes someone a capitalist is ownership of capital which is used to accumulate more capital. What makes a capitalist a socially powerful agent is *control* over capital and the ability to mobilize the power of money (cf. Harvey, 1985). Whether or not they own significant portions of their firm, top managers are, in a

[9] The gendered pronoun here seems to me appropriate – indeed, part of the point.

sense, honorary capitalists: they have the authority to allocate capital via their investment decisions.[10]

These decisions, in effect, define markets and the firm's position in them. They frame the material processes of production and competition and the social relations and ways of thinking involved in them. Though top managers may not be immune from later sanctions, they have the authority to risk the existence of the firm even if they do not own it, a power summed up in the widely used phrase "to bet the company."

High-level managers also, needless to say, have generally high incomes and are relatively wealthy. The titles attached to their corporate and civic positions, moreover, mark them as powerful agents in the perceptions of others – including other powerful people. This reflection of their status in the eyes of others, particularly as this implies a shared yet unspoken sense of recognition with others of their type, feeds back upon and reinforces the sense of power derived from purely material sources.

Differential access to educational capital (a university education or, better, graduate degrees in business, finance, or technical disciplines, especially from the "right" schools) provides another kind of support that can function in various ways. In some cases, it is the educational capital itself that is mobilized to gain access to economic capital in the first place (as when an MBA from Harvard provides entrée to a managerial position despite the inexperience or humble origins of the person in question). Academic credentials also provide a tacit guarantee of the general suitability of a person for a managerial career – that is, a career as a socially powerful actor – that goes beyond the specific competences formally attested to by the degree itself. That is to say, while the Harvard MBA only formally guarantees that the holder is well versed in the latest management techniques, the aura of the degree confers a broader social acceptability and a tacit marker of the social power of the individual (cf. Bourdieu, 1984).[11]

Following Bourdieu, we may also expect that economic and educational capital can be mobilized to reinforce one's control of cultural capital (referring here to culture as literary and artistic productions). This can be expressed in particular forms of cultural consumption (taste, judgment) and a particular relationship to cultural production

---

[10] For a different view of the class status of managers, see Wright, 1985.

[11] Even the case of the "self-made man" who rises to corporate leadership from an early career in the mailroom is not altogether anomalous in this context. In a kind of inversion of the basic point, the reinforcement of the sense of power comes from having actual power over all the highly credentialled people just below him in the corporate hierarchy.

(such as collecting, patronage, or personal and corporate philanthropy). Privileged access to cultural capital in turn provides another form of validation of the sense of social power derived from economic and educational capital.

We can see this fusion of different forms of social capital at work in the participation by corporate leaders (and/or their spouses) in support of cultural institutions (museums, the opera, etc.), often in their headquarters' cities. The point, however, is not about control of cultural production, but rather about the way in which different forms of social capital reinforce each other and provide a coherent substrate to the sense of social power.

One presumably does not need to amass large quantities of statistical data to claim that most high-level managers in the US are white males (but see *Fortune*, 1990, 1992). They are also typically American, and rose to their positions in the postwar period of global American economic and military dominance. Race, gender, geography, and historical moment combine as well to foster a generalized sense of power.

Here it can be seen too how the position of top managers differs from that of, say, other white American males in being reinforced on all fronts. The white male blue-collar worker may feel himself empowered within the family or among his peers. He may feel himself entitled to look down upon women, minorities, or immigrants, not to mention the Japanese or the Germans, who, after all, lost the war. But this sense of power is more likely to be contradicted, hence qualified, in other settings, as when he applies for a loan at the bank, for example, or when he writes to his senator and receives a form letter in response, or when he enters the workplace.

We can also note the considerable political capital that the manager is likely to enjoy. He does get a real response from the senator when he writes, or he may be asked to lead the local public/private partnership to revitalize the downtown. If his firm is sufficiently important at a national level, he may be asked to travel to Japan with the president to discuss trade barriers or to participate in the latest national commission on competitiveness (or, for that matter, on health policy or environmental problems).

It is important to recall, however, that these seemingly disconnected aspects of the sense of power are not so disconnected in fact. They are generally anchored by the position of top manager as (honorary) capitalist – head of the firm (or close to it) and the person with final authority over the disposition of real assets.

If the position of top manager is, in some sense, about power (cf. Pfeffer, 1992), then two things follow. The first is that power and the sense of power are central to the manager's own sense of identity. The second is that the real power he possesses is both a source of strength and an area of great vulnerability – a challenge to the manager's power is not only a threat to his position and his control over resources, but also represents a challenge to his identity, his sense of self.

Power and resistance

We need, then, to ask what are the most important powers that a manager possesses in his role as manager in order to understand where these vulnerabilities most directly come into play. This will provide valuable clues to what kinds of challenge to the status quo – in short, what kinds of change – will be most strenuously resisted.

One conventional candidate would be immediate power over other people: the ability directly to tell others what to do, what their status and position in the division of labor are, what their rights and responsibilities are. But I would like to suggest that, for the highest levels of management, this power of being the boss is less vital than others of a more conceptual and strategic nature.[12]

More centrally involved is the exercise of a strategic imagination. By this I mean the power to envision how the world should be and to establish the processes of valuation by which both the manager himself and all others are measured. This also includes how different expressions of power will be valued.

The arena of the strategic imagination may be quite broad. It certainly includes the mission and the strategy of the firm. But it extends to

---

[12] It might also be argued that this power of being the boss is less possible for the very highest levels of management of large corporations. Lou Galambos offers an insightful analysis of the changing scope and orientation of top managerial authority and responsibility in the large American firm during the course of the twentieth century. Focusing on the CEO, he points out that the increasing complexity of the firm's operations and the decentralized organizational structure implemented to manage this complexity (that is, the M-form organization) meant that the CEO's practical ability to make operational decisions was increasingly constrained. By the same token, the information reaching the CEO was increasingly condensed and abstract and his most important internal function was increasingly adjudicating the competition for resources within the firm. As Galambos writes, "The CEO now specialized in handling strategic decision-making, relationships with the board of directors, and personnel decisions involving top executives." He offers this analogy: "the CEO had become the business counterpart of the feudal lord. In order to run a successful organization, he or she had to depend upon the executives in the two levels of management below the top office in a way that in effect limited the range of actions the CEO could take" (Galambos, 1995:6–7). While Galambos is stressing here the practical limits of feudal lordliness, I think we must also remember that they weren't called lords for nothing. Feudal lords (and their most important vassals – the next two levels of management below the top) did have real social and political power in their society.

envisioning how markets and competition should work, who qualifies as an eligible competitor (and who, therefore, must be taken seriously), and how the outside world should see the firm. In short, it embraces the envisioning of a social and cultural order.

These kinds of power are, by definition, extremely scarce in the firm as in the society at large. Most of us do not, in fact, have the power to effectively envision the way the world (or at least our part of it) should be ordered. This scarcity anchors and guarantees the value of these powers, and raises the stakes in protecting them.

Second, since they operate at precisely the intersection between the real conditions of existence of the manager and his sense of identity, his understanding of himself as a social agent in the world, the stakes are extraordinarily high. These are the powers that must be protected at all costs.

Taking into account this pervasive and auto-reinforcing sense of power already suggests explanations for some commonly observed phenomena in analyses of corporate change. It has been noted, for example, that the strongest resistance to empowerment strategies comes from the ranks of middle management and line supervisors (Kanter, 1983). This might seem odd, since top managers have more power to give up, as it were, as authority is decentralized to operating units and further to the shop floor. By the same token, however, they can "afford" to give up certain expressions of power since they have so many others to draw upon. Their identity as powerful agents is not called into question by this sort of change.

Middle managers, by contrast, have more at stake in defending the particular powers of oversight and control they have been used to possessing, since they are less able to compensate by drawing upon other social assets. Their sense of themselves as powerful persons is thereby directly challenged.

The argument can be restated somewhat less mechanically, however. What sets top managers apart from other persons in the firm is that they possess the power to define what counts as power. In effect, they have the capacity to assign values to different expressions of power and, in doing so, to ensure that the powers they presently have are valued highly.

Obviously, this implies also the capacity to devalue other expressions of power. Empowerment strategies, for example, effectively devalue the power to tell other people what to do and to monitor their work, which was traditionally the main asset of middle managers and supervisors. As Bourdieu has shown in another context, the victims of such a devaluation will mobilize to defend the prior asset-valuation structure or to reposition themselves favorably in the emerging one (Bourdieu,

1984:125–68). But since the devaluation of their former powers is proceeding in tandem with a significant reduction in their actual numbers, the possibility of a successful reconversion strategy within the firm is limited. There is a very real sense in which the new management strategies, as they operate through strong devaluations of existing social assets, constitute a crisis for large numbers of people within the firm; hence their resistance.

Talk of social asset devaluations in the case of middle managers may seem superfluous since their immediate problem is survival, which simplifies many things in its starkness. Still, it offers some clues as to how and on what terrain resistance is likely to be mounted. This seems preferable to invoking the drag of custom and habit, which should work universally if it is to work at all, in the sense that all changes should be equally resisted if they contravene long-standing traditions. Yet these are the same people who successfully carry forward the implementation of new technologies on the shop floor, learn to deal with matrix reporting structures, and have long adapted to being shifted around organizationally and geographically within the firm. Again, newness, *per se*, is not the problem.

The threat to the position and identity of top managers is different. As suggested, it has more to do with the power to conceptualize identity and social order, the capacity to establish the rules of the game and construct processes of valuation, and the ability to exercise strategic imagination.

The threat to these powers arises most acutely in competition with others of their type – those who run competing firms (or, in some cases, dissident factions within their own firm). Here again, the immediate material problem is obviously survival; firms that are uncompetitive fail or are absorbed by others. The top executives no longer have anything to run and, hence, lose their power base. But on the way to this outcome, if we want to understand which kinds of change are likely to be embraced or resisted, it may be useful to recast the problem as a struggle over the power to construct and defend identities, to establish processes of valuation, and to define the way in which the world will be ordered.

The problem of identity is here a tricky one since it involves both the identity of the manager and the identity of the firm.[13] Regarding specifically the firm, what I want to suggest by invoking the term is that the problem of corporate transformation is not, in the first instance, a problem of figuring out what to do – what actions to take – although this is

---

[13] I don't think it implausible to suggest that many top managers see the firm as an extension of their identity, but this is not crucial to the argument.

the issue that receives most of our attention. The prior problem, arguably, is figuring out who and what the firm should be. Firms whose commitments are tied up in the network, mass production, mainframe computers, etc., will have difficulty adapting to a world in which these commitments and identities are no longer valid. The people who run those firms need to realign these commitments, but in order to do that, they must rethink their own identities.

Identity can also be represented as a kind of sunk cost. It was proposed above that the real asset structure of the firm is, in a sense, shadowed by the manager's own social asset structure, which is internalized as identity. These shadow assets only have a guaranteed value in the circumstances which produced them and risk being devalued in a different context. Both sets of assets must be defended in order for either to have value, but this task may, in particular historical moments, become deeply contradictory.

The threat posed by competing firms organized on a different model and around a different strategy (flexible mass production, personal computers, cooperation, or whatever) is, then, not only loss of markets and devaluation of the real assets of the firm, but also loss of identity and devaluation of the asset structures of those managers. The alternative models assert, in effect, that it no longer counts to be in charge of a large, mass production firm, a mainframe computer firm, or whatever. They challenge managerial identities in tandem with fundamental conceptions about what the firm may be and how it can operate in the world. This includes deeply entrenched understandings concerning the rules of the game (how competition takes place, who the eligible players are, what the point of the game is, etc.), as well as conventions governing the relationship between the firm and its external environment (markets, suppliers, government) and relations internal to the firm, especially with labor (cf. Storper, 1993).

To cite one example, there is a world of difference in the Fordist conception of labor as a cost that must be minimized, and the view of labor as creative human beings with individual value which may underlie the flexible specialization model (Piore and Sabel, 1984). The competition proceeds in the market and also in the sphere of who has the power to value or devalue different constructions of identity and different expressions of power.

In this context, the problem is not that managers don't understand or cannot adapt to alternative, demonstrably more competitive models because they don't "get" the Japanese or the Germans, say, or because they are blinded by tradition. In light of the reams of "how-to" material published in the business press and retailed by consultants, it seems improbable that the impediments to change revolve around not knowing what to do or being unable to alter one's habits simply because they are habits. The alternative is to suppose that managers are, understandably, defending their own asset structures – the power to construct identities, to impose one's own world view, and to define what kind of power counts.

As managers seek, then, to reassert their own asset structures, certain kinds of strategy, however appropriate, may be foreclosed. That is to say, information or knowledge about what to do to remain competitive may be available but not usable, to the degree that using it requires acceding to alternative (and unfavorable) processes of valuation of one's own assets. In this way, the manager's need to defend his own world view and sense of self may come seriously into conflict with his need to defend the competitive position of the firm.[14]

Social position and situated knowledge

The idea that our interpretation of the world depends on our social, historical, and cultural position in it arises in a number of intellectual traditions, from Marxian political economy to philosophical hermeneutics, as well as in feminist and anti-imperialist critiques (cf. Harvey, 1989; Williams, 1977; Gadamer, 1976; Ricoeur, 1974; Haraway, 1991; Rosaldo, 1989). In various ways it is particularly important in contemporary ethnography (cf. Geertz, 1973; Bourdieu, 1977; Godelier, 1986; Rosaldo, 1989; Fox, 1985). In this view, knowledge is socially constituted, relational, contestable, and mutable rather than objective, universal, and fixed. Further, as Rosaldo puts it, different social positions give rise to "a distinctive mix of insight and blindness" (Rosaldo, 1989:19).

Here it is perhaps useful to note a contrast with the argument of Kuhn, in which it is the paradigm that effectively constitutes the constraining social reality from which those raised within it cannot free themselves (Kuhn, 1970). In this line of thinking, by contrast, one's social reality (social position, material circumstances, history, etc.) tends to produce the interpretive schema through which all information is processed. Information is, thus, transformed into knowledge, but this knowledge is structured by the position of the knower. As knowledge within the firm is transformed into strategy, these structured constraints narrow the available terrain for action. In this way, certain kinds of initiative become more available than others.

This argument rests on the complicated intersection between material

---

[14] Similar struggles, of course, may also take place internally as competing groups within the firm seek to impose conflicting visions of the corporation's mission, strategy, and character.

circumstances and mental constructs. It supposes that social position and social identity shape our interpretations of the information available to us and influence our ability to act on that knowledge. And it suggests that the need to transform the firm in order to remain competitive may encounter one of its most serious obstacles in the social being, position, and perceptions of the people who run it.

Romance and aesthetics

It is worth taking a brief look at two other aspects of managerial commitments that are not too often directly broached: the romantic and the aesthetic. That is to say, we need to reckon with the degree to which managers fall in love with the products and the structures that they have created, and the degree to which they find them beautiful.[15]

These categories, of course, are not innocent of power relations, social position, gender, or cultural formation. What we find desirable is by no means innate in the mind or the eye. How, then, can we understand the power of the romantic and the aesthetic to shape managerial decisions and behavior?

I became abruptly aware of this issue in the process of recounting a story that I had heard from an executive of one firm to an executive (actually one of the founders, then retired) of another firm, a tactic I sometimes employ in interviews as a way of vetting my own interpretations or prompting discussions. Both men were engineers and both happened to be British.

The first executive, whom I shall call Mr Thorpe, described a laser-based cutting machine which his firm sold to companies that made cardboard cartons. The machine replaced a complicated band-saw arrangement which required a lot of labor input to reset for different kinds or sizes of carton. However, Mr Thorpe's laser equipment was quite expensive and the band-saws were cheap, so much so that the carton companies didn't save any money by switching to the more advanced equipment, even given the substantial labor savings involved. Actually, their cartons were more expensive.

How, then, did they sell the things, I wondered. Mr Thorpe's answer was that because the laser cuts were cleaner, more accurate, and more

---

[15] In one of the earliest management classics, *The Functions of the Executive*, Chester Barnard argues that executive processes are only in part a matter of logical analysis. Management, as he writes, "transcends the capacity of merely intellectual methods, and the techniques of discriminating the factors of the situation. The terms pertinent to it are 'feeling,' 'judgment,' 'sense,' 'proportion,' 'balance,' 'appropriateness.' It is a matter of art rather than science, and is aesthetic rather than logical" (Barnard, 1968[1938]:235).

consistent, the companies that *bought* the cartons were able to run their packaging machines much faster. *That* was where the significant cost savings came from. These firms would pay more for the cartons, which justified the purchase of the expensive cutting equipment.

I liked this story a lot because it seemed an excellent illustration of how ambiguous the issue of costs can be in business practice as opposed to economic theory. But when I recounted the story to the second executive, whom I will name Mr Lawrence, his reaction was something close to sympathetic delight at my innocence. Not to put too fine a point on it, he thought I'd been had.

Mr Lawrence pointed out that it was extremely unlikely that the companies that bought the laser equipment had any sound basis *a priori* for projecting the eventual costs and prices of their product. Mr Thorpe's story was altogether too neat and too rational, from his point of view. Rather, he felt, the decision to buy was made, in significant measure, because the buyer fell in love with the equipment. The buyer, in short, just wanted it – because it was more modern, because it was a particularly seductive technology (remember how awesome and mysterious lasers used to seem before they started showing up in our living rooms?), and because it made the buyer feel better about himself to be running a plant filled with this kind of equipment. Any economic justifications would be made after the fact. They might even turn out to be accurate, but they would still have nothing to do with the decision.

This is not news, of course. Stories such as this are what allow us all to understand references to "bells and whistles." Is there a way, though, that we can understand this as something other than the irrational at work?

Michael Roper (1991) provides some interesting insights in an analysis of the commitments of a group of British managers (again, all male and mostly engineers) who are of the generation that entered their firms just after the war. Roper was particularly struck by the emotional commitment that these men had to their company's products, often filling their offices and homes with models or components. But he is able to construct a link between this emotional commitment, the manager's individual identity, and the management culture of the firm as a whole.

Roper notes that while the possibility of creative fulfillment in making things has been steadily eroded for production workers in a refined division of labor, the same is not true for managers. In this sense, he points out, such functions as design, production, marketing, and sales are not merely administrative categories but work experiences providing control over products and processes, opportunities for creativity, and investment of personality. Control and power over other people, he argues, are not the only source of motivation for managers. What also counts is privileged access to the creative aspect of making things. The manager's identity is expressed through and caught up in the things that he makes.[16]

Roper argues that this is a highly gendered process and that industrial production can also be understood as an expression and validation of masculinity. The product, in this context, is feminized and aestheticized, leading to a protective, affective attachment to it. He suggests further that having an attractive product may be satisfying not only because it provides the firm a larger share of the market, but also "because possession of it transforms the possessor in the eyes of other men" (Roper, 1991:203).

However, as Roper notes, the desire to make beautiful products may be in conflict with the corporate need to maximize profits; or, perhaps more accurately, the commitment to a specific romantic/aesthetic ideal may impair the firm's ability to adjust to new circumstances and requirements. Needless to say, the things that managers make are not restricted to individual products. They make production processes, organizational forms, and the firm itself.

Michael Piore also provides some insight into the role of aesthetic *cum* professional sensibilities in shaping real outcomes (Piore, 1968). In an analysis of how production processes were designed in a number of manufacturing firms (including equipment design or selection and job design), he notes that apparently rigorous formal economic analyses were prepared beforehand to justify particular design decisions, but that the numbers used (for instance, for labor rates) were almost astoundingly arbitrary and had nothing to do with any likely cost outcomes. What seemed to underlie the actual decisions, at least in part, was a kind of engineering aesthetic which favored machinery but which saw unpredictable human bodies as awkward clutter. The design, in effect, would be driven by the desire to minimize clutter, although this might not be a sure guide to minimizing costs.

A couple of points emerge here which I think it useful to underscore. First is the extent to which commitments are not merely intellectual (a product of specific ways of thinking or thought worlds), but also aesthetic and emotional. Their power, then, is anchored in multiple sources.

Second is the strong suggestion that we know ourselves through what

[16] This might seem to be a point that applies only to engineers, or at any rate to people somehow involved in the actual work of designing and making things. But I think it must also be the case that the identity and sense of creativeness of accountants are caught up in the accounting systems that they devise. Even economists, after all, routinely speak of the "elegance" of their mathematics.

we create. Meanings and values aren't merely disembodied cultural arti-
facts; they are produced through what we make and how we make
things. Top managers, of course, don't often make discrete products
with their own hands. But their work is creative in the sense that it con-
tributes to the definition of organizational forms and processes, the
principles underlying social relations within the firm, and the firm's
understanding of itself in the world. In this way also, managerial identities are closely linked to corporate identities and cultures.

Summary

The argument here represents only a small and very partial start to
untangling the complexities arising from the fact that corporations are
run by real people. It claims that in order to understand corporate
strategies, we need to understand something about corporate strategists.
Specifically, we need to consider what shapes their interpretations of the
world and their ability to act in it. To put this another way, we need to
understand the origins of their commitments and the (selective) power
that these commitments have in shaping their strategic decisions.

To that end, it was proposed that the fact and sense of social power
are crucial constituents of managerial identities. The importance of
identity in this schema is that it provides a terrain on which the failure
to act appropriately despite accessible and accurate knowledge about
what to do becomes explicable. It does so by providing a grounding for
the extraordinary power of people's commitments to the way things
are, despite the danger those commitments pose to the very people who
hold them. The only thing more dangerous, in effect, than the failure of
one's firm, is having one's own sense of self demolished. This sheds
some light on the odd impasse that can arise when defending the assets
and competitive position of the firm comes into conflict with the manager's need to defend his own social assets and sense of self, even
though these are, in the first instance, dependent on the existence of the
firm.[17]

In parallel, a focus on the power of the manager allows us to consider the ways in which social position affects the constitution of
knowledge and one's interpretation of how the world is and how it

---

[17] It would be useful in this context to investigate the fates of managers who have
presided over the decline of their firms. To the degree that they emerge with their
wealth more or less intact or even capable of moving to a similar managerial position
at another firm, their impulse to defend themselves at the expense of the firm becomes
even more plausible. The many golden parachutes offered to ousted executives in the
past decade hint at some such underlying rationality.

ought to be. Again, this helps us to understand the origins of the commitments that guide the strategists' actions, and why some kinds of evidence, however clear and convincing to the disinterested observer, cannot be made use of, not matter what the consequences.

This partial argument needs to be linked back to the more general problem of cultural production and cultural change within the firm. What I want to show is that the problem is not, as much of the business literature would have it, how to *adapt* corporate cultures to (new) corporate strategies, but rather to show how culture *produces* strategy at the same time it is shaped by the history and strategic trajectory of the firm.

Corporate Culture and Strategy

Corporate strategies are usually viewed as a product of the decision-making processes of firms. The sequence might be described as follows: information about the state of the world (the firm's environment) is gathered, it is assessed in light of the existing capacities of the firm, it is then filtered through a set of implicit or explicit decision rules (such as return-on-investment criteria), and the outcome of the decision-making process is the strategy. In effect, the strategy is simply a particular kind of decision, broader in scope and implications and more future-oriented than most, as, for example, the decision to enter a new market or change the firm's approach to existing markets, and so on.

The strategy/decision then produces requirements. Thus, the strategy may require altering the existing skills base or capacities of the firm. This could include developing expertise in software engineering in a firm that has traditionally produced only hardware, or building strengths in electronics in a firm whose products have heretofore been electro-mechanical. It could include developing the in-house capability to codesign products with a customer, buying into a promising new technological arena, or developing the capacity to produce overseas. Yet again, the strategy may require the firm to offer a more flexible range of products, to increase product quality, to cut the development time of new products, and/or to be more responsive to the needs of customers.

Many kinds of strategic initiative require a number of related changes in order to be effectively implemented. Increasing product quality may imply a parallel strategy of worker empowerment. Or reducing time to market may entail organizational decentralization and breaking down barriers between research, engineering, and manufacturing.

Many of these strategic and operational initiatives will, again, often require a change in the culture, hence a shift in the underlying values and, consequently, a shift in the behaviors that these values produce. It may even be felt that any significant strategic realignment unavoidably requires a change in the culture. But the culture remains, nevertheless, the handmaiden of the strategy: a produced requirement that will allow the strategy to be implemented.

Take, for example, the case of a firm that has adopted a strategy to move out of its traditional commodity markets and reorient itself to higher-value-added, more specialized markets, where competition is less price sensitive and more responsive to product quality, performance, and service. One example would be a shift from a reliance on bulk hydrocarbon-based chemicals, where scale economies, capacity utilization rates, and, possibly, distribution networks define the competitive terrain, to more research-intensive and specialized products such as agricultural chemicals or paints and coatings. Another would be a reorientation away from standardized memories to logic chips or application-specific devices.

In the conventional view, this kind of strategy shift produces an associated set of operational and cultural requirements. R&D gets bigger, relations between engineering and manufacturing have to be improved, marketing becomes more important, new relations with suppliers and customers have to be forged, and values centered on quantity and costs must be realigned to stress quality and service. But these operational and cultural requirements are, in effect, read off from the strategy.

I want to propose a different view of what strategy is that may allow us to see the relationship between strategy and culture in a different light. Strategy, in this view, is not so much about decisions as about knowledge – what the firm knows, or what it thinks it knows well enough to bet on. This knowledge, in turn, reflects the firm's interpretations of how the world is and how it could be (alternatively, how it *ought* to be). Necessarily, this includes also the firm's knowledge and interpretation of who and what it is, and who and what it could be or ought to be in such a world. Strategy is the way firms envision a social order and their position in it.

This also means that strategy is unavoidably and deeply influenced by culture, since it is in and through its culture that the firm constructs interpretations of the world and understands itself. As new problems are produced or new states of the environment are encountered, the firm's culture will shape the kinds of strategic response it is able to develop. Yet we can also note that the firm's culture embraces the practices, relations, and ideas associated with the past strategic trajectory of the firm. The two are mutually constitutive categories.

Here it is useful to revisit the question of identity and commitments as a way of linking the firm to the people in it, or more particularly, the strategy to the strategists. The proposition is that managerial identities and commitments are closely entwined with, although not identical to, corporate identities and commitments. This is not because managers can't tell the difference between themselves and the firm, but because who and what the firm understands itself to be are produced in and through the actions and interpretations of the people in the firm, especially those of top management. The influence is reciprocal, though, insofar as the identity of the firm also influences identity formation on the part of these same individuals.

The relationships among the various categories of culture, identity, and strategy are sketched out in figure 5.2. But I want to stress that they should be seen as mutually constitutive processes rather than circular and endlessly self-reproducing states. Further, the relationships, though determining, are not determinate. A given culture doesn't necessarily and uniquely produce a specific corresponding strategy.

These processes produce change. They do so because they themselves embrace tensions and contradictions and because they take place in a contradictory environment that constantly generates new predicaments for the firm. In those brief moments of history when the dominant firms can collectively establish and defend a common social order in which the environment is relatively stabilized (as was the case for mass production firms in the immediate postwar decades), the changes generated may be largely evolutionary: adjustments and intensifications along an existing trajectory.

But this situation is untenable in the long run. The social order itself generates pressures and problems that cannot be resolved within its

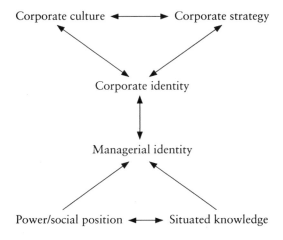

Figure 5.2 Identity, culture, and strategy

own framework. Markets become saturated, technologies and organizational forms hit their productive limits, social relations become intractable and the old ideas limiting. At the same time, new competitors embodying an alternative culture and social order emerge to challenge the dominant firms.

It is through contradictions and tensions of this sort that the most significant kinds of change are likely to occur. But as we have seen, the old social order embodies a whole range of specialized material, social and cultural assets, and specific power relations that are at risk of devaluation depending on the kinds of change that are undertaken. This implies that the process of cultural and strategic change and the possibility of corporate transformation are arenas of struggle. The outcome of this struggle will determine the kinds of change that are selected or resisted. In order to understand why firms do what they do in the face of particular kinds of contradiction and challenge, we need to pay close attention to how the struggle takes place.

6

Culture, Identity, and Corporate Transformations

Case Studies

Introduction

In this chapter I want to explore in some detail two stories of corporate cultural and strategic realignment. The stories concern two large and highly successful firms, Lockheed and Xerox, that, at a particular moment in their histories, confront sharply altered competitive and market environments and new organizational and technical challenges. For both, this period is marked by internal conflict over who and what the firm is or ought to be and how it will operate in a changed world. For both, strategic shifts are worked out *as part of* struggles over culture and identity.

The notion of culture and cultural change put forward in the previous chapter does not provide a precisely enumerated list of indicators against which to measure the various elements of the case studies undertaken here. But it does focus attention on certain features and underlying processes at issue in these stories that are related to the categories of material practices, social relations, and ways of thinking.

In both stories, for example, work is a central point of contention. The issue arises in a variety of ways: what work should be done and what not, who gets to organize it and carry it out, and how work is valued within the firm (even in such basic ways as what *counts* as work and what doesn't).

But work is a social process, so these questions shade into the problem of social relations within the firm: how rights and responsibilities are allocated and contested, how this process is legitimated, how the boundaries between my work and yours are determined and defended, who is really part of the corporate community (who is "us" vs. "them"), whose vision of the present and future of the corporation is validated and how, and who gets to decide what is important and what is not.

These issues are unavoidably worked out through culturally marked processes of interpretation and knowledge creation that are affected by the position or situation of the interpreters. How do these people understand their world, how do they select what things to think about and what to ignore, what does the firm and their own position in it mean to them, and how do they think about what could be and what ought to be?

This also brings us back to the problem that corporations both are and are not the individuals who populate them. We need to pay attention as well to questions of identity and how the individual's social capital is variously bolstered or threatened by particular kinds of change.

In the narratives which follow, I will try to show how these questions and others arose and were resolved at significant turning points in the histories of the two firms. For Lockheed, the story concerns the traumatic (though ultimately successful) move into the missiles and space business in the 1950s. The Xerox case involves the firm's response to Japanese competition in the 1970s and 1980s, and also its attempt to move into the computer business during the same period.

Lockheed

This story, in brief outline, concerns a large, well-established firm, a technically progressive leader in its traditional field, that is faced with the necessity of making itself, at least in part, into another kind of firm in another kind of business.[1] The shift involved, from aircraft to missiles and space, was technically challenging but it occurred within a stable orientation to the defense market with which Lockheed had an enduring and deep familiarity. Although the signals from this "market" were

---

[1] This study grows out of a larger collaborative research project with my colleagues Robert Kargon and Stuart W. Leslie of the History of Science Department at the Johns Hopkins University. Both were centrally involved in conceptualizing the research and provided invaluable help in refining the arguments presented here. In addition, several of the interviews were conducted jointly. The information presented here has been drawn from corporate histories and other internal documentation from Lockheed, contemporary press accounts and other secondary sources, and a series of oral histories conducted with some of the key Lockheed personnel involved at the time. In what follows, only the documentary material will be referenced in the text, whether it provides new information or confirms information drawn from the oral histories. Other detail is derived from the oral histories themselves.

exceptionally clear, Lockheed management resisted the move for quite some time. When the firm finally committed itself to the new project, the shift unleashed a period of great turmoil which almost killed the initiative before it was fairly launched.

To undertake a transformation of this sort, the firm clearly needed to resolve important technical and organizational problems. But I want to argue that the real impediment to change, for Lockheed, had to do with the firm's culture and identity and that conflict revolved around divergent conceptions of who and what the firm was and ought to be, what it ought to do, and how it ought to do it.

Early history

Lockheed was founded in 1913 in San Francisco. The next twenty years were rather turbulent as the firm moved progressively down the coast and went in and out of business several times. In 1928, it settled in Burbank, just north of Los Angeles, which became the headquarters and heart of the Lockheed Corporation.[2]

This early period, despite the moving around, is marked by several strongly consistent features. The firm always made aircraft, in those days primarily for the civilian market. It employed a series of famous aircraft designers, including John K. Northrop and Gerard Vultee, who went on to found firms of their own. And it built its reputation on aerodynamically advanced, fast planes.

Lockheed was acquired in 1929 (just before the Crash) by a Detroit-based holding company which aimed to become the General Motors of the air. Failing in this ambition, it went bankrupt in 1931. The following year, a group headed by a San Francisco-based investment banker, Robert E. Gross, bought Lockheed for $40,000.

Gross had originally become involved in the aircraft business working with Stearman Aircraft in Wichita, Kansas. Lloyd Stearman was named president of the newly reorganized corporation, although he would be succeeded by Gross in 1934. Stearman brought with him a young MIT aeronautical engineering graduate, Hall Hibbard, who soon rose to the position of chief engineer (*Lockheed Horizons*, 1983; Biddle, 1991; R. Anderson, 1983).

The first product of this venture was the twin-engine Model 10 Electra. Wind-tunnel tests for the plane were conducted at the University of Michigan, which provided the introduction between Lockheed and another famed aircraft designer, Clarence L. "Kelly"

---

[2] Since the 1995 merger with Martin Marietta, the headquarters of the new Lockheed Martin have been shifted to Bethesda, Maryland.

Johnson, in 1933. The connection with the university proved a durable one, and a number of its engineering graduates followed Johnson to Lockheed.

The period of explosive growth for the firm began in 1938 with a contract to produce Hudson bombers for the RAF. It was at the time the largest single order ever for a US aircraft manufacturer. That same year, Lockheed won an Army Air Corps design competition with the twin-tailed P-38 Lightning designed by Kelly Johnson and Hall Hibbard. Over 10,000 were eventually produced. Subsequently, the firm began mass production of B-17 Flying Fortresses. In 1941, employment was just shy of 17,000 (Francillon, 1982; *Lockheed Horizons*, 1983; Yenne, 1987).

Wartime design and production demands led to two significant initiatives. Formal research laboratories, including a large subsonic wind tunnel, were established at Burbank in 1940. In 1944, the firm began building production facilities on a new 77-acre site in nearby Van Nuys.

Lockheed accounted for 9 percent of total US military aircraft production during the war. Employment peaked in 1943 at 94,329. The end of the war, however, inevitably brought drastic reductions. In January 1945, employment stood at 60,000. By September of the same year, it had fallen to 35,000. By 1946, it was down to 17,000. Meanwhile, net sales, which reached $602 million in 1944, fell to $112 million in 1946. Operating losses were recorded in both 1946 and 1947 (*Lockheed Horizons*, 1983; Francillon, 1982; *Business Week*, 1951).

Lockheed's situation in the early post-war years was neither uncommon nor dire, although the company was criticized for its slowness in scaling down and rationalizing operations compared with other aircraft manufacturers (cf. Stekler, 1965; Woods, 1946). In many respects, the firm continued to be quite successful.[3] Sales and employment turned up during the Korean War, peaking at $802 million and 51,500 respectively.

A major disappointment for the firm, however, was that it was

---

[3] For example, Lockheed won the contract for the USAAF's first operational jet aircraft, the P-80 Shooting Star, although plans for large-scale manufacturing were cut back. While some 8500 (in various versions) were eventually produced, this was over a period of nearly fifteen years (Francillon, 1982). In 1950, Lockheed was asked to modernize B-29s for service in Korea at an old Bell manufacturing facility in Marietta, Georgia. This site was later used for production of the B-47 Stratojet bomber. Employment in Georgia rose to 10,000 by 1951. Other major defense contracts included the F-104 (which made its first flight in 1954) and the U-2, which first flew in 1955 (*Lockheed Horizons*, 1983; Francillon, 1982).

consistently outflanked in the civilian market by Douglas and Boeing.[4] Despite its best efforts, it remained heavily dependent on the military: defense contracts accounted for 85 percent or more of total sales from 1950 through 1954 (Stekler, 1965; Francillon, 1982).

In sum, then, although Lockheed was by no means on the brink of extinction, it quite clearly faced the question of where secure and stable growth would come from in the future. The same question confronted all the major airframe producers whose business had contracted following the war, but given Lockheed's military dependence, it was especially pressing. It turns out, however, that an answer to this question was available and, moreover, it was widely known.

Missiles and space

By the late 1940s, it was already apparent to many in the military and in the aircraft business that the real growth arena for future defense spending was going to be missiles and space. Studies for the air force had been underway since 1946 at Project RAND, then part of Douglas, to identify the key technological innovations that would be needed to place a satellite in orbit. In the meanwhile, the military was funding a number of different missile development projects (Schriever, 1958; Funk, 1958; Gatland, 1952).

Unlike most of its major competitors, however, Lockheed was remarkably slow to react to the new direction in military priorities, and this despite the fact that the military was practically its only customer. The company is utterly conspicuous by its absence from the lists of major contractors for all of the significant missile development projects from the end of the war to the mid-1950s (Schriever, 1958; Funk, 1958; Root, 1980). According to a number of high-level Lockheed personnel from that era, this was not because they tried and failed to win such contracts, but because they never tried.

Lockheed's only venture in this line for quite some time involved a modest contract for a supersonic ramjet test vehicle for the air force, known as the X-7. The project was developed in Lockheed's preliminary design department, then headed by Willis Hawkins, an

---

[4] The civilian air-transport market was, in any case, hampered in the early post-war period by the availability of converted military transports and, overseas, by the dollar shortage. Lockheed had some success with civilian versions of the Constellation and the subsequent Super Constellation (introduced in 1951). The L-188 Electra turboprop, introduced in 1956, was a costly disaster for the firm, however, plagued with technical problems and accidents. That plane and the long-range Starliner (1957) were effectively eclipsed by the introduction of civilian jet transports in 1958 (Yenne, 1987; Francillon, 1982; Stekler, 1965; *Aviation Week*, 1953).

aeronautical engineer who had been recruited from the University of Michigan by Kelly Johnson.

According to Hawkins, the technical demands posed by the X-7 were generally within Lockheed's existing capabilities, and that was the reason they bid for this particular contract. The X-7 needed to fly fast, which was Lockheed's traditional strength, but the guidance and control requirements were relatively unsophisticated. Since there was no organizational home for it within the corporation, the project stayed in the preliminary design department, which at the time employed only ten to fifteen people.

In sum, Lockheed's main market, the military, was very publicly announcing immediately following the war that missiles and space would be the new priority. All of Lockheed's major competitors in the airframe business, plus a large number of firms in other sectors such as electronics and automobiles, were trying to position themselves in this new business.[5] In this sense, there was absolutely no secret about what a firm such as Lockheed should be doing at this point in history.

Recall further that Lockheed, on its traditional terrain, had proved itself to be very technically progressive and innovative. In short, the knowledge of what to do was in hand, and knowledge about how to do it (including how to master the new technologies that would be needed) was as available to Lockheed as it was to anyone else. Yet the firm refused to engage itself in this new industry, and adhered to this decision until 1953.

By the time Lockheed decided to enter the market, it was already rather late in the game. The risks of late entry were high, especially in terms of assembling the technical personnel whose presence would guarantee *a priori* the competence of the firm – no small issue in contract competitions (cf. Stekler, 1965). What, then, accounts for this reluctance to adapt despite certain and accurate information about the new state of the firm's environment?

Redefining the firm: impediments to change

As Lockheed began belatedly to reorient itself to the demands of the new growth sector, it faced a number of apparently distinct problems

---

[5] An internal Lockheed memo from 1955 includes a lengthy list of firms that were jockeying for position in missiles and space. These included not only the obvious suspects such as aircraft, electronics, and the new systems firms such as Ramo-Wooldridge, or even plausible candidates such as automobile and tire companies, but breakfast-cereal makers and Bing Crosby Industries. It is hard to avoid the conclusion that if Bing Crosby knew about the growth potential of missiles and space, then Lockheed also knew (Quesada, 1955; cf. also *Aviation Week*, 1960).

that turned out to be closely interrelated. The most obvious of these, common to everyone in the business, was technological. Particularly pressing were problems of guidance and control, and Lockheed at the time lacked expertise in guidance especially. But the outstanding technical issues were intertwined at Lockheed with questions of corporate culture and identity – especially as these bore on the issues of labor recruitment and management. In short, Lockheed needed to resolve some important questions about what and who it was as a firm before it could enter fully into the Space Age.

Lockheed, from its birth in 1913 to the early 1950s, had a very consistent and well-defined sense of its identity. It was an airframe producer: that is, it designed and assembled structures that flew under human guidance. The corporate culture was necessarily embodied in the people who ran the firm, and these people were nearly exclusively aeronautical engineers who had spent their careers designing and producing aircraft. Robert Gross, though not an engineer, was apparently equally committed to the idea of manned flight. As Hall Hibbard, who was at the time Lockheed's senior vice president for engineering, put it:

> You take Bob Gross and [me]. We couldn't give a damn about missiles. We didn't like missiles. We wanted airplanes! ... The top guys at Lockheed were all airplane guys. They weren't missile guys. They're entirely different. The problems are entirely different and what you do with them is different. So you can either be in that field or you can be in this field. Bob Gross and I always wanted to be in this field – flying. We liked flying.

There is a strong element of what I have referred to as romantic and aesthetic commitments here as well. Many of these men had entered the business during the 1920s and 1930s, when aircraft and flying suggested the height of adventure and romance. Hall Hibbard was a friend of Howard Hughes and had flown with him on a record-breaking coast-to-coast speed trial. Their names were linked with planes of quite daring design and considerable beauty, from the P-38 Lightning to the Constellation. Arguably, in the late 1940s and early 1950s, missiles and satellites represented a new romantic frontier, but the old commitments were not so easily abandoned. In any case, the aesthetic value of missiles would require quite a different style of appreciation.

Entering into the missiles and space business meant redefining Lockheed's mission and commitments. It also mean a shift from a straight engineering orientation to more science-based R&D. Accordingly, the technical population of the firm (which is to say its elite and most influential stratum), until then composed entirely of engineers, would have to be reconstituted in favor of scientists, especially physicists. Finally, the move into missiles and space meant rethinking the firm as a systems integrator rather than a designer and assembler of airframes.[6] These distinctions might appear subtle, but the conflict and ambivalence they engendered within the firm were not.

In the case of Lockheed, as we have seen, there was no shortage of "objective" knowledge about what to do, and the firm had no reason to believe itself any less capable technically than its competition. The impediment to change was not lack of information or uncertainty. Neither is there any reason to believe that the people who ran Lockheed were irrational, excessively shackled by received tradition, or paralyzed by an encrusted bureaucracy that thwarted top management's strategic will. Lockheed management resisted this change because they did not want to be what (or who) the change implied. The adaptations that would be required of the company in order to enter into the new industry constituted a serious threat to a stable, yet by no means stagnant, culture and self-conception. In this context, the famed Lockheed "skunkworks" under the leadership of Kelly Johnson could be enthusiastically mobilized around crash development programs for strategic reconnaissance *aircraft* such as the U-2, but a very clear military mandate to undertake development of strategic reconnaissance satellites and ballistic missiles drew a colder response.

Pressures for change and the establishment of the Lockheed Missile Systems Division

Lockheed nevertheless faced growing pressures from without and within the company that were increasingly hard to resist. The external pressure came from the firm's most important market, the military, whose needs and desires were presumably of great importance to the firm. At the same time, Lockheed had started to recruit a number of people in the early 1950s who came out of the military planning apparatus – a not uncommon strategy for a defense-dependent firm. These new recruits began to lobby internally for a commitment to a change in strategy.

Key personnel in this effort included L. Eugene Root, a Cal-Tech-trained aeronautical engineer who worked on the initial satellite

---

[6] Although the military aircraft market functioned differently from the civilian one, the technological demands they generated had not been vastly dissimilar up to that time. Military aircraft were weapons platforms, not integrated weapons systems in the way that missiles were. And, obviously, subtracting the pilot meant integrating the guidance and control into the machine. The resulting technical complexity created the demand for a new type of actor – the systems integrator.

feasibility study at RAND and then moved to the air force's directorate for development planning. He was recruited by Hall Hibbard in 1953 to set up a development planning operation at Lockheed.[7]

Meanwhile, Robert Gross had recruited a retired air-force general, Ellwood R. "Pete" Quesada, to Lockheed's board of directors in 1952. Quesada, in the course of a colorful military career, had spent part of the war as air force liaison to MIT's Radiation Laboratories, where he learned, from the military's side, about the new forms of government–industry–university cooperation being worked out there (Leslie, 1993a).

The internal lobbyists had impeccable credentials. In any case, their message was exactly the same as that being received from the outside: Lockheed had to commit itself seriously to missiles and space. Although the top officers of Lockheed remained deeply ambivalent about the shift, when they finally conceded they did so with a very public display of decisiveness, establishing immediately an organizationally separate division. But, as will become clear, the ambivalence remained.

The Lockheed Missile Systems Division (LMSD; later Missiles and Space Division) was born on January 1, 1954. It inherited from the parent corporation the old X-7 contract, some engineers under the leadership of Willis Hawkins, and temporary offices at Burbank. Total employment at the outset came to sixty-five people. Pete Quesada was named general manager.

The decision to establish a formal organizational structure ahead of any actual business reflects both external pressures and internal divisions. It was a way of signaling to the military that, however long it had taken to get there, Lockheed was now making a serious and durable commitment to the new strategy. Further, it demonstrated to the customer that within Lockheed there would be no question as to the status of the operation, which was formally equal to the aircraft side. Appointing Pete Quesada to run the division was almost certainly a reinforcement of that message. A flamboyant outsider by local standards and a non-engineer, he nevertheless had excellent connections and high status with the military.

But the firm's ambivalence about the new commitment also appears to have come into play in this context. Both Robert Gross and Gene Root are reported to have favored organizational separation, although

---

[7] Root was followed a year later by his RAND colleague Robert Salter, who was the author or co-author of nearly every major RAND report on satellite feasibility. When he joined Lockheed, Salter had just coedited the report on Project FEEDBACK, which essentially set the specifications for the Agena/Discoverer reconnaissance satellite program. Salter would play a crucial role in securing Lockheed Missile Systems Division's initial satellite contract (cf. York and Greb, 1977).

for different reasons. Gross, in effect, didn't quite know what to make of the new business and worried about it getting in the way of the "real" Lockheed. Hall Hibbard recalls him as being of the view that "getting those missiles mixed up with our airplanes is no damn good. We ought to move them out." Root, meanwhile, is said to have been convinced that the new operation needed to be sheltered from the parent in order to succeed. In effect, he was worried about the "real" Lockheed getting in the way of the missiles and space effort.

Labor recruitment and management at LMSD

The new division's engineering staff was rapidly built up, almost entirely through internal recruitment within Lockheed. Although Kelly Johnson is said to have remained opposed to the new venture, Willis Hawkins had considerable prestige within the organization in his own right, and was able to persuade a sufficient number of his engineering colleagues to cross over.

Meanwhile, Pete Quesada went on what can only be described as a shopping spree in the market for physicists in order to rapidly acquire expertise in guidance, computers, and radar. Whatever top management's ambivalence, the corporation was willing to provide the necessary start-up financing. Given Lockheed's extremely belated entry into the field, the firm had a lot of catching up to do and this would be costly.

The scientists were recruited principally from universities and government research laboratories. Ernst Krause, who was named chief scientist, was brought in from the Naval Research Labs. Louis Ridenour, a brilliant computer scientist who first met Quesada at the Rad Labs during the war and who had also consulted on the RAND satellite study before becoming chief scientist of the air force, joined in 1954.

Quesada's recruitment strategy was simple and, on the whole, effective. He was convinced that scientists worked differently than other people; they needed, he thought, an absolutely free rein to develop their ideas. In a 1954 *Time* magazine interview, he promised to run the new division "more like a university than a hard-headed business" because "scientists function best when they know they can work without dictation and develop theories irrespective of military contracts" (*Time*, 1954). At that point, Quesada envisioned establishing an 80-acre campus in Van Nuys where scientists would be invited to "wander through" the problems that interested them and to "soak up academic atmosphere" by teaching at local universities (ibid). This freedom, along with high salaries and abundant resources, is what Quesada offered to the scientists he recruited.

By the end of 1954, sales from the inherited ramjet contract amounted to $24 million and employment had soared to 2800, of which 800 were in research and engineering. The division had outgrown its first home in Burbank and was shifted to Van Nuys, where the construction of new research labs, dedicated to LMSD, was started. In 1955, the firm won another modest contract, the X-17, to explore re-entry problems for the air force (*Lockheed Horizons*, 1983; Francillon, 1982).

This again was not an extremely demanding project technically. The X-17 was essentially a test bed for the evaluation of ballistic missile nose-cone materials that would have to withstand the extreme conditions of re-entry into the atmosphere. A small rocket, it would be launched into the upper atmosphere, the engine would be cut, the rocket would flip over and reignite, and it would be powered back down through the atmosphere at extremely high speed.

As the division grew in numbers, it entered a period of great turmoil. Almost immediately, the new scientists coming in from the outside came into conflict with the old Lockheed hands in engineering. Tensions were described as constant and cute, amounting nearly to fisticuffs in the hallways. Pete Quesada, who was convinced that the new technologies would advance primarily through the work of the scientists rather than that of the aeronautical engineers, acknowledged that he made no secret of whose side he was on.

But Quesada's position within the firm was increasingly tenuous, despite the fact that he was the only division head who also sat on the board of directors. In a remarkable 29-page memo to Lockheed Vice President Courtlandt Gross dated March 1, 1955, Quesada made an impassioned plea for a stronger corporate commitment to missiles and space.[8]

In this memo, Quesada first warned that Lockheed's fears that it would be seen as invading the avionics market in competition with important suppliers, thus risking the loss of access to new technologies, were misplaced. If anything, according to Quesada, the invasion was going the other way, and Lockheed was at risk of "being relegated to the role of airframe subcontractor" (Quesada, 1955:14).

Second, Quesada argued that Lockheed had to become a systems integrator because its chief customer, the military, demanded it. He described the military as quite eager to help the airframe companies make this transition, particularly in view of the relatively limited budget for new aircraft, but reported that they were also quite critical of the efforts that these firms had made to date. Quesada drove home his

[8] Courtlandt Gross was Robert Gross's brother.

point about what the transition really entailed in a way that directly challenged Lockheed's view of what and who, literally, it was:

> In a technical sense, the aircraft industry was dominated by those versed in the aeronautical sciences ... Assuring you that I have no lack of appreciation for the talent and skills of the aeronautical engineer, it is my firm conviction – unqualified – that they alone are not capable of advancing the state of the art.... Though I express this view as my own, it is likewise the view of the Air Force in general and those who have borne the burden of disappointment in particular.... The influential and knowledgeable elements of the Air Force are disappointed because the large aircraft companies, to whom were given the major burdens of developing our future weapons, failed to change with the trend and attempted to solve the new and novel requirements without new and novel people and skills. (ibid:19–20)

Quesada cited Hughes Aircraft as a company that had successfully "made a nearly complete change from whatever it was to what it is" because "they recognized the problem to be severe; they recognized the problem to be basically one of *physics*; they attracted the most capable people in that field and they were successful" (ibid:28, emphasis in original). The final, extraordinary sentence, indicative of Quesada's awareness of his equivocal position within the firm, is: "I do have one request – I beg that you don't get mad at me!"

It is worth noting that Quesada's characterization of the military's disappointment in the aircraft community echoes the 1954 report by the scientific advisory committee for the Atlas missile, headed by John von Neumann, which concluded that no aircraft company was sufficiently strong scientifically to manage the program (US Congress, 1959, cited in Stekler, 1965). Further, Quesada's belief that top Lockheed management was insufficiently committed to missiles and space was apparently shared by the air force. This is reflected in two confidential, unsigned Lockheed memoranda dated October 26 and October 31, 1955, which report on conversations held with several high-level air-force officials, including General Bernard Schriever, who headed the air-force missile development program. These conversations were undertaken by the company as part of a post-mortem evaluation of why Lockheed had failed to win the Atlas contract. The air-force sources clearly indicated concern over divisions within the Lockheed missile group and the evident lack of strong support from the top. Despite Lockheed's best efforts at presenting itself to the outside world as whole-heartedly committed to its new strategy, word of internal conflict and corporate ambivalence had evidently spread to the military development community.

The rebellion of the scientists

LMSD was organized into separate research and engineering departments under the leadership of Ernst Krause and Willis Hawkins, respectively. Hawkins, who would spend his entire career at Lockheed, was supervising a staff of aeronautical engineers who were used to working in a highly focused and scheduled way on clearly defined projects and contracts. As noted, virtually the entire engineering staff had transferred over from the aircraft side of Lockheed. For these engineers, the principal interest appears to have been missiles.

Although the scientists were by no means new to the priorities and exigencies of defense-related research, they were understandably less experienced in orienting their work to specific products and timetables and to the requirements of corporate profitability. In any case, they had been recruited on the specific promise that they did not have to pay attention to these constraints. The interests of Krause and the scientists closest to him were described as "esoteric" by Dr Walter B. LaBerge, who spent part of his career at Lockheed and who worked closely with Krause and his team in later years. The scientists were, on the whole, more interested in the space side of the business.

The first two years at LMSD were marked by increasingly open conflict between the engineers and the scientists. This conflict involved a bitter struggle for control of how work was to be carried out, the division of labor between the two groups, and whose priorities would shape the research agenda of the division.

From the engineers' point of view, the scientists at Lockheed appeared entirely unorganized in their work and detached from pressing current realities. As Willis Hawkins recalled it, they "never managed to get together and work on what we had contracts to work on or build the background to work on the next one." Something of the nature and magnitude of the gulf between the two camps, which involved quite divergent views of what counted as serious work, is suggested by Hall Hibbard's remark that "the scientists ... thought the engineers were a bunch of dumbheads, and the engineers thought the scientists were nuts. The thinking was different."

In other words, a key issue dividing the scientists and the engineers was how work would be valued: what would be seen as important work, how you judged which work processes were productive vs. those that weren't, and which work identities were seen to represent the core of a complex social effort. The aggrieved engineers felt that the scientists looked upon them as the people who kept the machines running. Meanwhile, from the engineers' perspective, the scientists might well be engaged in a lot of *activity*, but it was not obvious that all this effort produced much in the way of value.

Tensions multiplied when the scientists sought to extend their reach out of the labs into program management. This was resisted by the highest levels of the Lockheed corporate hierarchy. In a curious twist of the usual story, it is here the conceivers who are protesting at being deprived of the right to execute their ideas. Hall Hibbard is quoted in a late-1955 *Business Week* article as saying:

> Our position is that this type of work must be conceived and developed by scientists. That is why we have them. They think once the design is complete, they should carry it through the shop and be responsible for it until it is delivered to the troops. We think that there comes a time when the conceivers should give up their projects to the manufacturers and turn their attention to something new and startling. . . . Our scientists, however, are not content to be just scientists. They want to be managers, too. (*Business Week*, 1955)

In this article, the scientists' position is represented by a near-verbatim but unattributed extract from Pete Quesada's memo to Courtlandt Gross.

Finally, divergent priorities for the development agenda of the division took their toll. Though there were many technological overlaps between missiles and satellites, the differences were also great. Placing a satellite in orbit and stabilizing it there, for example, was a tremendous technical problem that didn't enter into the missile project. Thus, the choice of focus between missiles and space further divided the two groups.

By the end of 1955, the situation had become untenable. On November 9, Courtlandt Gross forced Pete Quesada's resignation. One month later, Ernst Krause led a walk-out of the top scientists in the division, including the directors of all five scientific research laboratories and a number of subsection chiefs. They immediately set up a new firm, the Systems Research Group, then a year later reformed themselves as Aeronutronic Systems, Inc., which was subsequently acquired by Ford Aerospace.

The so-called rebellion of the scientists received considerable coverage in the business and trade press at the time (cf. *Business Week*, 1955; *Newsweek*, 1955; *Aviation Week*, 1955). The extent of the real damage done to Lockheed's research program and capabilities is impossible to estimate. In Willis Hawkins's recollection, "it didn't look so bad, but then I was on the wrong side of that fence." Hall Hibbard remembers it more bleakly: "We'd been badly hurt because we lost those brains."

Perhaps more serious, however, was the impression that this open revolt would make on outsiders, specifically the division's only customer, the military. Only two years old, LMSD appeared to be in complete disarray. Lockheed's whole strategy of catching up in the business was predicated on demonstrating a solid commitment to the market and the technical resources to back it up. These were now very publicly thrown into doubt. Contemporary press accounts went so far as to hint that the Pentagon might intervene directly to restore order (*Aviation Week*, 1955).

The company moved rapidly to rebuild confidence. Hall Hibbard was named to head the division for a year until a suitable replacement could be found. This would be Gene Root. Louis Ridenour, who had established an excellent working relationship with Willis Hawkins on the engineering side, replaced Krause as chief scientist.

A home away from home: the move to Sunnyvale

As tensions were building in the course of 1955, Lockheed management decided on another major change for its troublesome division. Just a few days prior to Quesada's resignation, the company announced the purchase of a 275-acre site in Sunnyvale, California, just south of San Francisco, which would become the new home of LMSD. A few months later, the firm signed a lease for 25 acres in the then almost uninhabited Stanford Industrial Park a few miles north of the Sunnyvale headquarters. This site would house the research laboratories for the division. A final purchase of 4000 acres in the nearby Santa Cruz mountains would be used for static tests of rocket engines.

In many ways, the decision to move the division was a strikingly curious one. For one thing, the company had recently held festive groundbreaking ceremonies for the division's new facilities in Van Nuys, attended by an impressive array of military brass.[9] More significantly, southern California was not only Lockheed's home, it was also the headquarters of many of Lockheed's chief competitors. The region had a well-developed infrastructure of suppliers and a good source of newly trained technical labor from local universities such as UCLA and Cal Tech, with which Lockheed had excellent relations. The region would, indeed, go on to develop into the world's foremost center of the

---

[9] Some of whom were nearly killed when the *pièce de résistance* of the ceremony backfired. Someone had had the clever idea of planting a charge which would be triggered by a signal from Los Alamos as a high-tech substitute for a shovel. But the charge had been buried upside down, and erupted from the earth, headed towards the grandstand, when the signal was received. Fortunately, no one was injured.

aerospace business (A. Scott, 1991). An outside observer might plausibly suppose that a move away risked a kind of isolation and early death for the fledgling enterprise.

Moreover, moving to Sunnyvale in 1955 was a much more adventurous gambit than it would have appeared only a few years later. The explosive growth associated with the shift into solid state that gave Silicon Valley its name was still some ways in the future. Granted, the existing industrial and technical infrastructure was by no means negligible. It included Stanford University, which, at the time, was putting into place its model of university–industry cooperation under the guidance of Engineering Dean Frederick Terman (Kargon et al., 1992) and a small but healthy microwave tube-based electronics industry (Leslie, 1993b). Moffett Field Naval Air Station and NASA's Ames Research Center were adjacent to the new Lockheed headquarters and the University of California and Lawrence Laboratories were across the bay in Berkeley. But there is very little sense in which the area was an obvious site for an aerospace firm.

The decision to leave southern California seems to have been prompted by several factors. One was concern about space. Although LMSD was still small, the space available for future growth at Van Nuys was constrained and the Burbank headquarters was fully built up. Any major expansion in the Los Angeles area would have been, it was felt, a very costly endeavor.

Still, it is noteworthy that the decision to move was taken well before the division received any of the major contracts that would fuel its subsequent growth. In this it parallels the decision to set up the division itself well ahead of any significant business in order to demonstrate the firm's commitment to the market. The potential value of such an expensive demonstration would be difficult to quantify *ex ante*, but in the world of military contracting could be enormous. Lockheed at this time was still playing catch-up and needed to make its presence felt, especially to the degree that an initial contract award would improve its position for all the follow-on projects to come. Pete Quesada, for example, attributed the loss of the Atlas missile contract in 1955 in part to Lockheed's failure to promise a new, dedicated facility for the project.[10] The apparent lesson of this failure was that Lockheed had to be prepared to invest – and take considerable risks – up front. The commitment to the Sunnyvale venture was, arguably, such a risk.

Second, the military was in favor of decentralizing the aerospace industry for strategic reasons and was particularly concerned about the heavy concentration in southern California. The air force had even,

---

[10] Quesada's recollection is confirmed in the confidential memoranda described above.

temporarily, imposed a requirement that new facilities be placed inland (*Aviation Week*, 1956). This requirement was subsequently dropped, but not before Lockheed personnel had scouted several potential locations in the center of the country.

Several respondents also placed Gene Root at the center of this decision, for two main reasons. Root is reported to have been extremely concerned about the long-run availability of technical labor in southern California in view of all the competition there from aerospace firms. Thus, although the region had one of the world's largest concentrations of specialized technical personnel in the aerospace industry, Root was persuaded that excess demand locally could impair Lockheed's recruitment strategy. Note, however, that at the time, Lockheed's technical labor requirements were nothing like what they would become and gave little hint that an eventual shortage of labor would be a particular problem. Further, if the labor supply was really a problem, then relocating to Sunnyvale was not an obvious solution, since the technical labor supply there was still rather small and specialized around tube-based electronics. Whatever else it accomplished, the move northward changed Lockheed's labor-supply problem from recruiting in a very competitive local market to creating a labor supply virtually *de novo*.

Root was also reportedly convinced that it would be healthier for LMSD to be not only organizationally but geographically separate from the parent firm. Distance from headquarters would provide a buffer permitting LMSD to, in effect, create its own identity and culture.

In short, space and cost considerations, accommodating the customer, the availability of technical labor, and internal corporate relations seem all to have prompted the decision to move. The next issue was where the new operation would go.

Once the air force's geographic constraint was lifted, the Bay Area rapidly emerged as a leading candidate. Everyone connected with the decision agrees, in hindsight at least, that being near a good technical university was a major criterion. MIT and Princeton, for example, were seen as plausible early candidates, but each posed the problem that the areas around them were already developed industrially. The space and cost issues still pressed, as did the issue of local competition for the resources of those universities, especially students and faculty consulting time.

The degree to which a thriving regional economy based on high-tech industries was a locational *deterrent* to LMSD is striking. The company evidently desired privileged access to local resources, even at the cost of creating those resources itself. This would also shape its choice of location within the Bay Area and the way in which it engaged with other local high-tech institutions.

Lockheed and Stanford

The University of California at Berkeley is also a leading educational institution in the Bay Area, much larger than Stanford, and it had the further advantage of being located near the nuclear-weapons laboratories that the university managed. Nevertheless, it appears never to have exerted any serious pull on Lockheed management. This is, in part, because it was seen to be less oriented to the particular technical specialities that interested Lockheed. While it had a strong reputation in physics, for example, the university was less well known in electronics. Further, it appeared to be relatively uninterested in engaging directly with the firm.

Stanford, on the other hand, was extremely eager to establish a relationship with Lockheed, and it had good reason to be. Its once-renowned department of aeronautical engineering was by then virtually moribund, and Lockheed made clear its willingness to support the program and deepen its expertise in astronautical engineering (Kargon et al., 1992).

In preliminary discussions with Frederick Terman, the basic ground rules were easily agreed upon. Particularly important to Lockheed were the availability of faculty for consulting, and the ability to use Stanford for training its own technical personnel in a variety of disciplines, especially physics, electronics, and computer science. In return, Lockheed was instrumental in rebuilding the aeronautical engineering department, providing its own employees as part-time faculty, and going so far as to guarantee consulting work to particular individuals to enable Stanford to lure them away from other universities with better financial offers.

Contrary to the conventional history, which identifies Stanford as a beacon of strength around which fledgling high-tech firms simply clustered, it was arguably as much Stanford's weaknesses as its strengths which proved attractive to Lockheed. Its weaknesses stimulated its willingness to accommodate its own teaching and research agenda to the needs of the firm and guaranteed Lockheed a role in shaping the technological trajectory of the school (Kargon et al., 1992; Leslie, 1993a).[11] This influence was all the more secure in that competing claims on Stanford's attention from industry were still, in those early days, fairly modest.

The second advantage of the peninsula was that land was not only available in abundance, it was cheap. This reduced the costs and risks

---

[11] Lockheed personnel were frequently called upon to sit on various advisory committees within the Engineering School, for example. Consulting faculty, obviously, were engaged in the sort of work that was interesting to the company.

of the investment, and was a valuable recruiting tool. A Lockheed recruiting publication from that era promotes the favorable working conditions in the firm and then goes on to extol the advantages of the local housing market along with the climate and clean air (Lockheed, n.d.).[12]

Fortunately for Lockheed, the decision to expand the division through moving was validated by the award, in April 1956, of what would become the Polaris missile. This was followed in October by the contract for the air force's Weapon System 117L, which became the Agena/Discoverer reconnaissance satellite program.

It would be wrong to suppose, however, that Lockheed based its decision to move on the solid expectation of receiving huge contracts that were already, as it were, in the works before the decision was made. Both Polaris and Agena/Discoverer started small. The idea of a sea-based intermediate range ballistic missile (IRBM) was only accepted in 1955, and even then was supposed merely to be an adaptation of the army's liquid-fueled Jupiter rocket for surface firing. In 1956, the navy was authorized to proceed with a solid-fuel adaptation, the Jupiter S, on the theory that it would be less risky for shipboard handling. This was the original Lockheed contract. It was only in December of that year that the navy finally prevailed with an independent missile development program of its own; thus was the sub-based Polaris born (Fuhrman, 1978). Similarly, the Agena/Discoverer program was so small at the outset that Lockheed personnel were crestfallen when they learned that they had won that contract instead of a rocket project for which they were also bidding. The launch of Sputnik a year later would change that.

LMSD takes off

The Polaris program would have assured the future of the division by itself. In tandem with the Agena/Discoverer program, the division, reorganized as the Lockheed Missiles and Space Company (LMSC) in 1961, entered a period of spectacular growth.[13] In 1957, the division had sales

[12] Although undated, the publication appears to have been produced in the late 1950s or very early 1960s. It particularly stresses the extraordinary freedom enjoyed by researchers at Lockheed. In effect, Quesada's model of the way scientists work was at least partially vindicated after the fact. Curiously, the one photograph of idyllic campus life, included as an additional lure, features not Standford's landmark Hoover Tower, but the Campanile at UC Berkeley.

[13] Polaris went through three generations before being replaced by Poseidon and then by Trident, all Lockheed contracts. The Agena/Discoverer, along with Lockheed's U-2 reconnaissance plane, was the heart of the US strategic reconnaissance system for at least two decades. Moreover, since the military satellite programs provided most of the technical and industrial foundation for the later US space programs, Lockheed was extremely well positioned to participate in those efforts (cf. York and Greb, 1977).

of roughly $75 million, with employment of just over 5000. By 1961, LMSC accounted for just over half of Lockheed's total business. By 1962, sales had reached $824 million and employment was up to approximately 30,000 (*Aviation Week*, 1957; *Aviation Week and Space Technology*, 1961; *Fortune*, 1965).

Here we need to pick up some of the loose threads from the earlier part of the story. It appears that, following the rebellion of the scientists, relations among the remaining scientists and engineers improved dramatically. This may be partly due to the fact that a relatively small proportion of Lockheed engineers made the move to the Bay Area with the division. Most of them transferred back into aircraft instead. In any event, the extremely rapid scaling up of the operation meant that the newcomers (including engineers) soon outnumbered by a wide margin holdovers from the aircraft business. LMSD was bringing in thousands of young engineers who did not have to adapt to the changing identity and culture of the business since it was theirs from the start. Further, the research labs were organizationally and geographically separate from the main facilities at Sunnyvale. This was a deliberate strategy to keep the scientists out of the path of the day-to-day operational demands of contract work. Finally, the new chief scientist, Louis Ridenour, was able to work much more smoothly with the engineering side than had his predecessor.

Labor recruitment, on the other hand, suddenly became a very imposing issue. Moving to the Bay Area may have allowed Lockheed to escape fierce competition in the Los Angeles labor market, but it put the division in an area where local supplies were not abundant. Whatever the capacities of Stanford and UC Berkeley to provide young engineering and scientific talent, Lockheed's tremendous growth demanded even more.

The firm's principal strategy was recruitment from outside the region.[14] If local competition for graduates of southern California and the leading East Coast schools was too intense, Lockheed could focus on the large midwestern land-grant schools, whose graduates were more easily lured away.

Lockheed possessed a signal advantage in stabilizing its internal labor market once it had devoted the resources to building it up. Gene Root was right: there was practically no local competition for Lockheed

---

[14] Lockheed also devoted resources to local schools besides Stanford, such as San Jose State University and the junior college system which was then coming into being. These eventually became important sources of technical labor at various levels of qualification for Lockheed and other area firms. At the same time, LMSC personnel were active in other local infrastructure-building activities, such as promoting bonds for highway construction and the importation of water.

employees. Even after Silicon Valley came into its own with the growth of the semiconductor industry, the aerospace and electronics labor markets remained distinct. While the electronics industry in the region is noted for the hypermobility of its technical workers (Angel, 1994), there were only a few alternative aerospace employers in the area, and none that rivaled Lockheed in size.

In any case, to bolster its position, Lockheed developed a very careful and thorough recruitment and retention strategy under the leadership of LMSD's administrative chief, Herschel Brown. This strategy emphasized the freedom and autonomy provided to high-level research staff. The recruitment pamphlet mentioned above states: "Probably nowhere in industry is the research scientist given more freedom, recognition and opportunity to explore than at Lockheed Missile Systems" (Lockheed, n.d.:11). This represents, in effect, a validation of Quesada's vision, made possible by the new entente between the scientists and the engineers. LMSD researchers were encouraged to publish, and their efforts were recognized in internal company publications. The division organized internal seminars and reproduced the papers presented in Lockheed publications to encourage scientific exchange across disciplinary boundaries within the operation.

Lower-level technical staff were similarly encouraged. Lockheed, as noted, financed their pursuit of advanced degrees and allowed them to work part-time while doing so. Further, the flow of contract work through the division was carefully managed (for example, in decisions regarding what would be subcontracted out and what would be retained in-house) to stabilize the demand for labor. The aim was to avoid staffing up for particular bits of work if the company could not foresee how those employees would later be absorbed on other projects.

Lockheed was by no means unique in these attributes and there was no question that it was acting in its own interest.[15] Further, it is easier to put such a strategy in place during periods of robust growth. Nevertheless, that it was a strategy, carefully considered and on the whole successful, seems clear.

In sum, although LMSD had removed itself from the center of the largest specialized aerospace labor market in the world, it possessed the resources (courtesy of its parent and, to a non-trivial degree, its customer) to create its own. Indeed, the degree to which Lockheed was able to create or strengthen a local technical and social infrastructure to

---

[15] On the other hand, these conditions were not universal in the aerospace sector. Dr William Frye, who came to Lockheed from North American, bitterly recalls having to clock in and obtain a written pass to leave the premises during the day at North American.

support the explosive growth of the missiles and space division is remarkable.

Finally, Root's intuition that a geographical buffer was necessary to protect LMSD from the parent and allow it to establish its own identity and culture was confirmed, at least in retrospect, by several well-positioned observers Dr. Walter B. LaBerge, who had long experience of Lockheed from the inside and the outside, is quite explicit on this point:[16]

> [Lockheed was] slow off the block, but the move up to this area with a decentralized management was very effectively implemented. The early people who came up here were very strong and were allowed to have their own way.... They did in fact do well and changed the culture very substantially. Because the place has always been profitable, it was never as much battered by help from the corporate headquarters as were the aircraft divisions which were right down in the same set of offices.... So there was a tremendous [amount of] nitpicking that Lockheed did on its aircraft business, but it substantially left the missile business alone. In part because all of the senior executives were drawn from the aircraft business, so they all felt that they knew the thing that they had been promoted from and continued to overburden it with help. [Since they didn't] know anything about the missile business, they didn't bother it.... They were essentially left to develop their own futures and to hire a whole pile of very, very good people.

Robert Fuhrman, who was formerly president of LMSC and who spent nearly thirty years with the firm, concluded:

> The sense of experimentation we have incorporated into our program management in Sunnyvale couldn't have occurred if we had kept our operations in Burbank. There was a spirit of experimentation, a willingness to engage in new, decentralized programs here. That was counter-culture to the conservative defense industry in Los Angeles, but was natural here in Sunnyvale. (cited in Delbecq and Weiss, 1988:28).

The local management style was worked out in a context of explosive growth, which may also have favored a looser, more experimental approach. Growth was accompanied by a certain amount of organizational chaos as management structures and lines of authority were continually juggled. Daniel DeBra, at the time a newly minted engineer,

---

[16] Prior to Lockheed, Dr LaBerge worked at Philco, which was involved in developing the ground-support network for the satellite program and which had located its Western Development Laboratories a short distance from Lockheed's Sunnyvale plant. In between stints at Lockheed, he spent some time as undersecretary of the air force.

reports that he changed offices eleven times during his first year at Lockheed, counting as moves only those changes that took him across town lines. A standing joke from those days, he recalls, was to say to the secretary on the way to lunch, "If the boss calls, be sure to get his name." His impression from those years was that the staff was generally so young that there was hardly anyone around who was old enough to be in middle management.[17]

Whatever its causes, the "counter-culture" management style seems to have worked. The missiles and space group, indeed, has remained profitable to this day. The parent, on the other hand, only escaped bankruptcy in 1971 with federal government assistance (US Congress, 1971a, 1971b).

Time, space, and technology

LMSD's impressive second debut in the missiles and space effort took place in remarkable geographical and organizational isolation. As suggested above, the new division had to create its own technical and social infrastructure in order to accomplish its mission. Yet, within a few years, the division found itself surrounded by a thriving and vibrant solid-state electronics community.

By all accounts, the young Silicon Valley was an open and free-wheeling place. Spin-offs and new start-ups proliferated, the local technical labor market was extremely fluid, and information circulated easily, carried about as firms spun off, workers changed jobs, or researchers traded stories at local bars. Many observers contend that this openness and sense of a larger community and shared culture outside any specific firm contributed crucially to the Valley's success (cf. Saxenian, 1994).

The drive to miniaturization which led to the development of integrated circuits was, of course, propelled by the requirements of the missiles and space program. In the early years of Silicon Valley, defense programs were the principle market for the new devices (Flamm, 1988; Markusen et al., 1992).

Given these circumstances, one might have expected Lockheed to develop intimate and far-reaching ties with the other denizens of this emerging industrial district, expressed in subcontracting, joint development efforts, the trading back and forth of technical personnel, and so on. In this way, Lockheed, the largest inhabitant of this "new industrial

[17] DeBra, like many of his counterparts at the time, completed his PhD at Stanford while working part-time at Lockheed. He later joined the Stanford faculty and became head of the revived Department of Aeronautical and Astronautical Engineering.

space" (cf. A. Scott, 1988), would also have been an active participant in its vibrant local culture. This seems, however, not to have been the case to any great degree, at least according to the best recollections of the people interviewed. Lockheed certainly bought a lot of components, instruments, and the like from local suppliers, and was occasionally involved in the development of customized chips, but the extent of its local engagement appears, on the whole, to have been rather limited.

The reasons for this have to do with Lockheed's position as a systems integrator and the nature of the pressures involved in meeting the technological requirements of Polaris and Agena/Discoverer. With a few exceptions, these pushed the firm in the direction of establishing and deepening extra-regional ties with distant firms and laboratories. Lockheed, for example, was actively engaged in joint development work with certain kinds of supplier – namely, the suppliers of subsystems such as guidance or communications. But these tended not to be located in the area. One major exception was Philco's Western Development Laboratories (WDL), which were involved in work on ground stations for the satellite effort. Philco established WDL in the area precisely to be close to Lockheed. But the more usual pattern of engagement did not rely on proximity.

The subcontract for developing the guidance and on-orbit stabilization systems for the Agena program, for example, was given to the Draper Laboratories at MIT, which proposed AC Sparkplug in Milwaukee to do the actual manufacturing. The Draper Labs also developed the guidance system for Polaris. At the time, the only other plausible subcontractor for this task, in terms of technological competence, would have' been the Autonetics Division of North American Aviation in southern California. The decision in favor of the Draper Labs partly hinged on the perception that Lockheed would have more control over the process, especially since the design was separated from manufacturing. Autonetics insisted on doing both. Work on the Agena's photographic payload, meanwhile, was handled by Eastman Kodak in New York.

In contrast to its close work with subsystem suppliers, which involved a lot of travel back and forth or the temporary basing of technical teams on site, Lockheed was much less inclined to become directly involved in the development of specific components, which was Silicon Valley's speciality. In part this is because Lockheed's main preoccupation was with systems engineering and integration rather than components development *per se*. But here also the nature of technology development in both the Polaris and Agena programs is at issue.

There is no doubt that the technical challenges posed by launching an IRBM from a submarine or putting a satellite in orbit were very great.

But if the programs taken as a whole involved major technological advances, Lockheed was consistently conservative in defining the elements of the individual subsystems. The ruling maxim appeared to be to develop the system on the basis of technologies that could be expected with considerable confidence to be available in time for deployment (cf. Fuhrman, 1978).

Two constraints were particularly pressing: time and reliability. The Polaris program schedule had been drastically compressed. In 1955, the initial deployment of a submarine-launched missile was envisaged for January 1965. This date was brought forward in multiple iterations and the Polaris A1 was actually deployed in November 1960, only four years after Lockheed started work on it (Fuhrman, 1978). The Agena program was similarly sharply accelerated following the launch of Sputnik. The Discoverer I was successfully placed in polar orbit in February 1959 (*Lockheed Horizons*, 1983).

System reliability was also a high priority, for obvious reasons. Both programs had their share of spectacular failures during development, but successful deployment, especially for satellites, would depend on good functioning with little or no human intervention to correct errors or breakdowns. Taken together, these constraints steered Lockheed in the direction of the simplest technologies available for a given task, and ones with proven capabilities and reliability.

Frequently, time pressures forced Lockheed and its subsystems suppliers to abandon more technically adventurous designs and opt for simpler solutions in mid-course. The original, extremely sophisticated design concepts for the Agena's guidance and on-orbit stabilization systems were scrapped following Sputnik, for example, in favor of designs that were somewhat less accurate but could be developed more rapidly. Due to their relative simplicity, they were also more likely to be reliable. A contract for an electronic intervalometer for the satellite, to initiate and stop various tasks that the satellite would perform on orbit, was let to Boeing and then cancelled when it was decided that an electro-mechanical system being developed in-house as a back-up would work adequately with less risk of failure. This system was based on the counters one used to find in gas pumps, and was used for years, even after electronic alternatives became available, because it never failed.

At the same time, a sophisticated photographic transmission system under development at Eastman Kodak, which would have involved developing the film on board the satellite and then transmitting the image to earth, was also deferred. Instead, the undeveloped film would be ejected in a capsule and recovered in mid-air, reducing the on-board requirements to the still camera alone.

Similar decisions were being made for Polaris along the way. These included, for example, reducing the amount and complexity of on-board computing that would be required for guidance and fire control (Fuhrman, 1978).

Time compression, reliability requirements, and Lockheed's specific mission as systems integrator, then, all conspired to put Lockheed at the center of a spatially extensive set of relations. At the same time, the industrial and technical space it had constructed for itself in Sunnyvale and Palo Alto was in, but not really part of, the local high-tech industrial community. Its ties with Stanford notwithstanding, Lockheed's orientation remained largely extra-regional.

Conclusion

There are just a few features of this story that I want to highlight at this point. One has to do with the relationship between culture and strategy. The Lockheed case seems to me a particularly clear example of the point that major strategic shifts cannot be separated from processes of cultural conflict and change. The stubborn resistance to adopting the new strategy in the first place was deeply rooted in the ensemble of material practices, social relations, and ways of thinking that marked Lockheed as a designer and producer of aircraft. The individual identities and commitments of the people responsible for making strategy were bound up in a particular conception of who and what Lockheed was in the world. In the confrontation with a changed environment and new ways of thinking within the firm, the stakes involved in defending this culture and the identities and commitments tied to it were high – so high that the company risked missing out altogether on an extremely profitable new line of business.

The problem here was not access to information, but rather how available information could be used given the commitments of the firm's dominant culture and its interpretive possibilities. Once the formal decision to enter into missiles and space had been made, its effective realization still depended on the outcome of ongoing struggles. It is worth stressing that the conflict was played out within the elite stratum of the firm and revolved around incompatible conceptions of who and what Lockheed could be or ought to be.

Arguably, organizational and geographic separation were a necessary component of the eventual resolution of these struggles, allowing divergent cultures and identities to coexist within the larger firm. One might be tempted to conclude that it would have been better all around if the part of Lockheed that was interested in missiles and space had simply been spun off as an independent entity to begin with, to make its own way in the world. But the costs of entry into this new world were high, and it's hard to see how the entry could have been made without the resources of the parent. So the links between the old and the new parts of the firm needed to be preserved, but structured in such a way that the new division had an opportunity to create itself. The geographical shift, by buffering the new organization from the old, helped accomplish this.

The Lockheed case also illuminates the selective power of "tradition." The dominant culture was perfectly capable of embracing all manner of innovation in aircraft design. There is no sign of any particular anguish, for example, accompanying the transition to jet-powered air transport, although the technical requirements and experience of jet propulsion are different from propeller-based transport. The tradition that counted in this story was the tradition of manned flight. If manufacturing engineers may be thought to view human bodies as an impediment to a beautifully functioning system, Lockheed engineers saw the presence of a body – the pilot – in control of the machine as an essential feature of their work and their world. A new mission that displaced the pilot from this central role could not be highly valued by the dominant culture.

Much of this story, in fact, circles around conflicting processes of valuation embodied in the conflicting versions of who and what Lockheed should be. They underlie the conception of an appropriate mission for the firm, and help to define who is part of the corporate "us" and who is not. They are again at issue in divergent notions of what counts as productive and important work and how you recognize productive work practices when you see them. In sum, they both are a product of and, at the same time, help to structure the practical consciousness of the firm, and as such are deeply implicated in processes of cultural development and change.

Finally, I would like to draw attention to how temporal and spatial processes are intertwined with this story of strategic and cultural change. In the first place, the impulse to geographical separation reflects rigidities internal to the firm and not problems characteristic of the region (see chapter 4). The Los Angeles area was undeniably a good place to be for a firm in the aerospace industry. Being close to the parent, however, was not a good place for the young LMSD. Moving to northern California and constructing an independent technical and social space, in this light, was a way of accelerating the strategic and cultural transition that would allow the division to fulfill its mission.

Once there, however, a curious feature of the story is that while LMSD occupied the same geographical location as Silicon Valley, the division's operational space mapped quite differently. Its strongest ties linked it to places and processes outside of the region. As we have seen, this was a product of the particular nature of LMSD's mission as a systems integrator and they dynamics of time compression in carrying out that mission.

The same sorts of process and issue are at stake in the case of Xerox. In some respects the way they are worked out in practice will strongly echo the Lockheed story. In other ways, the trajectories of the two firms are quite different.

Xerox

Xerox's origins have the status of American corporate legend.[18] The xerographic process was developed by Chester Carlson, a Cal-Tech-trained physicist working in the New York patent office of a small midwestern electrical company. Frustrated by the tedious necessity of copying drawings and specifications, he developed an ingenious (but as yet primitive) new method of making copies in the late 1930s. Rebuffed over a number of years by a series of major corporations, he finally found financial backing from the Battelle Memorial Institute in Ohio with which to continue the development process.

It was not until 1945 that a company acquired the rights to the new technology with a view to bringing it to market. This was the tiny Haloid Company, a photographic supplies manufacturer based in Rochester, New York, home of Eastman Kodak. Haloid was interested in xerography as a way to counter a post-war sales slump. It was also afraid that its giant neighbor, Kodak, could annihilate the company any time it bothered to do so, and saw the move into a new business as a way of staying alive.

Haloid's early attempts to market products based on the technology failed repeatedly. Yet despite the high costs of development and a string of failures, the small company, under the inspiring leadership of Joe Wilson and Peter McColough, persevered. Along the way, Wilson negotiated a joint venture with the Rank Organization in England in order to protect its patent rights in Europe, despite the fact that there was still no product to sell there or, indeed, anywhere.

It was not until 1959 that production models of the 914, the first user-friendly, plain-paper office copier, became available. But the firm's

[18] This section owes a great deal to the hard work, energy, intelligence, and skills of my research assistant Elizabeth Dunn, who organized and carried out interviews with Xerox personnel. As a special bonus, she was able to enlist the cooperation of her grandfather, Robert P. Aex, the former city manager of Rochester, New York, for whose insights and help I am also grateful. The early history is based on Kearns and Nadler, 1992; D. K. Smith and Alexander, 1988; and Jacobson and Hillkirk, 1986.

single-mindedness and patience paid off richly. Haloid, renamed the Xerox Corporation, exceeded $1 billion in sales within a decade.

Xerox's position in the market it had created was apparently impregnable. The technology was protected by a formidable wall of patents. And because the machines themselves were so expensive, Wilson and McColough had hit upon the idea of leasing rather than selling them, with a fixed rate for a minimum number of copies per month and a per copy charge thereafter. Xerox, in effect, sold copies rather than copiers and, as the volume of copies made exploded, the company became immensely rich, with abundant resources available for further research and development. As larger, higher-volume products became available, users could easily replace their leased machines with new models. At the same time, even fully depreciated equipment continued to yield high revenues.

But Xerox wasn't just about revenues and profits. Joe Wilson, who was by all accounts revered within the firm, wanted to do good in the world and saw in xerography a way to do so. Anyone who could press a button now had control over the distribution of information. Wilson's commitments were shared by others amongst the firm's leadership. As David Kearns, former Xerox CEO, observes: "Senior managers believed they were making the world a little better by bringing about the democratization of information. Steadily, a culture was nourished of pioneers building something destined to become immensely powerful yet also something dedicated to the greater good" (Kearns and Nadler, 1992:37).

Whatever one may think about the liberatory potential of office copiers, the character of this self-image merits serious attention. The people who ran Xerox, unlike most of us, could see themselves as having real power to change the world in tangible ways. For quite a while, they were the only ones who had this ability, at least in this field, so the sense of specialness ("a culture ... of pioneers") was reinforced. This power and this self-understanding were inextricably linked to a product – the easy-to-use plain-paper copier.

In any case, it is easy to imagine the sheer exhilaration of being in this position. Wilson and his colleagues had mastered an intricate and challenging technology, they eventually had something like unlimited resources with which to further its development, and they achieved astounding success – by their own standards and in the eyes of others. We catch a glimpse here of the way commitments and identities are constructed and reinforced. All of this is tied to the homely 914 and its successors.

One can recognize here strong echoes from both sides of the Lockheed organization. On the aircraft side, commitments and identities were bound up in the aerodynamically advanced, elegant planes for which Lockheed was justly famous. On the missiles side, under the inspirational leadership of Gene Root, the mission was perceived as vital to national security, the technological challenges were immense, the resources with which to confront them were also vast, and their efforts met with stunning success. Nearly everyone I spoke with about the early development efforts in missiles and space recalled that time as intense and exhausting, even chaotic, but also tremendously exciting – the sort of experience, perhaps akin to war or other major historical moments, that strongly marks one's view of the world and one's sense of self.

David Kearns also remarks upon the sense of exhilaration and purpose that infused these years, something that he is able to know about only because so many people who were there at the time wanted to tell him what it was like: "the 1960s were incredibly heady times. I have heard plenty of stories about what the climate was like. Everyone felt there was a mission to be accomplished, and so everyone worked late but never complained. The Xerox offices buzzed with energy and purpose" (Kearns and Nadler, 1992:37).

Xerox reigns supreme – and worries about it

Throughout the sixties, Xerox grew by the proverbial leaps and bounds. By 1966, employment had reached 24,000, up from 600 in 1959 (Kearns and Nadler, 1992:45).

As with LMSD, this extraordinary growth brought with it a certain amount of organizational chaos and general confusion. The company was moving into large-scale production without adequate systems in place to keep track of costs or revenues, billing was a mess, and no one was very sure of what anyone else was doing. Top management increasingly felt that it was losing control of the situation, and decided that it had to introduce a new style of discipline in both the financial and operational sides of the business. To do so, it decided to recruit managers experienced in the systems of internal monitoring and regulation that had been so highly developed in mass production industries. The most important cadre of new recruits, including future Xerox president Archie McCardell, came from Ford.

There are a couple of observations one can make about this move on the part of Xerox strategists. First, it would be hard to argue that this was, on the face of it, a silly idea. Ford certainly appeared to be a company that knew what it was doing and its management had a strong reputation for devising and implementing effective management systems. At that time, any number of former Ford managers were reputedly reorganizing the Defense Department under the leadership of ex-Ford president Robert McNamara. Moreover, the Ford people, if McNamara was any example, were supremely self-confident about their ability to rationalize and discipline the most unwieldy organization. In his memoirs, McNamara, though diffident about his expertise in defense strategy issues when he first became Secretary of Defense, gives no evidence of any doubt that he could master the intricate processes and politics of the Pentagon (McNamara with Van De Mark, 1995). We can suppose, I think, that the Ford managers were convincing in their expertise.

Second, it seems clear that top Xerox managers were not so beguiled by their success that they were unable to evaluate their weaknesses in an environment that had been drastically altered by that very achievement. Moreover, they proved themselves willing to promote real change to compensate for these weaknesses by exposing a free-wheeling "culture of pioneers" to the disciplinary standards of established mass production industry. But the voluntary recruitment of an alien culture into the highest levels of Xerox management would, as in the case of Lockheed, trigger considerable conflict and turmoil. As David Kearns describes it:

> The old-timers didn't feel the auto people shared the same values. The eager Ford Men had manifest ambition, but they were not copier men. They were not rooted in the business and instilled with an adoration of the 914. . . . Their knowledge was about management systems and processes. . . . Their language was the peculiar mumbo-jumbo of financial wizards. Among other things, the Ford Men introduced rigid controls and a sense of authoritarianism that didn't exist before. A very hierarchical structure was put into place that had been unknown. . . . As a result, a rather severe culture clash, which would grow in intensity, developed between the Ford Men and the Xerox people. (Kearns and Nadler, 1992:54)

In Kearns's memoirs, the sense that cultural change is a deeply conflictual and power-laden process is extremely clear. He goes on to write: "[T]he Ford Men never really assimilated. Rather than buy into the culture that was there, the Ford Men began to change it. . . . the rigid managerial structure they subscribed to was driven by cost savings and not by what the customer wanted. . . . [T]he genetic code of the place changed" (ibid:56). Of course, the Ford Men were brought in precisely to change the culture in ways that were thought to be extremely important by Xerox management. In the long run, this strategy, though apparently salutary, would lead the company into serious difficulties.

Nevertheless, during the 1960s, the company continued to grow and forcefully expanded its international presence. Already in 1962, through

Rank-Xerox, it had entered into a joint venture in Japan with Fuji (not coincidentally, a competitor to Kodak). Xerox's early and aggressive internationalism also paid off handsomely. In 1972, Rank-Xerox and Fuji-Xerox accounted for 45 percent of total earnings. In that year also, Xerox machines were responsible for some 95 percent of the copies made in the world (D. K. Smith and Alexander, 1988:120, 189).

Perhaps surprisingly, this virtual monopoly did not lead to the smug conviction that nothing could ever go wrong for Xerox. David Kearns reports that top management was haunted by the fear that a competing technology would one day make xerography suddenly and irretrievably obsolete (Kearns and Nadler, 1992:46–7). Wilson and McColough were also nervous about the prospect of increasing competition within the plain-paper copier market. This competition, it was thought, would come from IBM and Kodak (D. K. Smith and Alexander, 1988:23–4).

In response to these concerns, the company started diversifying as early as 1962 when it acquired University Microfilms (Jacobson and Hillkirk, 1986:67). But over the course of the next two years, a consensus was formed within Xerox that secure growth in the long run would depend on a move into digital computing. The only disagreement, according to Peter McColough, was whether this capability should be developed internally or acquired (cited in Jacobson and Hillkird, 1986:214).

In the event, the company did both. After being rebuffed over the next several years by putative candidates such as DEC, Control Data, and Burroughs, Xerox expensively acquired Scientific Data Systems (SDS), a small, southern-California-based computer company, in 1969. This venture ended ingloriously, however, and SDS was liquidated in 1974, for a total reported loss of $1.3 billion (D. K. Smith and Alexander, 1988:128).

Of more enduring significance was the decision, also taken in 1969, to establish a research center devoted to the development of digital technologies. The Xerox Palo Alto Research Center (Xerox PARC) was born in June, 1970. The brainchild of Jack Goldman, a physicist and ex-Ford researcher who had become head of research at Xerox, it would be run by his old friend George Pake, also a physicist, who came from Washington University.

Xerox PARC

The first issue that had to be settled was where the labs would actually be located. Goldman was in favor of New Haven, on the theory that they would be far enough away from the corporate labs near Rochester to shield the new work from the traditional preoccupations of copier people, but still close enough that the new researchers would remain sensitive to the needs of the company. In a memo to Peter McColough, he wrote:

> If the new research center is too isolated from a Xerox environment and Xerox thinking, the chances of relevant coupling to Xerox's needs and practices will be severely diminished. . . . [O]ne area normally considered as an ideal research environment, Palo Alto, is eliminated only because of the absence of any nearby major Xerox facility. (cited in D. K. Smith and Alexander, 1988:56)

Pake, however, who had taught at Stanford in the 1950s, was precisely in favor of Palo Alto since it was at the center of so much relevant research and was, he thought, attractive to the kinds of researcher the labs would need. In the event, Pake prevailed and began a major recruiting drive that would result in what came to be seen as one of the most productive and creative computer research centers in the country.

Pake recruited his researchers from universities, including nearby Stanford and the University of California at Berkeley, and from the government research apparatus. Two key staffers, Bob Taylor and Alan Kay, had spent part of their careers at the Defense Department's Advanced Research Projects Administration (ARPA), which was heavily involved in funding advanced computer research.

Pake's recruiting strategy was remarkably similar to Pete Quesada's: he offered good salaries, abundant resources, and the freedom to work on whatever seemed interesting. In a 1971 memo describing the role of his researchers, Pake wrote: "I will hire them for their competence and their judgment how best to do that research" (quoted in D. K. Smith and Alexander, 1988:146). As David Kearns describes it, "The scientists were extremely well-paid and given plenty of freedom to function in a university-type of environment" (Kearns and Nadler, 1992:47). According to Alan Kay, "Xerox offered 10 years of blank-check funding. They never promised to make the stuff into products; that wasn't the charter" (quoted in Perry and Wallich, 1985:65).

We can detect echoes of the Lockheed story here as well. PARC researchers were largely recruited from the outside and had no experience of the history or culture of the "real" Xerox. Unlike the engineers back at the corporate research labs, they were given carte blanche to work on whatever ideas they found interesting. Further, in this case, the local style was aggressive about ideas yet laid back in demeanor, nonhierarchical, and, not to put too fine a point on it, scruffy.

It would be wrong, however, to say that PARC staffers had no sense of mission. In fact, they were strongly committed to an ideal of real-time interactive computing based on one machine, one user.[19] But their way of working was incomprehensible to the "outsiders" from Xerox and seemed dangerously divorced from corporate needs and priorities. There is more than a hint that PARC staffers' deepest loyalties lay primarily with the technology rather than the corporation *per se*, and they certainly didn't involve any commitment to copiers.[20]

In sum, Xerox PARC was a very un-Xerox kind of place. As Kearns notes, "From the beginning, a culture distinct from that at the rest of Xerox flourished at PARC" (Kearns and Nadler, 1992:101). Yet we should recall that this was the point. Xerox was trying to move into another kind of business altogether, and needed new kinds of people and new ideas in order to do so. But in practice, the tensions that this process created became increasingly alarming to the people at headquarters, who saw their new creation as wayward and undisciplined. In a way that recalls Willis Hawkins's assessment of the Lockheed scientists, Kearns stresses that "the work there was not connected to a firm business strategy.... The place just sort of drifted along on its own course" (Kearns and Nadler, 1992:103).

And yet, PARC researchers were actually doing what they were hired to do. In 1970, Peter McColough had publicly articulated Xerox's new guiding mission, which was to develop the "architecture of information" that would revolutionize the way businesses developed and handled information. The office would, in effect, become an integrated system in which information coursed through an array of linked, decentralized, easy-to-use machines (Kearns and Nadler, 1992:96–7; D. K. Smith and Alexander, 1988:48–50). PARC staffers, in a remarkably short time, developed many of the essential hardware and software components of such a system. These included personal computers, graphics interfaces, laser printers, WYSIWYG (what you see is what you get) word-processing programs, and networking capability.

By 1975, the whole system was operational inside the labs at PARC (Pake, 1985:58). Yet, famously, Xerox failed to commercialize nearly all of these technologies until after competitors such as Apple had

---

[19] In 1970, this vision may have appeared highly unrealistic to many competent observers, but it was nonetheless the guiding mission of Bob Taylor, Alan Kay, and a number of other key PARC staffers (D. K. Smith and Alexander, 1988:8–2; Davidson, 1993).

[20] As Pake recalled, "In the early days, I can't remember any of the scientists wanting anything to do with copiers, even though they all knew the copier business was paying everybody's salary" (quoted in Jacobson and Hillkirk, 1986:257). On the other hand, they were hired to develop computers, not to improve copiers. For an illuminating analysis of how loyalties to the technology and local community may conflict with loyalty to the firm and its priorities, see AnnaLee Saxenian's discussion of DEC's Palo-Alto-based research laboratories (Saxenian, 1994).

caught up with them and brought them to market – and made billions of dollars in doing so.

We can acknowledge the many uncertainties surrounding the possibility of commercializing PARC innovations. The technology went against conventional wisdom in the early 1970s, which was focused on improving the performance of larger, multi-user computers through faster batch processing and time sharing (Davidson, 1993; Varian, 1991). No market for distributed personal computing was known to exist. The products that came out of the labs were still of artisanal construction, and no one had done the work to figure out how to transfer them to a production environment (cf. Perry and Wallich, 1985). Although the PARC team was counting (correctly) on steady declines in component costs, prototype models were very expensive and eventual production costs were hard to forecast.

On the other hand, many of the same objections could have been voiced at Haloid at any time during the 1950s, yet the firm persisted in its apparently quixotic endeavor. Moreover, the development cycles at PARC were astonishingly compressed. The first working Alto, the original single-user computer, was available by April of 1973, roughly four months after development work had begun in earnest and some three years before the first Apple was built (Perry and Wallich, 1985). Within three years, the labs produced the third-generation Alto III. The Ethernet, linking Altos together, was also in use by the spring of 1973. The laser printer had been rapidly developed on an existing Xerox copier platform, but plans to sell five of them to the Lawrence Livermore National Laboratory were quashed by headquarters out of fear that service costs on the new equipment would escalate out of all proportion to revenues. Xerox decided to wait until the introduction of the 9000 series in 1977 before offering a laser printer option (Perry and Wallich, 1985:65-8; D. K. Smith and Alexander, 1988:158).

It seems likely that not many people below top management at Xerox knew very much about what was going on at PARC, and this may help to account for the overall lack of interest in PARC research. But this changed at Xerox's 1977 World Conference, held at Boca Raton. At that meeting, Peter McColough delivered what was known as his "Real World" talk, in which he concluded: "We are now faced with the urgent need for change within this company" (Kearns and Nadler, 1992:100). As it happened, PARC researchers had brought their equipment with them, and were able to introduce their products more widely in the Xerox community – apparently to great effect. Yet despite McColough's exhortations and the product evidence at hand, no real commitments to the new technology were immediately forthcoming (Perry and Wallich, 1985; D. K. Smith and Alexander, 1986).

Backing from the top would await the departure of several of the more reluctant managers, including most of the cohort that had been brought in from Ford. They were replaced by people more sympathetic to the project, including David Kearns, who became CEO in 1977, and Don Massaro, who took over the non-copier business in Dallas. Massaro, who had founded a disk-drive company before joining Xerox, understood the technology and strongly supported the Alto (D. K. Smith and Alexander, 1988:229).

Nevertheless, the Alto, renamed the Star, was not released until 1981. Not only was it late to market, it was based on a proprietary architecture at a time when the market was strongly signaling a preference for open systems. Disillusioned, and feeling increasingly constrained by headquarters' efforts to exert control over the operation, many PARC researchers began to leave. Bob Taylor moved to DEC's new Palo Alto laboratories in 1983, taking several PARC researchers with him (Kearns and Nadler, 1992:103; D. K. Smith and Alexander, 1988:254). Others ended up at IBM and Apple. Xerox had lost its market opportunity and now began to lose the talent that had made that opportunity possible.

This is a remarkable story because Xerox, in effect, *did* all the right things for all the right reasons. Foreseeing a day when its copier franchise would be eroded, it developed (well in advance of its eventual crisis) a vision of what the company could become, repeatedly reaffirmed its commitment to that vision,[21] and provided abundant resources to fulfill it. Top management made clear at the outset its willingness to allow PARC researchers to figure out their own way and, despite definite concerns, accepted the need to separate the computer labs from the rest of the company to ensure that they would not be overshadowed by the copier people.[22] It hired new people for the new kind of work and, judging from the results, this strategy worked brilliantly in developing the desired technologies. Yet Xerox didn't *become* a computer company. It remained very profoundly a copier company.

We have to suppose that there are many reasons for such an outcome. It certainly seems to be the case, however, that organizational and geographic separation played an important – although paradoxical

---

[21] A 1974 strategic review specifically reaffirmed Xerox's commitment to the office-of-the-future/architecture-of-information orientation, highlighting the contributions of PARC (D. K. Smith and Alexander, 1988:136–41).

[22] The decision to move corporate headquarters to Stamford, Connecticut, in 1970 was made in the same spirit. McColough wanted to reduce the status and resource disparities between the copier and non-copier sides of the business and thought that moving the headquarters away from the center of the copier business in Rochester would help balance the scales (D. K. Smith and Alexander, 1988:46).

– role. On the one hand, distance from the center arguably did protect the labs from the company's dominant culture and allowed them to develop into the sort of place that could produce these innovations. On the other hand, it helped ensure that news from the labs would not diffuse rapidly or widely within the rest of Xerox, reducing the chance that PARC technologies would become part of the practical consciousness back at headquarters.

There was little institutional connection between Xerox central and the labs (cf. D. K. Smith and Alexander, 1988; Perry and Wallich, 1985). This meant that there was no consistent way for the labs' ideas to be fed back to headquarters as they were emerging, and thus no way either for headquarters to shape the trajectory in a way that made sense to them or to be educated and brought around to the labs' way of thinking. Instead, two quite divergent thought collectives, to borrow Fleck's phrase, coexisted unproductively within the firm. And since PARC, unlike LMSD, had no brief and no capacity to carry its ideas into production independent of the activities of the parent firm, the impasse was essentially total.

Apart from organizational and geographical distance, it is possible to detect the elements of a deep cultural divide. Xerox and PARC, for example, had decidedly different ways of working and different styles of social relations within the organization. PARC researchers came and went according to their own internal clocks (Alan Kay famously did his most productive thinking between four and eight in the morning) and worked on what they found interesting rather than according to priorities defined by the center. The management hierarchy at the labs was very flat and a great deal of emphasis was placed on developing a broad consensus around the trajectory the research should take – so much so that the process had a name: Tom Sawyering. According to former PARC staffer James Mitchell, "Someone would decide that a certain thing was really important to do. They would start working on it, give some structure to it, and then try to convince other people to come whitewash this fence with them" (quoted in Perry and Wallich, 1985:62–4; cf. also Pake, 1985). While others have described this intense pressure for consensus as frequently coercive (cf. D. K. Smith and Alexander, 1988), there seems little doubt that the PARC researchers saw the process of developing a research program as a collegial and inclusive endeavor. Such a self-image implies that the building of commitments is seen explicitly as an ongoing social process rather than a matter of signing on to a pre-existing and authoritative set of values and norms.

Beyond that, the labs had a very different way of thinking about the world and Xerox's place in it – a different sense of how things could be and how things ought to be. It can be suggested, for example, that it wasn't merely the technological preoccupations (computers vs. copiers) that divided the two camps. PARC technologies represented a new way of thinking not only about document production but about how *information* would be produced and who would use the machines involved.[23] In Xerox's world, thinking and writing were separate activities from document production (typing and copying) and they were done by different people in a long-established (and highly gendered) division of labor between thinkers/managers and executors/secretaries. In the world envisioned by PARC, composing, document preparation, and even printing were collapsed into a unified process that could be performed by the writer at his or her terminal. PARC technologies, in effect, proposed a dramatic overhaul in the material practices and social relations involved in office work. While this sounds as though it exactly fits the bill of the new architecture of information sought by Peter McColough, it simultaneously represented an abrupt shift of thinking for Xerox. Even the question of who exactly you were selling to within the client's firm and what you thought they were going to do with your products suddenly became murky.

Ironically, there are grounds to argue that PARC's sense of itself in the world had much more in common with the early days at Haloid than it did with 1970s-era Xerox. Most significantly, there was the same conviction that the technology being developed would change the world for the better by democratizing the control of information. As James Mitchell put it: "We really wanted to have an impact on the world. That was one reason we built things, that we made real things; we wanted to have a chance of making an impact" (quoted in Perry and Wallich, 1985:75).

By the 1970s, however, the "real" Xerox had come under the sway of the cadre of managers recruited from Ford to bring order and rationality to the company's chaotic management systems. Peter McColough, who had become chairman upon Joe Wilson's death in 1971, had a visionary if admittedly vague idea,[24] but he was soon to be distracted by an anti-trust action filed in 1972 by the Federal Trade Commission and the looming reality of competition in the copier business. Meanwhile, the rest of the firm was increasingly focused on classic Ford preoccupations: rationalizing systems, cutting manufacturing costs, attempting to quantify everything possible, and instituting complicated and unwieldy review processes for every idea.

---

[23] My thanks to Elizabeth Dunn for suggesting this idea.

[24] No one knows, for example, who thought of the phrase "architecture of information." McColough has attributed it to his speechwriter who later acknowledged that neither of them had any specific idea of what it meant (Perry and Wallich, 1985:62).

This, of course, made a lot of sense from the point of view of people who had been raised at Ford and brought to Xerox precisely to impart their Ford-style expertise. In their world, it was reasonable to celebrate as a major achievement a dollar reduction in the cost of a component of which you might need half a million in the course of a year. In their world also, numbers had the highest value as a source of information.[25] If it couldn't be quantified (for example, how big *is* the potential market for personal computers?), it didn't count as real information. Moreover, in a world of standardized mass production, big and/or rapid changes were anathema, as they threatened the premature devaluation of a tremendous amount of fixed capital and the write-off of large sunk costs. In that context, it was reasonable to subject any new ideas to exhaustive review and to kill those that did not conform to the decision-makers' analytical rules and standards.

In a sense, Xerox headquarters, in the person of McColough, had a vision for the company, but didn't really know what the substance of that vision should look like. At the same time, PARC had a vision of the technology, but had no particular idea about what the company should be – or at least no idea that it had the power to put into effect. If PARC was "us," the rest of Xerox was "them" and could not easily be incorporated into PARC's sense of itself in the world. How, then, could PARC use its vision to transform Xerox? Or, as David Kearns describes the stalemate:

> The copier-duplicator gang vehemently wouldn't accept outsiders. They viewed the West Coasters as people who spent their time coming up with sophisticated ideas that never made any money for the corporation. The West Coasters, on the other hand, regarded the copier people as the past, a group of stodgy individuals completely out of touch with the future path of the world. (Kearns and Nadler, 1992:104)

In the face of this stalemate, the ex-Ford managers, led by Archie McCardell as president, had the power to impose their own view of the world. This view, unluckily, was technically and financially conservative and led the firm to short-circuit the further development and commercialization of PARC inventions.

The picture that emerges of Xerox during these crucial years is of a firm that is riven by competing cultures, identities and commitments. As David Kearns recalls it: "These were confused years at Xerox. . . . The clash between the Ford Men and the Xerox veterans had been draining enough. Now a war intensified between the West Coast and East Coast

---

[25] Robert McNamara creates the strong impression in the early chapters of his memoirs of a near-total faith in the value of quantitative analysis as a guide to action.

segments of the corporation that, to Xerox people at least, seemed every bit as bitter as the Civil War" (Kearns and Nadler, 1992:101). In this three-way struggle, it is hard to avoid the conclusion that the wrong people won.

The copier wars

At the same time as the struggles over PARC were unfolding, Xerox's worst nightmares about competition in the plain-paper copier business were in the process of being realized. The company would see its market share slide from over 90 percent to just under 15 percent in the space of a decade (Kearns and Nadler, 1992:134–5). This was a true catastrophe and, by the early 1980s, CEO David Kearns was privately contemplating the possibility that Xerox would die (Kearns and Nadler, 1992).

When Xerox achieved its first billion dollars in sales within a decade, it was the first American corporation to do so. In this context, ten years is a very short space of time, and on the downside, careening toward oblivion, it must have seemed even shorter. On the other hand, it was ten years and the evidence that the firm was in serious trouble was accumulating forcefully and rapidly. From 1974 to 1977 alone, Xerox's share of units placed in the US, its home market, dropped from 82 percent to just over 50 percent (Jacobson and Hillkirk, 1986:136). A decade of disastrous news can't be written off as a market blip and it does afford considerable time for thinking about what to do.

Indeed, there was a lot of such thinking going on. McKinsey consultants were practically in permanent residence at Xerox, but reportedly felt that their expensive advice was not having much impact. According to McKinsey consultant Eddie Miller, when David Kearns requested yet another study in 1980, he replied: "we can't tell you anything new. You know everything we're going to tell you, and so does everyone else in this company. People have known what's wrong for a long time" (quoted in D. K. Smith and Alexander, 1988:220; cf. also Jacobson and Hillkirk, 1986:178–9).

Part of the competitive challenge that Xerox faced was what I described in chapter 5 as "normal competition:" competition that takes place within a common social order and which involves similar understandings of the market, production strategies, and the general rules of the game. It came, as expected, from Kodak and IBM. In other words, the competition came from known quarters – even very well known, as many Xerox managers (including David Kearns) had previously worked for one or another of these giants.

Further, it was competition on a common terrain. Both Kodak and

IBM focused their attention on the mid- to high-volume copiers that constituted the heart of Xerox's market strategy. Similarly, they leased rather than sold these large machines and supported their products in the field with large sales and service organizations.

The one major challenge to this conventional notion of what the copier market was really like came from Kodak, which pioneered document recirculation, contravening an ancient Xerox taboo. From its earliest days, the prime directive at Xerox had been "don't damage the original." This meant minimizing the degree to which the original document was handled by the machine. In the Xerox culture, the whole idea of document recirculation was scandalous. But the market, it turned out, liked it. So Kodak, also because of the high quality of its copiers' output, was a serious threat.

So, too, was IBM after some initial fumbling. Indeed, a company would have to be truly witless to be unconcerned by competition from such formidable rivals. Still, Kodak and IBM weren't the only serious intruders onto Xerox's terrain or even, as became increasingly clear, the most important. Yet Xerox central remained wholly preoccupied with its familiar competitors and their familiar style of competition, and failed to appreciate or respond to a new kind of competition from a new source until it was almost too late.

This competition, of course, came from Japan. It represented what I referred to earlier as competition between social orders, implying a very different understanding of what the market was like, the relationship of the firm to the market and to its competitors, how things are designed, how they are made, how they are sold, and the like. I argued above that this sort of competition is particularly difficult to respond to because it is hard to discern what the stakes are, and because it throws into question the value of the whole array of material practices, social and power relations, and ways of thinking that constitute an existing corporate culture (see chapter 5).

The Japanese entrants into the copier market focused their attention on developing small, low-volume, simple, cheap but reliable machines. In the world view of Xerox and its chief American rivals, this segment of the market had been written off as uninteresting. The dominant culture valued large, fast, technically elegant, and high-margin and, in the absence of any viable alternatives in the market, these commitments were unchallengeable. But even when viable alternatives appeared in the market, the commitments remained unchallenged. The parallels with the US automobile industry are striking and, given the importance of ex-Ford managers at Xerox, may have reflected similar processes of cultural formation.

In Japan, however, where space is scarce and extremely expensive, office machines that are so large that they require their own room are a problem. Moreover, the fastest route to the market was through dealers rather than a direct sales and service force. Since these machines were sold rather than leased, and since they were comparatively inexpensive, this was an eminently reasonable approach. It was also an economical one since the firms didn't have to invest in building a huge presence in the field.

The Japanese challenge came from outside the social order in another sense: it came from Japan. That was a problem not because the Japanese were so Japanese, but because they weren't supposed to be players in this particular game. Kodak and IBM – and their products – were culturally recognizable as competition in Xerox's world; Canon, Ricoh, and Sharp were not.

At one point, Xerox did actually approach Canon with the idea of licensing the copier technology that Canon had developed in the 1960s in order to avoid Xerox patents. But Jeff Kennard, who initiated the talks for Xerox, reports that "The most knowing people in the organization, the technologists, pooh-poohed the whole damn thing. Even when we saw it [in 1971], we didn't recognize it for what it was" (quoted in Jacobson and Hillkirk, 1986:143–4).

Such an inability to recognize what you can see in front of you reflects a cultural understanding that defines what has value, and can therefore be seen, and what does not. The Japanese machines might exist, but they were invisible to Xerox because they came from the wrong place – a place outside Xerox's understanding of the known world of competition. This seems the only way of explaining Xerox's continuing refusal to acknowledge this competitive threat despite abundant and excellent information that it existed and would rapidly grow worse. Catastrophic loss of market share is one kind of evidence. But since the number of copies made in the world continued to mushroom, Xerox's revenues actually continued to grow. Further, the company had started selling off its lease base, so profits remained high (cf. Jacobson and Hillkirk, 1986:170; D. K. Smith and Alexander, 1988:218). This eased the trauma considerably, but it couldn't entirely obscure the inevitability of decline. According to Eddie Miller, "They all knew what was going to happen ... The big earnings decline was no surprise to anybody in Xerox" (cited in Jacobson and Hillkirk, 1986:179).

In any case, years before earnings did turn down, Xerox had access to a great deal of accurate information about the Japanese threat from a wide range of sources. In 1970, for example, top Xerox managers met with James Abegglen, a well-known authority on Japanese industry. As Abegglen recalled the encounter: "I told them that here in Japan was the world's biggest market for copiers. That if you put out a small machine that pumped out copies slowly but effectively, there was going to be one helluva market." This advice was met with derision. According to Abegglen, Xerox President Archie McCardell "just giggled and ignored the Japanese threat" (cited in Jacobson and Hillkirk, 1986:124).

Xerox management didn't just ignore the advice of outsiders, however. There were two excellent sources of information within the firm that were also arguing strongly in favor of recognizing and responding to the Japanese threat, specifically by bringing out a small, low-volume, inexpensive machine. These sources were the Rank-Xerox organization in England, and the Fuji-Xerox joint venture in Japan.

In talks with individuals who held high-level positions in Xerox at home and abroad from the early 1970s to the early 1980s, a picture emerges of highly divergent subcultures developing on the basis of very different experiences in these different corporate locations. But there was ample opportunity for communications across these growing cultural divides, especially between headquarters and Rank-Xerox, where a number of American expatriate managers spent several years. But the struggle to transform information into knowledge that informed strategy at the center was a long one.

Xerox in Japan and in Europe

Fuji-Xerox had been established in the early 1960s to manufacture and sell Xerox products in Japan. But according to Jeff Kennard, who was the assistant to the president of Fuji-Xerox from 1977 to 1982, the joint venture was also meant to serve as Xerox's "window on Japan and Japanese competition ... [and the company's] primary source of competitive intelligence." In other words, Fuji-Xerox theoretically had an important role to play as a source of information for the rest of the company.

For a while, Fuji-Xerox did quite well in the Japanese market on the basis of Xerox products, market strategy, and ways of doing business. But in the 1970s, it found itself in a market in which the demand for smaller, cheaper machines was increasingly significant and was being served entirely by its emerging domestic rivals.

The competition had products that Fuji-Xerox couldn't match; it had low manufacturing costs, as a result of a highly refined production apparatus; and it had economies of scale based on a volume of production that was entirely outside the realm of possibility for Fuji-Xerox, given its product line. Moreover, the competition sold through dealers on the basis of price, quality, and reliability rather than direct on the promise of excellent field service when things went wrong. In Japan, selling a machine that was unlikely to break down afforded a stronger marketing position than promising to fix it quickly when it did break down. Such an approach to the market also reduced costs in the long run, allowing prices to remain low.

Fuji-Xerox, watching its market evaporate, decided it had to thoroughly overhaul its operations. As Jeff Kennard recalls it, the company rather rapidly concluded that "the culture had to change." The overhaul proceeded on two fronts: strategy toward the market and internal practices and relations.

This entailed, in the first instance, rapidly developing a line of smaller, lower-cost, and low-margin machines more suited to local demand. In short, Fuji-Xerox decided it had to follow its competition into the low end of the market despite the fact that this move went entirely counter to Xerox's view of what the market was like, how it would evolve, and how you made money in it. It also required Fuji-Xerox to take on for itself a more significant design and engineering role than it had traditionally held within the larger enterprise.

Fuji-Xerox had to move fast in order to restore its position, and this meant a dramatically compressed product development cycle compared with Xerox norms, which tended to run anywhere from five to eight years (cf. D. K. Smith and Alexander, 1988:202). As many firms have since discovered, such a compressed development cycle required adjusting relations within product design and across the design, engineering, and manufacturing functions. The first product of this accelerated effort, the 2200, appeared in 1972.

Fuji-Xerox also turned its attention to manufacturing practices internal to the firm, stressing a commitment to total quality management, employee participation, flexibility, and other features of the "Japanese style" of production that have become increasingly familiar to us. All in all, Fuji-Xerox's efforts met with considerable success. But what Fuji-Xerox termed "the New Xerox Movement" remained a local phenomenon for years, as Xerox central refused to acknowledge the validity of this departure.

This was not due to lack of information about what was going on at Fuji-Xerox or about how successful they were. As David Kearns makes clear in his memoirs, top Xerox managers were frequent visitors to Fuji-Xerox (cf. Kearns and Nadler, 1992). There was an expatriate manager on site during much of this period, and Fuji-Xerox head Yotaro (Tony) Kobayashi also traveled frequently to the States. In 1978, Xerox commissioned a study by McKinsey that enthusiastically supported the Fuji-Xerox strategy and recommended it to headquarters. Moreover, Fuji-Xerox had started supplying its small machines to Rank-Xerox and they were selling like hotcakes in Europe.

Rank-Xerox, by 1976, had acknowledged to itself that it was seriously in trouble in the European market. For a while, it had attributed declining sales to the state of the economy, but eventually it became clear to the top management that they were losing their market to the Japanese and needed to figure out some way of countering this loss.

Although many top positions at Rank-Xerox were held by American expatriate managers (such as Bill Glavin, Paul Allaire, and Wayland Hicks), the management style there was considerably more fluid and experimental than was characteristic of the US parent at the time. From interviews with some of the people involved, it seems clear that this was in significant measure a product of the fragmentation and diversity of the European market. There was simply no way to pretend that a single, unified strategy could be made applicable everywhere from Scandinavia to the Mediterranean. At the same time, there was also more space to experiment at relatively low cost. Initiatives could be tried out in one country and then, if successful, gradually expanded into other areas. If they were unsuccessful, then not much would have been lost.

Rank-Xerox's ability to focus on Japanese competition also benefited from the fact that Kodak was very slow in moving into international markets with its own products. Japanese firms, however, were entering in force, and so it was particularly clear in Europe that Xerox was highly vulnerable to the kind of competition that they represented.

In 1977, Rank-Xerox committed to buying 25,000 small copiers from Fuji-Xerox. They sold them within a year. As one of the participants at the time observed: "We had never sold anything like that, of one product, in the history of the company. [We] really stopped the Japanese for a period of time, with that product. . . . And we were the first ones to buy a product from Japan because the US organization just wouldn't buy products from Japan." Fuji-Xerox, in fact, had been offering to supply its small machines to the US since 1972 and had been steadily rebuffed. One respondent described the situation in this way:

> I'd been part of a meeting in 1972 . . . where the decision was made not to buy product from Fuji-Xerox which had, at that time, the 2200. [This] was probably the biggest strategic mistake that the Xerox corporation ever made in their history, in my opinion. . . . I went to this meeting . . . and they [the management group commissioned to study the proposal] got up and said, . . . "here's our charge, here's our conclusions, and here's our recommendations." And their recommendation was to do that [buy the 2200]. And Peter [McColough] said, "no, I can't do that." These people had worked six months on that project. What do you mean? "We're not going to buy product from Japan." That was it, the meeting was over.

It is worth stressing that the decision to buy from Fuji-Xerox was not blocked by unimaginative bureaucrats intent on reviewing all new ideas to death. In this case, the numbers were in, the analysis had been made, and the recommendation was unambiguous; the proposal had been evaluated by the company's norms and standards and had been found acceptable. Buying small machines from the Japanese was unacceptable, however, to Peter McColough.

This is a remarkable story given that the machine in question already existed. All Xerox had to do was sell the thing. Even after Rank-Xerox made the decision to buy in 1977 and had such extraordinary success, Xerox central continued to resist the product. Why?

There are grounds to argue that selling a small machine designed and made in Japan did not conform to Xerox's sense of who and what it was in the world. Xerox was the company that had invented xerography and set the technical and design standards for the market. Its commitments were to ever larger and faster machines, technical elegance and complexity, and a massive organizational presence in the market through its sales and service force. Its frame of reference included the possibility of technically strong competition from other, similar American firms, but it did not allow for real innovation from Japan, even from its own partner there. As one respondent put it:

> [P]eople in the United States, the engineers and manufacturing people, had a "not invented here" attitude, which said that the Japanese can't do anything very good because we taught them everything they know. So how could they make it any better than we can? And frankly, they did.... [T]he arrogance was, "We invented xerography, we're the only ones who can do it," and [as] I mentioned before, with Fuji-Xerox, even though they were our own company, "those people can't make a product they can sell in the rest of the world, because we taught them everything they know." ... [P]eople on the engineering and manufacturing side truly believed that.

Jeff Kennard phrased the problem in the same terms, describing Xerox central's attitude as "we taught them everything they know about copiers, how could they have anything to teach us?" In his judgment, "Xerox did not pay sufficient attention either to Japanese companies or to Fuji-Xerox ... [because they considered them] just little companies in Japan." Rather than "not invented here," Xerox central's attitude seems to have been "it couldn't have been invented there."

David Kearns, in his memoirs, asserts that "It's wrong ... to think that we were oblivious to the Japanese.... it wasn't a matter of Xerox not knowing about Japan. In fact, we predicted the Japanese would arrive sooner than they did" (Kearns and Nadler, 1992:75). He acknowledges, however, that Xerox did not anticipate the level of quality or the cost structure that the Japanese competition would offer. Further, at the outset, the Japanese were making coated-paper copiers, which really didn't count as competition in the eyes of Xerox, despite the fact that people bought them in droves. Nevertheless, Kearns argues that the information necessary to understand the Japanese threat was available, it just wasn't usable: "For a long time, we had been getting engineering reports on the Japanese cost structure and now we realized that they had been hopelessly wrong. And I was buying them. Was it bad analysis? I doubt that it was a case of the information not being available. I think it was purely a matter of denial" (Kearns and Nadler, 1992:122).

In Kearns's view, top management at Xerox was truly blinded by its own success and simply couldn't bring itself to believe that there were problems. As he writes:

> You see all the trappings that prove how successful the company has become and how successful you have become and what a big deal you are. This leads to your denying the data presented to you that show the company floundering. The trappings work against the actual situation and so you end up not believing it. After all, you don't see customers or hear from them. If the company were in sad shape, then the flowers ought to be dead. (Kearns and Nadler, 1992:270)

But this doesn't seem a wholly accurate representation of top management's way of thinking about its situation. The state of denial that Kearns invokes was highly selective. Management *was* worried about Kodak and IBM, and for good reason. But with abundant evidence about the existence of a different kind of competitive threat altogether, and with equally unambiguous evidence in hand about how it could be effectively responded to, Xerox central couldn't bring itself to acknowledge the nature and magnitude of the Japanese threat.

In this sense, Xerox could both "know" about the Japanese, as Kearns asserts, and at the same time not "know" about them, because the available information couldn't be interpreted – transformed into knowledge that could be acted upon – within the Xerox culture. The Japanese existed but couldn't be seen because they were not interpretable as eligible players in this particular game. Hence, a viable strategy that was quite literally on the table couldn't be adopted.

This story, as is well known, has a happy ending. But the process of arriving there was a long and arduous one. Repatriated managers from Rank-Xerox brought the fight more directly to headquarters. The last of the Ford people left in the early 1980s. Other internal lobbyists for change increased their pressure. As Kearns describes them, "They were mavericks and outlaws in the organization.... They were revolutionaries.... It was guerrilla warfare" (Kearns and Nadler, 1992:147).

Kearns himself, shaken by the realization that Xerox was on the brink of death, is widely credited (along with his successor, Paul Allaire) with promoting the deep changes in material practices (including what the firm made, how products were designed, and how they were made), social relations (decentralization of authority, worker participation, etc.), and ways of thinking (about markets, products, quality, pricing, competition, labor, and so on) that eventually turned the firm around. More recently, Xerox's approach to managing research and integrating it into the firm's operations has also been overhauled (cf. Webb, 1991; Corcoran, 1992).

The decisions that were taken were undeniably tough. The change in pricing structure led to a drop in profits of 50 percent from one year to the next. People were laid off for the first time in the company's history. Operations were drastically restructured. So the process of change was both costly and difficult – not to mention risky. Little wonder that the people involved would be loath to embark on such a course and would resist it in many ways.

Yet given that the alternative was total disaster, it seems insufficient to invoke inertia, or the blind adherence to tradition, or even simple arrogance as an explanation of why Xerox refused for so long to address its real problems. In a sense, what we have seen throughout this story is an ongoing struggle over which "traditions" and commitments in Xerox's culture would be validated. Thus, the firm's traditional mission as a company that did good in the world by democratizing information ran headlong into its traditional commitment to copiers, while its traditional emphasis on technical elegance and complexity eventually conflicted with its long-standing sense of who was able to define what the copier market was about. Management may have suffered from arrogance, but this arrogance was selective: Kodak and IBM inspired fear, while Canon and Ricoh elicited disdain. Even their own joint venture, Fuji-Xerox, didn't count as a force to be reckoned with. The stakes involved in how these conflicts and struggles were played out were very high indeed.

Reflections

On information, knowledge, and strategy

Robert McNamara, in his memoirs of the Vietnam War, describes the 1964 decision to launch air attacks against North Vietnam in this way:

The risk of Chinese escalation and the possibility that air attacks would neither break the will nor decisively reduce the ability of the North to continue supporting the insurgency in the South were recognized. But, because no better alternative appeared to exist, the majority of the group meeting in Saigon favored such attacks! This was the sort of desperate energy that would drive much of our Vietnam policy in the years ahead. Data and analysis showed that air attacks would not work, but there was such determination to do something, anything, to stop the Communists that discouraging reports were often ignored. (McNamara with VanDeMark, 1995:114)

In the fall of 1964, these discouraging reports were coming from such impeccable sources as Undersecretary of State George Ball; Admiral U.S. Grant Sharp, Jr., the head of naval operations in the Pacific; the CIA; and General William Westmoreland, head of the Military Assistance Command in Vietnam (McNamara with VanDeMark, 1995:156-9). McNamara laments the lack of knowledge about the culture and history of Vietnam that undermined their attempts to devise and implement an effective Vietnam policy overall, and criticizes the distorted information supplied by the government of South Vietnam. But the data to evaluate the military strategy adopted was not the problem. As he makes clear, the problem was the strategic decision-makers' inability to ask the right questions of the information they had in abundance, and their unwillingness to interrogate their own assumptions about what the situation in Vietnam really meant. The result was that more ordinance was dropped on Vietnam by the US than by all sides during the entire course of World War II (cf. Sheehan, 1988). Not only did this incredible destruction fail to achieve its announced objectives, it was undertaken despite the fact that the strategists had good reason to believe it *couldn't* achieve those objectives.

Conventional economic analysis treats information as a strategically important but fairly normal commodity in the sense that it has a price, its value is influenced by scarcity, and the resources committed to obtaining and processing it represent an opportunity cost for the firm. The main proviso is that the market for information is imperfect and its quality and availability are subject to the strategic behavior of economic agents. Further, information is inevitably compromised by uncertainty and an unanswerable question about how much information is enough to make satisfactory, if not optimal, decisions given its cost (cf. Akerlof, 1970; Cyert and March, 1963; Simon, 1961; Williamson, 1985). So information is a real problem for strategic decision-making.

But I have tried to show here that it is only one problem that affects the process of strategy formation, and not even necessarily the most difficult. The Lockheed and Xerox stories are interesting in this context precisely because they do not turn on faulty or incomplete information. They rest instead on the problem of how information is interpreted and transformed into knowledge that can provide the basis for an effective strategy.

This process of interpretation is unavoidably individual in that some set of persons must actually do the interpreting and devise the strategy. The interpretive possibilities, then, are shaped by the identities, commitments, experiences, and social, geographical, and historical position of those persons. The possibilities may also depend on the stakes involved in defending those identities and commitments.

At the same time, the interpretive process is deeply cultural. It grows out of the ensemble of material practices, social relations, and ways of thinking that mark the firm's practical consciousness and help to define the subset of interpretive possibilities that can be pursued or even actually thought by the people involved.

These processes are extraordinarily powerful. As we saw in the case of Xerox, they can render real things in the world invisible. At Lockheed, they silenced the voice of what was practically the company's only customer.

They also involve extraordinarily high stakes. For Lockheed and Xerox, they were measured in billions of dollars and thousands of actual or potential jobs. In Vietnam, the stakes were incalculably higher.

On power, conflict, and cultural change

The Lockheed and Xerox cases also illustrate the proposition that corporate cultures are not the source of resistance to change *tout court*. The Ford Men, after all, seem to have rapidly and profoundly changed Xerox during their relatively short tenure. Lockheed, for its part, made the transition from a primarily civilian aircraft producer to an overwhelmingly defense-oriented one with relative ease during the late thirties and into the war.

Corporate cultures do, however, shape the process of change. They are intimately involved in determining what kinds of change will be accepted and which refused, whatever their "objective" desirability. Corporate strategies, for this reason, cannot be understood apart from the cultural processes underlying their production.

These changes, moreover, play out through a highly conflictual process in which the power to define who and what the firm is in the world, how markets should be understood, how competition works, how different products and practices should be valued, and so on are all at stake. The strategic trajectory of the firm depends on how these conflicts are resolved.

In the case of Lockheed, these struggles were resolved through a fairly stable agreement to disagree, which involved the separation of the new venture from the larger organization. Lockheed, in effect, grew a new part of itself that had little to do operationally or culturally with the old. The parent firm certainly benefited from the stream of profits that LMSD generated. But the corporation as a whole remained insulated from the transformative processes at work in its own periphery – processes that it tolerated but did not embrace. It's impossible to know what this aloof stance may have cost it, but if the parent's near bankruptcy in the early 1970s is any indication, the price was high. One sign that the company may belatedly have decided to draw the two parts of the firm closer together is that its current chairman, Daniel Tellep, started his career in the missiles and space group.

Xerox also started down the path of geographical and organizational separation in its dealings with PARC. This approach was, to a degree, successful in that PARC was able to fulfill its task of developing the desired technologies. But in this case, since PARC remained dependent on the parent for the realization of its own mission and commitments, an agreement to disagree was not a viable solution. The outcome, instead, was a stalemate as competing definitions of the company and its world could not be reconciled. In this case, the power lay with those who would refuse what the new strategic orientation implied. The cost to Xerox was almost certainly billions of dollars in revenues that flowed, instead, to other firms.

On the copier side, meanwhile, commitments, identities, and processes of valuation, inclusion, and exclusion were also at stake. Xerox, in an important sense, had an easier time recognizing Kodak and IBM as a kind of "us" than it did with its own partner, Fuji-Xerox. Kodak and IBM could be seen as valid competitors, operating in the same kind of world and in the same way as Xerox. They were members of the larger social order inhabited by Xerox. The Japanese were excluded from this sense of the relevant world despite the fact that their presence was everywhere in evidence. Recognizing the Japanese meant accepting the implicit devaluation of a whole range of commitments, practices, and understandings by which Xerox recognized itself. That it took a kind of guerrilla warfare within the firm to effect the necessary changes gives some indication of how high the stakes were in preserving the firm's sense of itself in the world.

These struggles, in one way or another, all involve competing visions of the social order within the firm and the way it will relate to the outside world, including the market and other competitors. They also involve the power to defend or successfully challenge the appropriateness of the array of material practices, social relations, and ways of thinking that constitute a corporate culture and the individual identities and social assets tied up in it.

On case studies as a way of learning

These are two stories about the difficult process of corporate transformation. There is no way to present them as statistically generalizable accounts.

In the case of Lockheed, I have relied heavily on the recollections of people involved in the process. Memory is a notoriously unreliable document; and to tell the story at all, I have had to interpret the interpretations of participants who have their own stakes in how the story is told, and whose recollections are undoubtedly selective and partial. I have tried to deal with this by corroborating their stories with documentary evidence where available and by talking with a range of people located in different positions within the story to, in effect, triangulate in on a coherent and fair account.

The Xerox story is much better known and has been exhaustively analyzed by others. What I have tried to do in this case is offer my own interpretation of these accounts, supplemented by interviews with several participants. Again, the process has been one of developing an analysis that seems to me to make sense, to be fair, and to take into account the available information. But this kind of work is unavoidably an interpretive process.

The question still remains of why they should be taken as anything more than two more or less interesting stories of very particular processes. Can they, in fact, provide a basis for thinking about corporations more generally?

I think that they can. In the first place, both Lockheed and Xerox are places where these kinds of problem, in a sense, shouldn't have arisen. They were both technically progressive firms that had proved themselves eminently capable of devising and implementing important changes in their universes. Xerox in particular demonstrated an admirable ability to evaluate its own actual and potential weaknesses and act to counter them. In both cases, there was no shortage of good information about what to do. Yet despite these very favorable starting points, both firms had to pass through highly traumatic periods before they were able to fully commit themselves to the kinds of change they needed to make.

If firms that were so well positioned at the outset had such deep problems, then it seems reasonable to hypothesize that companies whose circumstances are less favorable to begin with must also resolve many of the same kinds of issue. There are many indications that this is so. Some such processes may plausibly be sought in explanation of GM's inability to internalize the lessons of NUMMI or Saturn (see chapter 4). DEC's refusal to acknowledge the threat to its minicomputer empire posed by computer workstations, despite the fact that they precisely mirrored the challenge DEC originally posed to IBM, also seems to hinge on similar factors (cf. Saxenian, 1994). IBM, for its part, strenuously resisted embracing time sharing and virtual machine systems despite the fact that the scientific and technical market that it was eager to break into was precisely interested in these capabilities, as IBM researchers who were close to these potential users repeatedly made clear (cf. Varian, 1991). AT&T's slow response to competition from other long-distance providers seems also to have involved the questions about commitments and identity that are featured here (cf. Galambos, 1993).

If the reader finds it unlikely that the case studies presented here have any resemblance to other stories of other firms that could be told, or if she or he finds my interpretation of these stories implausible, then they must be seen as idiosyncratic tales with no relevance to anything outside themselves. If, on the other hand, they do resonate in some compelling way with the reader's own experience or interpretation of similar stories, then perhaps it may be accepted that these case studies do speak to broader issues and that the approach to corporate culture argued for here does provide some guidance for understanding why firms do what they do in the world.

Part III

The Cultural Crisis of the Firm

7

The Cultural Crisis of the Firm

To fit in with the change of events, words, too, had to change their usual meanings.

Thucydides, *History of the Peloponnesian War*

Introduction

The sorts of cultural struggle that I've described in the previous chapters may be more or less pervasive in American corporate life, but they don't of themselves explain why so many firms ran into such similar troubles at roughly the same time, or how corporate culture might generally be implicated in this large-scale process. To get at this problem, I want to connect the argument about culture and strategy with the earlier discussion about time, space, and competition.

One task of this chapter is to show how historical transformations in time, space, and competition become general cultural problems – both disorienting and difficult to grasp, and the locus of struggles over the eventual character of a changing social order. Then I will try to construct the basis for the proposition that American corporations during the 1970s and 1980s were broadly confronted with an array of changes in their environment that, taken together, constituted a very deep challenge to their experience and understanding of time, space, and competition. These processes, in effect, provided the underpinnings of a geographically and historically specific but large-scale cultural crisis of the firm.

Phrased this way, however, the proposition suggests a very linear causal relationship in which the boundaries between structure and agent are too neatly drawn. The kind of picture I wish to portray is one in which firms are structuring social agents that must act within structural processes (of, for instance, competition) that their actions and very existence contribute to creating. Any effort to turn this story into something akin to a model with precisely delineated dependent and independent variables would simply be misleading. So the goal of this final chapter is not so much to bring closure, to tie all the themes of the book neatly together, as to open up ways of thinking about how these processes work in general by elaborating a hypothesis about how they may have worked in this highly traumatic historical period.

Transformations in Time, Space, and Competition as Cultural Problems

Time, space, and competition are oddly slippery concepts whose meaning and import are hard to keep track of. On the one hand, they can appear as natural, pre-given categories within which social processes take place: time passes, space is, and, in a capitalist society at least, firms must compete or die. They can also seem to be rather airy metaphysical abstractions: if you're trying to get product out the door, it doesn't seem worthwhile to philosophize about the nature of time or the role of space in structuring social life.

But in the same moment, they are abstractions with real power in our lives. Time *is* money and deadlines really count. Distance matters and having the power to construct a built environment that meets your needs is essential. Meanwhile, you really do have to figure out a way to beat the competition.

They are abstractions, moreover, that play a real part in our material practices and social relations. The moving assembly line perfected the transfer of control over the pace and intensity of labor from the worker to the machine. In doing so, it tied the worker firmly to a particular space on the shop floor, making it difficult to have social interactions with anyone more than a few feet away on the line. Competitive pressures which have promoted the uptake of just-in-time techniques have altered spatial arrangements in and between factories. Distance seems to matter more in production, even as it is being annihilated in the electronic circulation of financial capital. Meanwhile, exhausted at work, we heat takeout meals in microwave ovens and eat them in front of the television.

They are also abstractions with real power to shape our sense of living in the world, our way of thinking about it, and our expectations about what things will be like. We're all frantically short of time and beset by the nagging awareness that time seems to be speeding up in ways that we can't quite control. We often seem to need to be in two places at once, we fume in gridlock as we try to make our way from home to office, we live in a "global village" in which we have increasing

difficulty in defending our own personal space despite recourse to bur-
glar alarms and gated communities, and we are exhorted for our own
good in the future to be global and local at the same time, whatever
that might mean. Being competitive is the essential validation in a capitalist world, but no one knows whether it should be measured by profits, market share, return on investment, stock price, growth, or even,
lately, shrinkage.

The nub of the issue, I think, can be expressed in this way: time,
space, and competition are structural conditions shaping our lives and
our possibilities for action. At the same time, they are socially and culturally constructed, and as such they are arenas for social conflict where
struggles for control over how the world will work are played out.
Paradoxically, however, because these features of social life appear to
be "natural," and not part of the very social and cultural processes they
affect, it's often hard to discern what the struggle really is or should be
about and to strategize appropriately.

There is a substantial body of literature that analyzes time and space
as social and cultural categories (see Harvey, 1996, for a review and
elaboration). This is less true of competition, and so I treat the latter in
a separate section.

The culture of time and space

It is possible to identify periods in history when spatio-temporal sensibilities, meanings, and practices have shifted significantly, entraining an
array of social and cultural struggles and dislocations. Such shifts have
been an especially consistent feature of capitalist development processes
as they first took root and then expanded their field of dominance.
Although these changes often seem to be driven purely by technological
or organizational innovations (such as the mechanical clock, the steam
engine, the factory, or the telephone), what really counts is how they
enter into social practices and contribute to the generation of social and
cultural meanings.

Le Goff, for example, in his study of social and cultural change in the
fourteenth century, shows that it wasn't merely the invention of the
mechanical clock, but the transition from an ecclesiastical to a secular
division of time, one more suited to the needs of urban society and the
conditions of urban labor, that was really the source of conflict and
change (Le Goff, 1980; cf. also Landes, 1983). Coming into this period,
the "traditional" unit of labor time was the day, marked off according
to religious hours of devotion. But the needs of a rising class of urban
merchant capitalists created pressures in favor of nightwork and
increasing precision and harshness in the measurement and enforcing of

work times. Particularly in the major textile centers, the period saw a proliferation of bells to mark the periods of the working day, and uprisings which sought to silence them. As Le Goff notes, "This time indicated the dominance of a social category. It was the time of the new masters" (Le Goff, 1980:46).

There are a number of features of this transition worth drawing out. First, it was specifically a feature of urban manufacturing and commercial activity. The ability to precisely mark the passage of hours has little meaning in agricultural work, and relying on bells as public timekeepers would have little utility in the countryside. So the temporal change had a particular place.

Second, this place became the arena for social conflict, as the masters tried to impose new temporal and spatial practices on workers who sought to resist their power to do this. The new temporal rhythms were part of a redefinition of spatial practices and meanings, as workers faced new constraints on where they could be at any particular moment and how long they had to be there. By the same token, the masters were driven in their effort to develop new temporal practices by the realities of spatial competition (from merchants in other towns) and by the need to extend their reach to new markets.

Finally, changes in spatio-temporal practices were linked with transformations in social and cultural meanings or, as Le Goff describes it, "the disturbance of the chronological framework in the fourteenth century was also a mental and spiritual disturbance." Later, he adds: "The century of the clock was also the century of the cannon and of depth of field. For both scholar and merchant, time and space underwent joint transformation" (Le Goff, 1980:50).

In the late eighteenth and early nineteenth centuries, the transition from putting out to factory-based production was a spatial strategy aimed at exerting greater control over time, material practices, and social relations (cf. Thompson, 1963, 1967; Landes, 1970; Marglin, 1974; Engels, 1968). Cottage-based manufacturing was too easily interrupted by agricultural tasks or abandoned altogether when a sufficient family income was achieved. Collecting everyone together in a factory under direct supervision and tying work processes to the rhythms of water or steam-driven machinery enabled the owner to regulate the temporal rhythms of work, and to ensure that his capital stock was kept in motion to yield the maximum value possible. Factory-based production had the collateral effect of drawing women and children out of the home into a public work space, while segregating them within the factory according to tasks and a gender- and age-based division of labor. It had the further effect of drawing people out of the countryside into increasingly dense and degraded urban industrial and residential areas.

These temporal and spatial transformations, driven by competitive pressures, profoundly changed the way people lived. One doesn't need to romanticize rural life to appreciate that an entire ensemble of material practices, social relations, and ways of thinking – in short, an entire culture – was irrevocably altered by this shift.

These deep changes were also accompanied by considerable social conflict in which the power to define time, space, and social practices and relations was at stake. The Luddites are one kind of example. The struggles over the control of time and work in English textiles, described in chapter 2, are another.

That story also points to a different arena of struggle – one between groups of capitalists organized around competing models of control over time and space. The Lancashire cotton-textile producers, as we saw, substituted a strategy of control over space for one of control over time in their competition with their larger-scale, more productive rivals. This move was successful for a time, but ultimately doomed, as American and other producers eventually gained control over global markets. The fact that the British manufacturers continued to support free trade even when it was no longer in their interest to do so provides some evidence of the great power exerted by a set of identities, commitments, and ways of thinking that had been formed when these people had created and embodied *the* dominant culture in textile manufacturing. It may also suggest that the inability to respond to significant shifts in spatio-temporal practices and meanings – in part because space and time seem merely to be the natural backdrop to everyday life rather than strategically important social constructs – can invalidate an array of industrial practices, devalue material and social resources, and undermine a whole way of life.

The decades around the turn of the twentieth century mark a period when life came to be seen as "modern" and in which time and space were increasingly recognized explicitly as crucial features of social life and social theory. In effect, the sense of modernism was inextricably bound up in a sense of spatio-temporal transformation.

As Stephen Kern shows in *The Culture of Time and Space*, these changes reverberated across a range of social and cultural endeavors, from science to industrial practice, and from modes of consumption and private life to art, architecture, and music (Kern, 1983). This was the period in which time was standardized, first by American railroads (in 1883), which had to coordinate their activities across a huge territory. The International Conference on Time, held in Paris in 1912, globalized standard time, courtesy of the wireless telegraph (Kern, 1983:11–14).

Paradoxically, this was also the period in which the reigning Newtonian concept of absolute time was overthrown, starting with

Ernst Mach in 1883 and continuing through Einstein's general theory of relativity, published in 1916. Meanwhile, non-Euclidean geometry and the theory of relativity were also challenging conceptions of absolute space. Time and space were becoming both more homogeneous and more heterogeneous and relative (Kern, 1983:18–19, 136).

Traditional concepts of day and night, time and space, distance and speed, indoors and outdoors were disrupted by a steady stream of technical and organizational innovations. From Edison's invention of the electric light in 1879 through the advent of the bicycle, the automobile, escalators, elevators, air conditioning, the telegraph, the telephone, the airplane, and the machine gun, the experience of time and space seemed to be changing at an accelerating rate.

Work life changed as well. The time discipline underlying the principles of scientific management, elaborated by Frederick Taylor starting in 1883, was amplified by the moving assembly line, introduced by Ford in 1913. Office workers, meanwhile, learned to use typewriters.

These processes were reflected in and reinforced through a whole range of cultural productions. This was the period of the stream of consciousness novel, impressionist and Cubist painting, the cinema, jazz, urban planning, and a new attitude toward space in architecture (Kern 1983:118–24).

In geopolitics, imperial practice and ideology held sway even in the most "democratic" nations. The US, during this period, annexed Hawaii, Puerto Rico, Guam, and the Philippines. In 1898, American banker Charles A. Conant urged:

> The irresistible tendency to expansion, which leads the growing tree to burst every barrier, which drove the Goths, the Vandals, and finally our Saxon ancestors in successive and irresistible waves over the decadent provinces of Rome, seems again in operation, demanding new outlets for American capital and new opportunities for American enterprise. (cited in Kern, 1983:239)

In this way, increasing portions of the globe were parcelled out according to maps that had nothing to do with the lived experience of the people inhabiting those territories. And, as Kern argues, imperialist conflicts were "framed around shared values concerning the control of space" (Kern, 1983:236).

In the natural and the social sciences as well, new concepts of time and space came to the fore. Geological and paleontological discoveries provoked a new understanding of humans as a natural species, while archaeological and linguistic research located humans as ancient but familiar cultural beings. Historians increasingly differentiated between conceptions of cyclical or mythic time and linear/historical time in ancient civilizations (J. Smith, 1991). Meanwhile, sociologists and anthropologists such as Durkheim and Mauss established the basis for understanding the social origins and heterogeneity of time across cultures (cf. Kern, 1983:31–2).

So the "modern era" became the period in which time and space were not only transformed but seen to be transformed. The temptation, perhaps, was to ascribe these changes to new technologies which regularized and compressed time and space. Yet some, at least, certainly saw these technologies as expressive of deeper social processes. The quotation above from Conant, for example, avoids mentioning the technologies of imperialism and, while it seems to attribute the goal of territorial expansion to some inherent human or even natural force, in the end names the needs of capital for new investment and market outlets as the driving inspiration.

What does it mean to recognize that you live in a period in which time and space are changing? Undoubtedly it means many things, but one can speculate that eventually it comes to be seen as normal: time simply speeds up and space gets smaller. Time–space transformations, in other words, become a condition of modern life. As they do so, they come to seem less remarkable and more natural, and remarking upon them seems increasingly redundant. As the editor of the *Revue Scientifique* wrote in 1891: "to say that there are no longer distances is to utter a very banal truth" (quoted in Kern, 1983:229).

Another way of putting this is to suppose that at the very moment when we have learned to live by accelerated temporal rhythms and in apparently distanceless space, when the effects of time–space transformations are everywhere in evidence, they come to seem less and less rooted in social processes and more naturalized. Or at any rate, this becomes a workable hypothesis for daily life since, as individuals, we clearly can't control them.

This means we lose sight of the degree to which the value of material and social assets and the realities of social power are caught up in particular ways of envisioning and controlling temporal and spatial processes. And when a new model of spatio-temporal practices arises to challenge the old and threatens the value of the assets tied to it, it may be very difficult to discern what is at stake, even on the part of those whose own social power is most immediately at risk. Alternatively, *because* their social power is at risk, they may have every incentive to resist the new practices and everything they imply.

I don't need to argue here that time and space simply dropped out of social consciousness or that they were no longer deeply implicated in social struggles. The centuries-old conflict over the length and intensity of the working day continues still (cf. Roediger and Foner, 1989). Political battles and protectionist sentiments associated with the power of capital to relocate production offshore, or the perceived need to defend the national market against foreign encroachment, remain common. The hype surrounding the Internet or the billions poured into research to find ways to cram ever more circuitry onto a microchip testify to the power of spatio-temporal dynamics and the cultural upheavals they continue to spawn.

A key question, then, is whether contemporary spatio-temporal transformations represent "more of the same," just another stage along a normal trajectory, or reflect something qualitatively different. The answer, in a sense, is both. Spatio-temporal transformations are a normal feature of capitalist development processes. But, as I argued in chapter 2, the particular form they take and the particular problems they pose vary historically. This means that they can't always be responded to by means of "normal" adjustments along a given trajectory. They are strategic problems and require the putting into place of new practices, relations, and ways of thinking even at the price of devaluing the assets and power bases characteristic of the old order.

The culture of competition

Competition, like time and space, is often viewed as a natural feature of the social landscape. From Adam Smith's tendency to truck and barter to powerful analogies with the forces of natural selection and survival of the fittest, competition is located as an inherent aspect of human nature and of biological processes in general, lately right down to the genetic level (Dawkins, 1989).

The naturalization of competition has tremendous ideological power. In theory, competition in the market is the guarantor of fairness and of the efficient allocation of social resources to provide the maximum social product for all to share in proportion to the contribution of their own resources. So pervasive is this way of thinking that challenges to it are rather easily dismissed. Thus, a Polanyi who describes the extraordinary historical changes associated with the marketization of social relations, a Marx who identifies competition as a feature specifically of capitalist society, or any number of anthropological studies which portray cooperative social and economic relations in different societies, can be written off as "merely" historical, politically misguided, or quaint (cf. Polanyi, 1985; Marx, 1967a). The collapse of the former socialist states is seen as yet a further validation of the idea that societies based on competitive market relations are the truest expression of human nature.

A particularly important feature of the ideology of competition is that competitiveness reflects technical superiority (cf. Marglin, 1974). Whoever survives at the end of the day did so because they were more efficient than their rivals. The market, like nature, is impartial: survival of the fittest. So even if it is recognized that competition today looks quite different than it did a hundred years ago, this is seen as a "natural" evolutionary outcome which tends to the perfection of the system. Although the production and distribution of wealth are a deeply social process, its history is seen as the working out of an impersonal and largely technical trajectory. Questions of social relations, social power, strategy, culture, and identity have little place in such a story.

In this context, particular styles of competition at different periods are idealized as being appropriate to the technological conditions of the times.[1] Then they give way to technically superior models. Thus, for example, an idealized version of Marshallian competition, with small, specialized, interlinked firms organized in highly flexible industrial districts, is displaced historically by an equally idealized version of Chandlerian oligopolistic competition based on large-scale, capital-intensive, vertically integrated, high-output production systems whose historical superiority is cemented by economies of scale (cf. Piore and Sabel, 1984; Chandler, 1962, 1977).

This way of thinking is akin to models of ecological succession. No one asks what it means to the life and culture of grasses that they give way to forests. Nor does anyone expect grasses to try to become like trees in order to survive. Nor, for that matter, does anyone ask why trees become so tree-like or what they have against grass. By the same token, older competitive practices are naturally overcome by the new, and the social and material assets bound up with them quietly disappear from history.

What I want to get at is a way of talking about competition that recognizes it as a structural condition of capitalism that is also a deeply social and cultural process, in which real firms and people are engaged in defending and expanding the value of their material resources, culture, and identity. Historical shifts in the basis of competitiveness and the character of competitive practices, then, are bound to produce the sorts of social and cultural upheaval and dislocation that we saw in the case of time and space. This is, plainly, an arena of struggle, but what kind of struggle, on what terms, and involving what kinds of social agent?

The closest analogy would be to an analysis of class struggle, in which groups of people with differing command of material resources

---

[1] My thanks to Dick Walker for suggesting this.

and conflicting stakes in the social and political rules of the game seek to impose their view of an appropriate social order – that is to say, a social order which will protect and enhance the value of their material and social assets. Capitalists vs. labor is one obvious example, but a rising bourgeoisie vs. an old aristocracy would be even better for the present purposes.

In this kind of struggle, not only the value of material resources but an entire way of life are at stake. This involves everything that I have subsumed under the label of culture: material practices; social relations, including the allocation of rights, obligations, and responsibilities; and ways of thinking about the world and one's position in it. It involves the selection of which traditions to honor (for example, lavish hospitality vs. thrift, ancestry vs. hard work), processes of valuation (what counts as productive activity – landed estates vs. factories; or perhaps what counts as a desirable source of income – rent or profit), and processes of inclusion and exclusion (who is "us" and how do we recognize ourselves?). It also involves identities and the question of who has power and what it is used for. The struggle between aristocracy and bourgeoisie was hard fought historically and frequently a bloody affair. But then, the stakes were very high.

A struggle within the class of capitalists over whose version of the social order will prevail has far less historical drama about it. It is, nevertheless, important, since the fate of so many people and places are caught up in what happens to firms. When a large group of firms, which had played a dominant role in constructing a specific social order within the general framework of capitalism, fails to respond effectively to the challenge of a new competitive model, this failure has immense social impacts.

Where do different versions of a common capitalist social order that put whole groups of firms at risk come from? The sources are multiple, including changes in the social and technical infrastructure (such as improved transportation and communications or programmable automation) that create new or altered opportunities for firms. They are also generated by systemic pressures – problems produced by the normal workings of the system – such as chronic overcapacity. But not all firms take advantage of these opportunities, or they don't do so effectively, and not all firms are equally caught out by systemic problems. So something else must be going on.

That something else, it seems to me, must be the development, under specific historical and social circumstances, of divergent ensembles of material practices, social relations, and ways of thinking that lead certain firms, or groups of firms, to develop different interpretations of what markets are like or could be like, how firms can compete within them, and how production should be organized technically and socially. Different cultural trajectories create different interpretive and strategic possibilities in the face of the same technical and environmental conditions. But they also necessarily involve different processes of valuation of material and social assets and challenges to identities, commitments, and the bases of power characteristic of a particular cultural ensemble.

This is a very deep challenge. On a broad enough scale, it threatens, in effect, a whole way of life, much as a rising bourgeoisie threatened the material and social assets, identities, commitments, and power of aristocrats. Even though this process happens within the general framework of capitalist society, it involves a high-stakes struggle between competing versions of the social order.

Aristocrats, the old dominant culture, couldn't easily decide to join the winning side en masse by becoming industrialists. The material and social assets they commanded had little value in the new social order and their cultural formation was ill suited to the set of practices, relations, and ways of thinking on which the new order was built. It may have been theoretically possible for them to attempt such a transformation, and some individuals certainly did by, for example, opening coal mines on their estates or moving into steel production (Beynon and Austrin, 1994; D. Smith, 1982). But for the most part, this kind of self-renovation seems to have lain outside the set of interpretive and practical possibilities available to members of the aristocracy. They sought, instead, to defend their social position as aristocrats.

Competition between rival versions of the social order within capitalism doesn't threaten the existence of an entire class of people. But it does threaten specific groups within that class, and these groups may, under certain historical circumstances, be quite large. They might include, for example, specialized, small-scale manufacturers clustered in Marshallian industrial districts faced by competition from mass producers. Or the group might be those mass producers, engaged in a stable regime of oligopolistic competition, faced by a challenge from a proliferation of high-quality, high-volume, flexible manufacturers. The analogy with aristocrats is by no means perfect, but it does suggest why these groups would fight to defend their erstwhile dominant culture rather than accede to the processes of valuation implied in the rival social order.

I want to stress that this analysis does not mean that no change is possible once a particular dominant culture has established itself. But certain kinds of change – those that threaten the material and social assets validated by that dominant culture – are more difficult than others that tend to reaffirm that value. This allows us to understand better why certain trajectories of change, no matter how "objectively" beneficial, may be refused by whole groups of firms.

Transformations in time, space, and competition: the cultural crisis of the firm

Transformations in competitive regimes are akin to spatio-temporal transformations in that they are changes in the qualities of social life that are normally seen to be natural and enduring features of the human environment. Time passes, space is, and *Homo economicus*, like all species, competes for survival. They pervasively affect our lives, but we have no control over them as individuals. At the least, this naturalization makes it difficult to discern what is at stake in competitive and spatio-temporal transformations, and to strategize about them.

Time, space, and competition are, indeed, structural conditions of life in a capitalist society. But as I have tried to show, they are also social and cultural constructs. The particular forms and rhythms they take are created by the practices, relations, and ways of thinking of real social agents and vary historically, engendering new social and cultural practices and attitudes in the process.

These real social agents have conflicting stakes in how spatio-temporal and competitive practices and processes are structured. Their social and material assets are subject to different processes of valuation in different social orders. So they have powerful incentives to promote and defend specific constellations of spatio-temporal and competitive practices in order to protect the value of these assets, even when rival systems are demonstrably more competitive in changed circumstances.

The whole is made more complex and difficult when we recognize that time, space, and competition are profoundly interconnected. Changes along any single dimension generally imply changes in the others. New competitive practices entail and are part of spatio-temporal transformations. As these changes progress, corporate cultures and identities – indeed, whole ways of life – are powerfully challenged.

An example may help to clarify the argument. William Cronon, in *Nature's Metropolis*, traces the career of John Burrows, a leading merchant in Davenport, Iowa, in the middle of the nineteenth century (Cronon, 1991). In the pre-railroad era, Burrows's success was built on a very specific combination of resources, skills, and relationships. In a cash-short rural economy, merchants were generally paid in kind. In exchange for his goods, Burrows accepted grain, sides of pork, and other agricultural commodities. When he had amassed sufficient stock, he would transport the goods by river to St Louis or New Orleans, where agents would arrange reshipment to final markets in the east. Burrows, as the seller, retained ownership of the goods until they reached their final destination, possibly weeks later.

Even during the shipping season, Burrows had a high exposure to price fluctuations and devoted a great deal of time to analyzing market conditions along the river for a variety of goods. In winter, when shipping closed down, he had to be able to store large stocks of commodities and extend credit to farmers. By the standards of the time, his capital requirements were considerable, and he had developed a long-standing relationship with a family-owned network of wholesalers based in St Louis, New York, and New Orleans who provided credit to maintain his operation.

The arrival of the Chicago & Rock Island Railroad in 1854 changed Burrows's world. The railroad offered speed, reliable schedules, and year-round movement, but east to Chicago and not south to St Louis and New Orleans. Chicago rapidly became the center of the commodities trade. The technical requirements of rail transport (for example, shipping carloads rather than sacks of grain), increasing mechanization of commodities handling, and the institution of the Chicago Board of Trade, which standardized and homogenized the flow of commodities, transformed the legal and social basis of the commodities trade.

At the same time, the entry barriers into Burrows's business dropped significantly. Small lots of goods could be easily integrated into the general flow, and the need to store stocks over winter disappeared. Prices across geographically distant markets converged, and futures markets reduced the risk of price fluctuations. Large capital and credit resources, and the time, network of relationships, and specialized knowledge required to gather information and analyze heterogeneous market conditions, were no longer the price of entry into the trade. Burrows suddenly faced a proliferation of new competitors operating on the basis of a new set of practices, relationships, and understandings. His own material resources, skills, relationships, and ways of thinking were as suddenly devalued. As Cronon describes it:

> For Burrows, this was a disaster. Long accustomed to dominating the Davenport market, he suddenly found himself confronted with intense new competition from small dealers with much less money. The warehouse facilities that a few years before had enabled him to handle large quantities of agricultural produce now became a serious disadvantage, tying up his money while competitors without such investments could devote all their capital to buying and selling goods. "The opening of the Chicago & Rock Island Railroad," Burrows recalled, "rather bewildered me." (Cronon, 1991:326)

Bewildered though he may have been, Burrows tried to adapt in a variety of ways. He invested in new flour mills, a sawmill, and a reaper factory, and opened branches in other Iowa towns. But, as Cronon writes, "Nothing worked. The new structural conditions created by the railroad and by Chicago's metropolitan market were simply too alien to his familiar way of doing business" (Cronon, 1991:327). John Burrows was bankrupt by 1859, just five years after the railroad arrived.

Three points emerge particularly clearly from this story. First, spatio-temporal transformations and competitive transformations go together. As time and space were altered by new technologies and social practices, a whole way of doing business changed.

Second, time, space, and competition are both structural conditions and social constructs. Real social agents built the railroads, decided on the route structure, and developed new ways of handling commodities – processes whose own histories were marked by competitive rivalries between places and people. The technology alone doesn't determine the outcome; its power to change the landscape depends on how these social struggles are worked out. The disassembly line for meatpacking, for example, was invented in Cincinnati, but the eventual convergence of rail lines on Chicago eclipsed that city's apparent technical advantage in the business. Taken together, these social processes confronted John Burrows with new structural conditions of time, space, and competition in which he was unable to succeed.

Third, the changes that occurred constituted a thoroughgoing challenge to what can be thought of as a particular corporate culture. An entire ensemble of material practices, social relations, and ways of thinking, and the material and social assets tied up in them, were invalidated. The basis for Burrows's social position and social power as the "dominant" merchant in Davenport evaporated. As his plaintive comment suggests, the challenge extended to his sense of the world and of his place in it – in short, to his very identity.

There is no particular reason to lament the fate of John Burrows. His bankruptcy was an individual affair. It might even be thought cause for celebration that the market became more competitive and efficient, with a larger number of small participants. But when the John Burrowses of the world run firms that employ several hundred thousand people in specific places, what they do and what happens to them become important.

Conclusion

The history of capitalist industrial development is a history of change. Existing practices, relations, and ways of thinking are constantly challenged by new problems and opportunities, and a continuous stream of innovations and adaptations is propelled by the pressures of competition. In this sense, change is a normal feature of industrial culture.

There are some historical periods, however, that seem to be marked by such broad transformations that they lie outside the bounds of normal cultural change in industry. Henry Ford's achievement, for example, was not merely to put into place the moving assembly line. Ford's inspiration was based on the recognition that the market didn't want a cheap car – that had been tried and failed – but a functional, good-quality car that was also inexpensive.[2] A new way of thinking about the market went hand in hand with developing a new way of organizing production to serve it, and with conceiving of a new style of relationship with workers on the shop floor.

Ford, as we know, met with tremendous success and his new practices and ways of thinking eventually were taken up by a broad stratum of American industry. In effect, Ford inaugurated a new kind of industrial culture and a new social order in the US. Along the way, of course, hundreds of small firms in the auto business and, eventually, in many other sectors, organized according to the principles and practices of an older industrial culture, failed or were absorbed by more successful rivals.

This new industrial culture entailed substantial transformations in spatio-temporal rhythms and practices, competitive practices, processes of valuation, processes of inclusion and exclusion, the development of new traditions, and so on. Not surprisingly, this process was marked by tensions and trade-offs. Workers, for example, were paid more, but their "traditional" industrial skills were made redundant – devalued. Their possibilities for consumption expanded even as they were made appendages of the machinery in the factory, fixed to one spot on the floor while their work was regulated by the speed of the line.

In short, this new industrial culture transformed a way of life for workers, for managers, for consumers, and, of course, for Henry Ford himself. But this Schumpeterian process of creative destruction also implied the devaluation of the social and material assets that were constructed in and validated by the old social order. A whole range of practices, relations, ways of thinking, identities, and commitments had no value in this new world. Many people found that the basis of their social power and position had suddenly collapsed.

The new dominant culture was a very powerful one and lasted for many years. It changed, of course, along the way. New products and production technologies were introduced, new labor-management practices were worked out, new ways of thinking about markets and how firms compete in them were put into place. Some firms died and new ones came into being. But these were, arguably, normal changes within

2   My thanks to Bill Leslie for pointing this out to me enough times that I finally got it.

a common social order, changes that didn't fundamentally challenge the value of the material and social assets built up within it. They reflected intensifications and adjustments along a consistent cultural and strategic trajectory.

What about now? I argued in chapter 3 that American industry, starting in the 1970s and continuing today, has faced an array of challenges to its normal way of doing business. Taken together, they arguably amount to a major historical shift of the sort that was inaugurated by Henry Ford or that swamped John Burrows.

Some key markers of such a transition include the following. First, a reasonably stable oligopolistic regime was upset by a dramatic proliferation of new competitors. This meant that a commonly accepted style of engagement with the market and with competitors lost its effectiveness. A set of tacit understandings about the rules of the game and the list of eligible players was undermined.

Second, the new competition was based on deeply altered spatio-temporal practices within and across firms. Just-in-time practices, for example, subverted an entire, well-established way of organizing production. Just-in-time, needless to say, was developed in a resource and market environment that was ill suited to American-style just-in-case practices. It accordingly reflected a very different way of thinking about what markets were like and how firms should position themselves within them. Or, to put this another way, just-in-time practices make no sense unless the market is conceived of as highly fragmented or fragmentable and variable over time.

Third, these revised spatio-temporal and competitive practices, in order to be made effective, entail a very different style of social relations within and across firms. This style is associated with different processes of valuation and of inclusion/exclusion with regard to workers and suppliers at the least, and even with customers. This doesn't mean, say, coddling workers and making their work lives pleasant at all times. It does mean thinking about them – and valuing them – as knowledgeable individuals who are able to think productively and who can be relied on to monitor themselves. This could be dismissed as just another way of exploiting workers, but the main point is that it *is* another way that departs sharply from standard American industrial practice.

A final marker, of course, is the massive trauma inflicted on American industry and on the people and places whose fates are so strongly shaped by what firms do in the world. The inability to respond effectively to these new challenges and pressures on such a broad scale and for so long constituted a real collective failure of corporate decision-making.

Taken together, these changes seem to me to represent an historically significant challenge to the dominant industrial culture developed and embodied by a broad stratum of American firms. These companies tried to cope with the new competition chiefly by normal intensifications and adjustments of existing practices: rationalization, eliminating labor from the shop floor, intensifying the pace of work, moving more production offshore, trying to avoid or break unions, diversification and concentration (mergers and acquisitions), automation, cosmetic adjustments to product lines, more advertising, and the like.

All of this expensive activity, however, had little effect. In the first instance, one might suppose that this is because it is hard to tell the difference between competition within a social order and competition between social orders. As I've tried to suggest, the naturalization of time, space, and competition makes it hard to strategize about them and to recognize what is at issue.

Twenty-five years later, however, this argument wears thin, especially in the face of all the changes that firms did undertake and all the available evidence of the size and nature of the problem. Then we need to look more closely at how and why particular changes were selected and others resisted. This entails understanding how the value of material and social assets, identities, commitments, and social power are tied up in a particular constellation of material practices, social relations, and ways of thinking, and how they are threatened by the processes of valuation characteristic of a competing social order. Then we might better understand why massive resources can be mobilized in defense of an historical model of industrial practice whose ineffectiveness in changed circumstances has been so thoroughly and repeatedly demonstrated.

Such an approach seems to me preferable to invoking disembodied and sterile notions of culture as the obstacle to change. And, although there is much talk these days of the qualities of leadership and vision, there seems no particular reason to suppose that the problem was a lack of either. Leaders, as we know, can lead right over the edge of the cliff. And it seems far more likely that managers and strategists *did* have a vision: they envisioned preserving a social order that affirmed the value of their social and material assets and the basis of their social power, and they fought strenuously to make that vision a reality. In the course of that struggle, it seems fair to say, the burden of loss fell disproportionately on people who did not have the power to propose and realize their own vision of the social order.

How can we, as a society, guard against the adverse effects of such large-scale historical and cultural processes? There are, obviously, no simple prescriptions. It may seem tempting, for example, to conclude that companies should routinely purge the ranks of top management and replace them with new and/or young people whose minds are uncluttered by received tradition. Term limits, as with politicians, seem to promise automatic institutional renovation and a continually refreshed liberation from old commitments and practices.

This solution, however, idealizes the new and the young while mis-specifying the nature of social understanding and social change. Youth and newness are not in themselves automatic antidotes to the power of old understandings and old constellations of social and material assets. Youthfulness, for example, and new ideas about being aristocratic would not have saved the aristocracy. Similarly, the continual supply of new recruits to the Mamelukes were mowed down by gunfire as readily as their elders.

There are other avenues of thought that may be more productively explored, however. One applies to the world of the strategists them-selves while the other is concerned with the social context in which they operate. The arguments are different in focus and style, but in practice need to be linked.

Sandra Harding, in her critique of science, offers an intriguing dis-tinction between weak and strong objectivity. Weak objectivity, she argues, is the normal stance of scientists and the scientific project. That is to say, scientists strive for objectivity in analyzing the natural phe-nomena that they study. But they don't normally apply the same stan-dards of critical analysis to their own social and cultural location and the way these shape their practices, relations, and ways of thinking, along with the general trajectory of science. Strong objectivity, by con-trast, requires that the object of knowledge and the knower be subjected to the same critical scrutiny (Harding, 1991).

The scientist, in this view, needs to ask not only what is going on under the microscope or in the particle accelerator, but why certain kinds of scientific question have become more interesting than others, why the lab and the scientific team are structured in a particular way, why certain hypotheses seem more intuitively satisfying or elegant than others, and so on. Strong objectivity requires acknowledging that sci-ence and scientists are embedded in (at the same time as they shape) broader historical, social, and cultural processes, and trying to under-stand what meaning this has for the work that scientists do and for the way that they think.

Strong objectivity, needless to say, would not change the nature of quarks or T-cells. But it might change scientific trajectories and the practice of science. Very much to our purpose, it might facilitate negoti-ating the difficult path between paradigm shifts. By analogy, then, strong objectivity in business practice would not, of itself, change the nature of markets or competition. But by subjecting their own practices and ways of thinking to the same critical scrutiny they apply to market shifts and process technologies, managers might arrive at richer and more productive understandings of the broader social order in which they live and which they help to create, and the strategies appropriate to it.

Strong objectivity, as a normal part of business practice, would be a step in the right direction. But it does not seem a sufficient response to the problem at hand. For one thing, being very clear about how your own ensemble of material and social assets shapes your strategic choices doesn't neutralize the power of that particular asset configuration. Or, acknowledging that your own social and historical position may prevent you from seeing certain kinds of available option doesn't necessarily bring them into view. In short, individual enlightenment is better, but it's not enough. The strategists need help from others whose social and cultural locations and mix of social and material assets are different.

This implies a profound reordering of power relations within the firm and between the firm and other social actors (communities, unions, other firms, etc.). It also implies going well beyond such current ideas as recruiting more women and minorities into management to get a better sense of the segments of the market or the workforce they are thought to represent. By the same token, devolving the power and authority to make decisions about discrete problems on the shop floor is only a start. The kind of power that needs to be redistributed is the power to envision and construct the social order.

Bibliography

Abernathy, W.J., K.B. Clark, and A.H. Kantrow. 1984. *Industrial Renaissance: Producing a Competitive Future for America*. New York: Basic Books.

Aglietta, M. 1979. *A Theory of Capitalist Regulation*. London: New Left Books.

Aitken, H. 1985. *Scientific Management in Action: Taylorism at Watertown Arsenal*. Princeton, NJ: Princeton University Press.

Akerlof, G. 1970. "The market for 'lemons:' qualitative uncertainty and the market mechanism." *Quarterly Journal of Economics*, 84(August):488–500.

—— 1984. *An Economic Theorist's Book of Tales*. Cambridge: Cambridge University Press.

Aldcroft, D.H. 1968. "Introduction: British industry and foreign competition, 1875–1914." In D.H. Aldcroft, ed., *The Development of British Industry and Foreign Competition 1875–1914*. Toronto: University of Toronto Press.

Alford, B.W.E. 1981. "New industries for old? British industry between the wars." In R. Floud and D. McCloskey, eds, *The Economic History of Britain Since 1700. Vol. 2: 1860 to the 1970s*. Cambridge: Cambridge University Press.

Alonso, W. 1975. "Location theory." In J. Friedmann and W. Alonso, eds, *Regional Policy: Readings in Theory and Applications*. Cambridge, MA: MIT Press.

Altshuler, A., M. Anderson, D.T. Jones, D. Roos, and J.P. Womack. 1984. *The Future of the Automobile*. Cambridge, MA: MIT Press.

Anderson, B. 1981. *Imagined Communities*. Rev. edn. London: Verso.

Anderson, R. 1983. *A Look at Lockheed*. Exton, PA: Newcomen Society.

Angel, D. 1994. *Restructuring for Innovation: The Remaking of the US Semiconductor Industry*. New York: Guilford Press.

Aoki, M. 1984. *Economic Analysis of the Japanese Firm*. Amsterdam: North Holland.

—— 1994. *The Japanese Firm: The Sources of Competitive Strength*. Oxford: Oxford University Press.

Applebaum, H., ed. 1987. *Perspectives in Cultural Anthropology.* Albany, NY: State University of New York Press.

Argyris, C. and D. Schon, 1978. *Organizational Learning.* Reading, MA: Addison-Wesley.

Armstrong, P., A. Glyn, and J. Harrison. 1984. *Capitalism Since World War II: The Making and Breakup of the Great Boom.* London: Fontana.

Aviation Week. 1953. "Connie cutbacks." November 9:14–15.

Aviation Week. 1955. "Lockheed missile scientists quit." December 19:16.

Aviation Week. 1956. "Lockheed moving missile division into San Francisco Bay Area." February 6:34.

Aviation Week. 1957. "Lockheed, atune to USAF warning, plans expansion into avionics." July 8:29–30.

Aviation Week. 1960. "Lockheed diversifies for new markets." May 23:66–73.

Aviation Week and Space Technology. 1961. "Lockheed earnings may top $25 million." November 13:21.

Baran, P. and P. Sweezy. 1966. *Monopoly Capital.* New York: Monthly Review Press.

Barnard, C. 1968 [1938]. *The Functions of the Executive.* Cambridge, MA: Harvard University Press.

Baumol, W., J. Panzor, and R. Willig. 1988. *Contestable Markets and the Theory of Industry Structure.* 2nd edn. New York: Harcourt Brace Jovanovich.

Best, M. and J. Humphries. 1986. "The city and industrial decline." In B. Elbaum and W. Lazonick, eds, *The Decline of the British Economy.* Oxford: Clarendon Press.

Beynon, J. and T. Austrin. 1994. *Masters and Servants: Class and Patronage in the Making of a Labour Organisation.* London: Rivers Oram Press.

Biddle, W. 1991. *Barons of the Sky.* New York: Simon and Schuster.

Bluestone, B. and B. Harrison. 1982. *The Deindustrialization of America.* New York: Basic Books.

Bourdieu, P. 1977. *Outline of a Theory of Practice.* Cambridge: Cambridge University Press.

—— 1984. *Distinctions: A Social Critique of the Judgement of Taste.* Cambridge, MA: Harvard University Press.

Bowles, S., D. Gordon, and T. Weisskopf. 1983. *Beyond the Wasteland.* Garden City, NY: Anchor Press/Doubleday.

Boyer, R. 1990. *The Regulation School: A Critical Introduction.* New York: Columbia University Press.

Braverman, H. 1974. *Labor and Monopoly Capital.* New York: Monthly Review Press.

Brody, D. 1980. *Workers in Industrial America.* Oxford: Oxford University Press.

Brooks, F. 1982. *The Mythical Man-Month: Essays on Software Engineering.* Reading, MA: Addison-Wesley.

—— 1986. "No silver bullet: Essence and accidents of software engineering." Dept of Computer Science, University of North Carolina at Chapel Hill, NC.

Brown, C. and M. Reich. 1989. "When does union–management cooperation work? A look at NUMMI and GM-Van Nuys." *California Management Review*, 31(Spring):26–44.

Buckley, P. and M. Casson. 1979. *The Future of the Multinational Enterprise*. New York: Holmes and Meyer.

Burawoy, M. 1979. *Manufacturing Consent*. Chicago: University of Chicago Press.

Burke, K. 1954 [1933]. *Permanence and Change*. Los Altos, CA: Hermes.

Business Week. 1951. "Lockheed tools up for the jet age." February 3:55–60.

Business Week. 1955. "Where does the lab end and the plant start?" December 24:90–2.

Carney, J., R. Hudson, and J. Lewis, eds. 1980. *Regions in Crisis*. London: Croom Helm.

Caves, R. 1971. "International corporations: The industrial economics of foreign investment." *Economica*, 38:1–27.

—— 1974. "Industrial organization." In J. Dunning, ed., *Economic Analysis and the Multinational Enterprise*. New York: Praeger.

Chandler, A. 1962. *Strategy and Structure*. Cambridge, MA: MIT Press.

—— 1977. *The Visible Hand*. Cambridge, MA: Harvard University Press.

Chinitz, B. 1962. "Contrasts in agglomeration: New York and Pittsburgh." *American Economic Review, Papers and Proceedings*, 279–89.

Clark, G. 1981. "The employment relation and the spatial division of labour." *Annals of the Association of American Geographers*, 71:412–24.

—— 1989. *Unions and Communities under Siege: American Communities and the Crisis of Organized Labour*. Cambridge: Cambridge University Press.

—— 1994. "Strategy and structure: Corporate restructuring and the Scope and characteristics of sunk costs." *Environment and Planning A*, 26:9–32.

Clark, G., M. Gertler, and J. Whiteman. 1986. *Regional Dynamics: Studies in Adjustment Theory*. Boston: George Allen and Unwin.

Clark, K. and T. Fujimoto. 1992. *Product Development Performance: Strategy, Organization and Management in the World Automobile Industry*. Boston: Harvard Business School.

Cohen, S. and J. Zysman. 1987. *Manufacturing Matters: The Myth of the Post-industrial Economy*. New York: Basic Books.

Collis, D. 1991. "Organizational capability as a source of profit." Working Paper 91-046, Harvard Business School, March.

Corcoran, E. 1992. "Redesigning research." *Scientific American*, June:106–16.

Coriat, B. 1990. *L'atelier et le robot*. Paris: Christian Bourgois.

Cronon, W. 1991. *Nature's Metropolis*. New York: Norton

Cusumano, M. 1985. *The Japanese Automobile Industry*. Cambridge, MA: Harvard University Press.

Cyert, R.M. and J.G. March. 1963. *A Behavioral Theory of the Firm*. Englewood Cliffs, NJ: Prentice-Hall.

Davidson, C. 1993. "The man who made computers personal." *New Scientist*, June 19:18–22.

Dawkins, R. 1989. *The Selfish Gene*. Oxford: Oxford University Press.

Deal, T. and A. Kennedy. 1982. *Corporate Cultures*. Reading, MA: Addison-Wesley.

Delbecq, A. and J. Weiss. "The business culture of Silicon Valley: Is it a model for the future?" In J. Weiss, ed., *Regional Cultures, Managerial Behavior, and Entrepreneurship*. New York: Quorum Books.

Dertouzos, M.L., R.K. Lester, and R.M. Solow. 1989. *Made in America: Regaining the Productive Edge*. Cambridge, MA: MIT Press.

Dicken, P. 1992. *Global Shift*. 2nd edn. New York: Guilford Press.

DiMaggio, P. and W. Powell. 1991. "Introduction." In W. Powell and P. DiMaggio, eds, *The New Institutionalism in Organizational Analysis*. Chicago: Chicago University Press.

Dore, R. 1985. *Flexible Rigidities*. London: Athlone Press.

Drucker, P. 1971. "What we can learn from Japanese management." *Harvard Business Review*, March–April.

Drummond, I. 1981: "Britain and the world economy 1900–45." In R. Floud and D. McCloskey, eds, *The Economic History of Britain Since 1700. Vol. 2: 1860 to the 1970s*. Cambridge: Cambridge University Press.

Dunn, E. (forthcoming). "Transational production and new persons in Poland's transition from socialism." PhD dissertation, Department of Anthropology, Johns Hopkins University, Baltimore.

Dunning, J. 1981. *International Production and the Multinational Enterprise*. London: George Allen and Unwin.

Economist. 1985. "Rings of Saturn." August 3:61–2.

—— 1991. "When GM's robots ran amok." August 10:64–5.

—— 1992a. "The marriage of true minds." September 19:79–80.

—— 1992b. "A drive on the wild side." October 24:83.

—— 1992c. "IBM: Hardware and tear." December 19:61.

—— 1993. "Return of the stopwatch." January 23:69.

Edsall, T. 1984. *The New Politics of Inequality*. New York: Norton.

Edwards, R. 1979. *Contested Terrain*. New York: Basic Books.

Engels, F. 1968. *The Condition of the Working Class in England*. Stanford: Stanford University Press.

Farnie, D.A. 1979. *The English Cotton Industry and the World Market, 1815–1896*. Oxford: Clarendon Press.

Ferguson, C.H. and C.R. Morris. 1993. *Computer Wars: The Fall of IBM and the Future of Global Technology*. New York: Times Books.

Financial Times. 1991a. "IBM and Intel to develop new superchip." November 7:22.

—— 1991b. "Toshiba and Siemens in electronics agreement." November 10:9.

—— 1991c. "Philips and SGS-Thomson in deal." November 19:22.

—— 1991d. "Texas, Hitachi form joint chip venture." November 22:24.

—— 1991e. "Breaking barriers between 'us' and 'them.' " December 30:7.

—— 1992a. "From design studio to new car showroom." May 11:15.

—— 1992b. "Brother slims down bloated product range." June 22:15.

—— 1992c. "Milking profits by churning." June 26:11.

—— 1992d. "Partners thank each other for the memory." July 14:17.

—— 1992e. "A corporate marriage made to last." July 15:20.

—— 1992f. "Take your partners." July 17:11.

—— 1992g. "US Steel's dumping complaints sound familiar." July 22:6.

—— 1992h. "GM's revolution turns into a race against time." October 15:21.

—— 1992i. "Working in harmony." October 15:16.

—— 1992j. "Big Blue decides small is beautiful." October 23:23.

—— 1992k. "Strength through strategic alliances." (Toshiba advertisement). November 4:9.

—— 1992l. "GM to cut 18,000 staff and shut plants." December 4:23.

—— 1993. "Report shows US productivity is ahead of Japan's." October 22:1.

—— 1994a. "Hewlett Packard chips in with Intel." June 9:1.

—— 1994b. "Honda to spend extra £330 million at Swindon." June 11:7.

—— 1994c. "Promise of power." August 11:8.

Flamm, K. 1988. *Creating the Computer: Government, Industry and High Technology.* Washington, DC: Brookings Institution.

Fleck, L. 1979 [1935]. *Genesis and Development of a Scientific Fact.* Chicago: University of Chicago Press.

Fortune. 1965. "Lockheed scrambles for the battle of the primes." February:150–226.

—— 1990. "Why women still don't hit the top." July 30:40–62.

—— 1992. "When will women get to the top?" September 21:44–56.

Foster, R.N. 1988. "Timing technological transitions." In M.L. Tushman and W.L. Moore, eds, *Readings in the Management of Innovation.* 2nd edn. New York: HarperBusiness.

Fox, R.G. 1985. *Lions of the Punjab: Culture in the Making.* Berkeley, CA: University of California Press.

Francillon, R. 1982. *Lockheed.* London: Putnam.

Friedman, D. 1983. "Beyond the age of Ford: The strategic basis of the Japanese success in automobiles." In J. Zysman and L. Tyson, eds, *American Industry in International Competition.* Ithaca, NY: Cornell University Press.

Frobel, F., J. Heinrichs, and O. Kreye. 1980. *The New International Division of Labour.* Cambridge: Cambridge University Press.

Fruin, W.M. 1992. *The Japanese Enterprise System.* Oxford: Clarendon Press.

Fuhrman, R.A. 1978. "The fleet ballistic missile system: Polaris to Trident." Von Karman Lecture, Washington, DC: American Institute of Aeronautics and Astronautics.

Funk, Maj.-Gen. B.I. 1958. "Impact of the ballistic missile on industry, Part I: From the Air Force's viewpoint." In Lt.-Col. K.F. Gantz, ed., *The United States Air Force Report on the Ballistic Missile: Its Technology, Logistics and Strategy.* New York: Doubleday.

Gadamer, H.-G. 1976. *Philosophical Hermeneutics.* Berkeley, CA: University of California Press.

Galambos, L. 1993. "The innovative organization: Viewed from the shoulders of Schumpeter, Chandler, Lazonick, et al." *Business and Economic History,* 2nd series, 21:79–91.

—— 1995. "The authority and responsibility of the chief executive officer: Shifting patterns in large US enterprises in the twentieth century." *Industrial and Corporate Change,* 4(1):187–203.

Galbraith, J.K. 1956. *American Capitalism: The Concept of Countervailing Power.* White Plains, N.Y.: Sharpe.

Gatland, K.W. 1952. *Development of the Guided Missile*. London: Iliffe and Sons.

Geertz, C. 1973. *The Interpretation of Cultures: Selected Essays*. New York: Basic Books.

Gereffi, G. 1992. "Transational production systems and third world development: New trends and issues for the 1990s." Paper presented at a conference on the New International Context of Development, University of Wisconsin, Madison, April 24–5.

Gertler, M. 1993. "Implementing advanced manufacturing technologies in mature industrial regions: Towards a social model of technology production." *Regional Studies*, 27:665–80.

Glickman, N. and D. Woodward. 1989. *The New Competitors*. New York: Basic Books.

Godelier, M. 1986. *The Mental and the Material*. London: Verso.

Goodman, R. 1982. *The Last Entrepreneurs*. Boston: South End Press.

Gordon, D. 1977. "Class struggle and the stages of American urban development." In D. Perry and A. Watkins, eds, *The Rise of the Sunbelt Cities*. Beverly Hills: Sage.

Graham, M. 1986. *RCA and the Videodisc*. Cambridge: Cambridge University.

Gramsci, A. 1971. *Selections from the Prison Notebooks*. Ed. and trans. Q. Hoare and G. Nowell Smith. New York: International Publishers.

Greider, W. 1987. *Secrets of the Temple*. New York: Simon and Schuster.

Hampden-Turner, C. 1990. *Creating Corporate Culture: From Discord to Harmony*. Reading, MA: Addison-Wesley.

Haraway, D. 1991. *Simians, Cyborgs, and Women: The Reinvention of Nature*. New York: Routledge.

Harding, S. 1991. *Whose Science, Whose Knowledge?*. Ithaca, NY: Cornell University Press.

Hareven, T. 1982. *Family Time, Industrial Time*. Cambridge: Cambridge University Press.

Harley, C.K. and D.N. McCloskey. 1981. "Foreign trade: Competition and the expanding international economy." In R. Floud and D. McCloskey, eds, *The Economic History of Britain Since 1700. Vol. 2: 1860 to the 1970s*. Cambridge: Cambridge University Press.

Harrison, B. 1994. *Lean and Mean: The Changing Landscape of Corporate Power in the Age of Flexibility*. New York: Basic Books.

Harrison, B. and B. Bluestone. 1988. *The Great U-Turn: Corporate Restructuring, Laissez Faire and the Rise of Inequality in America*. New York: Basic Books.

Harvey, D. 1982. *The Limits to Capital*. Oxford: Blackwell.

—— 1985. "Money, time, space and the city." In *Consciousness and the Urban Experience*. Oxford: Blackwell.

—— 1988. "The geographical and geopolitical consequences of the transition from Fordist to flexible accumulation." In G. Sternlieb and J. Hughes, eds, *America's New Market Geography*. New Brunswick, NJ: Rutgers University, Center for Urban Policy Research.

—— 1989. *The Condition of Postmodernity*. Oxford: Blackwell.

—— 1992. "Class relations, social justice, and the politics of difference." Paper delivered to Wissenshaftliche Jahrestagung der Deutschen Gesellschaft für Amerikastudien, Berlin, June 12.

—— 1996. *Justice, Nature and the Geography of Difference*. Oxford: Blackwell.

Hatvany, N. and V. Pucik. 1988. "Japanese management: Practices and productivity." In M.L. Tushman and W.L. Moore, eds, *Readings in the Management of Information*. 2nd edn. New York: HarperBusiness.

Haugen, E. 1966. *Language Conflict and Language Planning: The Case of Modern Norwegian*. Cambridge, MA: Harvard University.

Hayes, R.H. and W.J. Abernathy. 1980. "Managing our way to economic decline." *Harvard Business Review*, July–August:67–77.

Hobsbawn, E. and T. Ranger. 1983. *The Invention of Tradition*. Cambridge: Cambridge University Press.

Holmes, J. 1983. "Industrial reorganization, capital restructuring and locational change: An analysis of the Canadian automobile industry in the 1960s." *Economic Geography*, 59(3):251–71.

—— 1988. "Industrial restructuring in a period of crisis: An analysis of the Canadian automobile industry, 1973–1983." *Antipode*, 20:19–51.

Hounshell, D. 1984. *From the American System to Mass Production, 1800–1932*. Baltimore: Johns Hopkins University Press.

Hymer, S. 1972. "The multinational corporation and the law of uneven development." In J. Bhagwati, ed., *Economics and World Order*. New York: Free Press.

—— 1976. *The International Operations of National Firms*. Cambridge, MA: MIT.

IEEE *Spectrum*. 1991. "Special report: concurrent engineering." July:22–38.

Jacobson, G. and J. Hillkirk. 1986. *Xerox: American Samurai*. New York: Collier Books.

Jewkes, J., D. Sawers, and R. Stillerman. 1959. *The Sources of Invention*. New York: St Martin's Press.

Johnson, H.T. 1991. "Managing by remote control: Recent management accounting practices in historical perspective." In P. Temin, ed., *Inside the Business Enterprise: Historical Perspectives on the Use of Information*. Chicago: University of Chicago Press.

Kanter, R.M. 1983. *The Changemasters*. New York: Simon and Schuster.

Kargon, R., S. Leslie, and E. Schoenberger. 1992. "Far beyond big science: Science regions and the organization of research and development." In P. Galison and B. Hevly, eds, *Big Science: The Growth of Large Scale Research*. Stanford: Stanford University Press.

Kearns, D. and D. Nadler. 1992. *Prophets in the Dark: How Xerox Reinvented Itself and Beat Back the Japanese*. New York: HarperBusiness.

Keegan, J. 1993. *A History of Warfare*. New York: Alfred A. Knopf.

Kelley, M. 1990. "New process technology, job design, and work organization: A contingency model." *American Sociological Review*, 55 (April):191–208.

Kelley, M. and H. Brooks. 1991. "External learning opportunities and the diffusion of process innovations to small firms: The case of programmable automation." *Technological Forecasting and Social Change*, 39 (March–April):103–25.

Kern, S. 1983. *The Culture of Time and Space, 1880–1918.* Cambridge, MA: Harvard University Press.

Knickerbocker, F. 1973. *Oligopolistic Reaction and Multinational Enterprises.* Boston: Harvard Business School.

Kochan, T., H. Katz, and R. McKersie. 1986. *The Transformation of American Industrial Relations.* New York: Basic Books.

Koopmans, T. 1957. *Three Essays on the State of Economic Science.* New York: McGraw-Hill.

Kotter, J.P. and J.L. Heskett. 1992. *Corporate Culture and Performance.* New York: Free Press.

Kuhn, T.S. 1970. *The Structure of Scientific Revolutions.* 2nd edn. Chicago: University of Chicago Press.

Kunda, G. 1992. *Engineering Culture.* Philadelphia: Temple University Press.

Landes, D. 1970. *The Unbound Prometheus.* London: Cambridge University Press.

—— 1983. *Revolution in Time.* Cambridge, MA: Harvard University Press.

Lawrence, R. 1984. *Can America Compete?* Washington, DC: Brookings Institution.

Lazonick, W. 1986. "The cotton industry." In B. Elbaum and W. Lazonick, eds, *The Decline of the British Economy.* Oxford: Clarendon Press.

—— 1990. *Competitive Advantage on the Shop Floor.* Cambridge, MA: Harvard University Press.

Le Goff, J. 1980. *Time, Work, and Culture in the Middle Ages.* Chicago: University of Chicago Press.

Leslie, S. 1983. *Boss Kettering.* New York: Columbia University Press.

—— 1993a. *The Cold War and American Science: The Military-Industrial-Academic Complex at MIT and Stanford.* New York: Columbia University.

—— 1993b. "How the west was won: The military and the making of Silicon Valley." In W. Aspray, ed., *Technological Competitiveness.* New York: IEEE Press.

Lewchuk, W. 1987. *American Technology and the British Vehicle Industry.* Cambridge: Cambridge University Press.

Lipietz, A. 1982. "Towards global Fordism." *New Left Review*, 132:22–37.

—— 1986. "New tendencies in the international division of labor: regimes of accumulation and modes of regulation." In A.J. Scott and M. Storper, eds, *Production, Work, Territory: The Geographical Anatomy of Industrial Capitalism.* Boston: George Allen and Unwin.

Lockheed. n.d. *Space . . . the New Frontier.* Sunnyvale, CA: Lockheed Missiles and Space Division.

Lockheed Horizons. 1983. *A History of Lockheed.* Issue 12. Sunnyvale, CA: Lockheed Missiles and Space.

Maidique, M. and R. Hayes. 1988. "The art of high-technology management." In M. Tushman and W. Moore, eds, *Readings in the Management of Innovation*, 2nd edn. New York: HarperBusiness.

Mair, A. 1991. "Just-in-time manufacturing and the spatial structure of the automobile industry: In theory, in Japan, in North America and in Western Europe." Unpublished paper, Dept of Geography, University of Durham, UK.

Mandel, E. 1974. *Late Capitalism*. London: New Left Books.

Marglin, S. 1974. "What do bosses do?" *Review of Radical Political Economy*, 6(2):60–92.

Markusen, A. 1985. *Profit Cycles, Oligopoly, and Regional Development*. Cambridge, MA: MIT Press.

Markusen, A., P. Hall, S. Campbell, and S. Detrick. 1992. *The Rise of the Gunbelt*. New York: Oxford University Press.

Martin, E. 1994. *Flexible Bodies*. Boston: Beacon Press.

Martin, J. 1992. *Cultures in Organizations*. Oxford: Oxford University Press.

Martin, R. and R. Rowthorn, eds. 1986. *The Geography of Deindustrialization*. London: Macmillan.

Marx, K. 1967a. *Capital. Vol. I*. New York: International Publishers.

—— 1967b. *Capital. Vol. II*. New York: International Publishers.

—— 1967c. *Capital. Vol. III*. New York: International Publishers.

Massey, D. 1984. *Spatial Divisions of Labour: Social Structures and the Geography of Production*. London: Macmillan.

Massey, D. and R. Meegan. 1982. *The Anatomy of Job Loss*. London: Methuen.

Matthews, R.C.O., C.H. Feinstein, and J.C. Odling-Smee. 1982. *British Economic Growth 1856–1973*. Oxford: Clarendon Press.

McAlinden, S.P. and B.C. Smith. 1993. "The changing structure of the US automotive parts industry." UMTRI93-6. Office for the Study of Automotive Transportation, University of Michigan, Transportation Research Institute.

McKinsey Global Institute. 1993. *Manufacturing Productivity*. Washington, DC: McKinsey.

McMillan, C. 1984. *The Japanese Industrial System*. New York: Walter de Gruyter.

McNamara, R.S. with Brian VanDeMark. 1995. *In Retrospect: The Tragedy and Lessons of Vietnam*. New York: Times Books.

Mintz, S. 1985. *Sweetness and Power*. New York: Penguin.

Mishel, L. and J. Bernstein. 1994. *The State of Working America, 1994–95*. Washington, DC: Economic Policy Institute.

MIT Commission on Industrial Productivity. 1989. *The US Automobile Industry in an Era of International Competition: Performance and Prospects*. Cambridge, MA: MIT Press.

Monden, Y. 1981. "What makes the Toyota production system really tick?" *Industrial Engineering*, January:36–46.

Montgomery, D. 1979. *Workers' Control in America*. Cambridge: Cambridge University Press.

Mutlu, S. 1979. "Interregional and international mobility of industrial capital: The case of the American automobile and electronics industries." PhD dissertation, University of California, Berkeley.

Nader, L. 1969. "Up the anthropologist – perspectives gained from studying up." In D. Hymes, ed., *Reinventing Anthropology*. New York: Random House.

Nelson, R. and S. Winter. 1982. *An Evolutionary Theory of Economic Change.* Cambridge, MA: Harvard University Press.

New York Times. 1985. "New GM plant site linked to shift in population." July 31:A1.

—— 1990a. "Study says Ford leads in efficiency." January 3:D5.

—— 1990b. "GM plans to shut up to 9 factories: Loses $1.98 billion." November 1:A1.

—— 1991a. "GM retrenchment to shut 21 plants, losing 70,000 jobs." December 19:A1.

—— 1991b. "Experts doubt cutbacks alone will save GM." December 23:A1.

—— 1992a. "Be it a whale or a dinosaur, can IBM really evolve?" September 6:10.

—— 1992b. "GM will consolidate engineering plants." October 24:17.

—— 1992c. "As GM tries to outrun past, critics ask: who's in charge?" October 26:A1.

—— 1992d. "GM to shut down 7 parts factories in strategy shift." December 4:A1.

—— 1994a. "Detroit struggles to learn another lesson from Japan." June 19:F5.

—— 1994b. "In supercomputers, bigger and faster means trouble." August 7:F5.

—— 1994c. "A back to basics U-turn in Japan." August 26:C1.

—— 1996. "Brake strike makes GM shut idle plants." March 12:A10.

Newsweek. 1955. "Scientists take a walk." December 26:60.

Noble, D. 1986. *Forces of Production: A Social History of Industrial Automation.* Oxford: Oxford University Press.

Nofal, M.B. 1983. "Dynamics of the motor vehicle industry in Argentina." PhD dissertation, Johns Hopkins University, Baltimore.

O'Toole, J. and J. Lewandowski. 1990. "Forming the future: The marriage of people and technology at Saturn." Paper presented at Stanford University, Dept of Industrial Engineering and Engineering Management, March 29.

Ohno, T. 1984. "How the Toyota production system was created." In K. Sato and Y. Hoshino, eds, *The Anatomy of Japanese Business.* New York: Croom Helm.

Ortner, S. 1984. "Theory in anthropology since the sixties." *Comparative Studies in Society and History,* 26(1):126–66.

Ouchi, W. 1981. *Theory Z: How American Business Can Meet the Japanese Challenge.* New York: Avon Books.

Pake, G.E. 1985. "Research at Xerox PARC: A founder's assessment." *IEEE Spectrum,* October:54–61.

Pascale, R.T. 1990. *Managing on the Edge.* New York: Simon and Schuster.

Peet, R. 1983. "Relations of production and the relocation of United States manufacturing industry since 1960." *Economic Geography,* 59 (April):112–43.

—— 1984. "Class struggle, the relocation of employment, and economic crisis." *Science and Society,* 48(1):38–51.

—— 1987. *International Capitalism and Industrial Restructuring.* Boston: Allen and Unwin.

Perrow, C. 1986. *Complex Organizations*. New York: Random House.

Perry, T.S. and P. Wallich. 1985. "Inside the PARC: The 'information architects.' " IEEE *Spectrum*, October:62–75.

Pfeffer, J. 1992. *Managing with Power*. Boston: Harvard Business School Press.

Phillips, K. 1984. *The Politics of Rich and Poor*. New York: Random House.

Piore, M. 1968. "The impact of the labor market upon the design and selection of productive techniques within the manufacturing plant." *Quarterly Journal of Economics*, 82:602–20.

Piore, M. and C. Sabel. 1984. *The Second Industrial Divide*. New York: Basic Books.

Polanyi, K. 1985. *The Great Transformation*. Boston: Beacon Press.

Porter, M. 1980. *Competitive Strategy*. New York: Free Press.

Pratt, J. and R. Zeckhauser, eds. 1985. *Principals and Agents*. Boston: Harvard Business School Press.

Quesada, E.R. 1955. Memo to C.S. Gross, March 1. In Papers of Lee DuBridge 111.2. California Institute of Technology Archives.

Rees, J., R. Briggs, and D. Hicks. 1985. "New technology in the US machinery industry." In A. Thwaites and R. Oakey, eds, *The Regional Economic Impact of Technological Change*. London: Frances Pinter.

Reich, L. 1985. *The Making of American Industrial Research*. Cambridge: Cambridge University Press.

Ricoeur, P. 1974. *The Conflict of Interpretations: Essays in Hermeneutics*. Evanston, IL: Northwestern University Press.

Roediger, D. and P. Foner. 1989. *Our Own Time: A History of American Labor and the Working Day*. London: Verso.

Root, L.E. 1980. Transcript of March 6 interview by Robert E. Burgess, Lockheed Missiles and Space Company, Sunnyvale, CA.

Roper, M. 1991. "Yesterday's model: Product fetishism and the British company man, 1945–85." In M. Roper and J. Tosh, eds, *Manful Assertions: Masculinities in Britain since 1800*. London: Routledge.

Rosaldo, R. 1989. *Culture and Truth: The Remaking of Social Analysis*. Boston: Beacon Press.

Roseberry, W. 1982. "Balinese cockfights and the seduction of anthropology." *Social Research*, 49(4):1013–28.

Rosen, 1991. In P. Frost, L. Moore, M. Louis, C. Lundbert, and J. Martin, eds, *Reframing Organizational Culture*. Beverly Hills: Sage.

Rosenbloom, R.S. and M.A. Cusumano. 1988. "Technological pioneering and competitive advantage: The birth of the VCR Industry." In M.L. Tushman and W.L. Moore, eds, *Readings in the Management of Innovation*. 2nd edn. New York: HarperBusiness.

Sabel, C. 1982. *Work and Politics*. Cambridge: Cambridge University Press.

—— 1989. "The re-emergence of regional economies." In P. Hirst and J. Zeitlin, eds, *Reversing Industrial Decline*. Oxford: Berg Press.

—— 1992. "Studied trust: Building new forms of cooperation in a volatile economy." *Human Relations*, 46 (September):1133–70.

Saxenian, A. 1994. *Regional Advantage*. Cambridge, MA: Harvard University Press.

Sayer, A. and R. Walker. 1992. *The New Social Economy*. Oxford: Blackwell.

Schein, E. 1992. *Organizational Culture and Leadership*. 2nd edn. San Francisco: Jossey-Bass.

Schoenberger, E. 1985. "Foreign manufacturing investments in the United States: Competitive strategies and international location." *Economic Geography*, 61(3):241–59.

—— 1988. "From Fordism to flexible accumulation: Technology, competitive strategies and international location." *Environment and Planning D: Society and Space*, 6:245–62.

—— 1989a. "Multinational corporations and the new international division of labor: A critical appraisal." In S. Wood, ed., *Work Transformed?*. London: Unwin Hyman.

—— 1989b. "Some dilemmas of automation: Strategic and operational aspects of technological change in production." *Economic Geography*, 65(4):232–47.

—— 1990. "US manufacturing investments in Western Europe: Markets, corporate strategy and competitive environment." *Annals of the American Association of Geographers*, 80(3):379–93.

—— 1991. "The corporate interview as a research method in economic geography." *Professional Geographer*, 43(2):180–9.

Schonberger, R. 1982. *Japanese Manufacturing Techniques*. New York: Free Press.

Schriever, Maj.-Gen. B.A. 1958. "The USAF Ballistic Missile Program." In Lt.-Col. K.F. Gantz, ed., *The United States Air Force Report on the Ballistic Missile: Its Technology, Logistics and Strategy*. New York: Doubleday.

Scott, A. 1988. *New Industrial Spaces*. London: Pion.

—— 1991. "The aerospace–electronics industrial complex of Southern California: The formative years, 1940–60." *Research Policy*, 20(5):439–56.

Scott, R. 1981. *Organizations*. Englewood Cliffs, NJ: Prentice-Hall.

Sculley, J. with J. Byrne. 1987. *Odyssey: Pepsi to Apple ... The Journey of a Marketing Impresario*. New York: Perennial Library, Harper and Row.

Shaiken, H. and S. Herzenberg. 1987. *Automation and Global Production: Automobile Engine Production in Mexico, the United States and Canada*. San Diego: Center for US–Mexican Studies, University of California.

Sheehan, N. 1988. *A Bright Shining Lie: John Paul Vann and America in Vietnam*. New York: Random House.

Simon, H. 1961. *Administrative Behavior*. 2nd edn. New York: Macmillan.

Smith, D. 1982. *Conflict and Compromise: Class Formation in English Society, 1830–1914*. London: Routledge and Kegan Paul.

Smith, D.K. and R.C. Alexander. 1988. *Fumbling the Future: How Xerox Invented, then Ignored, the First Personal Computer*. New York: William Morrow.

Smith, J. 1991. "A slip in time saves nine: prestigious origins again." In J. Bender and D. Wellbery, eds, *Chronotypes: The Construction of Time*. Stanford: Stanford University Press.

Smith, N. 1984. *Uneven Development*. Oxford: Blackwell.

Smith, P. and D. Reinertsen. 1991. *Developing Products in Half the Time*. New York: Van Nostrand.

Stalk, G. and T. Hout. 1990. *Competing Against Time.* New York: Free Press.

Stekler, H.O. 1965. *The Structure and Performance of the Aerospace Industry.* Berkeley, CA: University of California Press.

Stinchcombe, A. 1990. *Information and Organizations.* Berkeley, CA: University of California Press.

Storper, M. 1985. "Oligopoly and the product cycle: Essentialism in economic geography." *Economic Geography,* 61(3):260–82.

—— 1993. "Systems of innovation as forms of collective action: Worlds of production." Paper presented at the annual meeting of the Association of American Geographers, Atlanta, Georgia, April 6–10.

Storper, M. and R. Walker. 1989. *The Capitalist Imperative: Territory, Technology and Industrial Growth.* Oxford: Blackwell.

Sugimori, Y., K. Kusunoki, F. Cho, and S. Uchikawa. 1977. "Toyota production system and Kanban system: Materialization of just-in-time and respect-for-human system." *International Journal of Production Research,* 15:553–64.

Swyngedouw, E. 1989. "The production of space." PhD dissertation, Dept of Geography and Environmental Engineering, Johns Hopkins University, Baltimore.

Tabb, W. and L. Sawer, eds. 1984. *Sunbelt/Snowbelt.* New York: Oxford University Press.

Taplin, I. 1994. "Strategic reorientation of US apparel firms." In G. Gereffi and M. Korzeniewicz, eds, *Commodity Chains and Global Capitalism.* Westport, CT: Greenwood Press.

Taylor, W. 1992. "The logic of global business: An interview with ABB's Percy Barnevik." In W. Bennis, ed., *Leaders on Leadership.* Boston: Harvard Business Review.

Teece, D. 1981. "The multinational enterprise: market failure and market power considerations." *Sloan management Review,* 22:3–17.

Thompson, E.P. 1963. *The Making of the English Working Class.* New York: Pantheon.

—— 1967. "Time, work-discipline, and industrial capitalism." *Past and Present,* 38:56–97.

Thwaites, A. and R. Oakey, eds. 1985. *The Regional Economic Impact of Technological Change.* London: Frances Pinter.

Tichy, N. and R. Charan. 1992. "Speed, simplicity, self-confidence: An interview with Jack Welch." In W. Bennis, ed., *Leaders on Leadership.* Boston: Harvard Business Review.

Time. 1954. "The general's laboratory." August 23:66–7.

Togo, Y. and W. Wartman. 1993. *Against All Odds.* New York: St Martin's.

Trice, H. and J. Beyer. 1993. *The Cultures of Work Organizations.* Englewood Cliffs, NJ: Prentice-Hall.

Tyson, R.E. 1968. "The cotton industry." In D.H. Alford, ed., *The Development of British Industry and Foreign Competition 1875–1914.* Toronto: University of Toronto Press.

US Congress (Subcommittee of Committee on Government Operations). 1959. Hearings, organization and management of missile programs. 86th Congress, 1st Sess., February 4 to March 20. Washington, DC: GPO.

—— (Committee on Banking, Housing and Urban Affairs, Senate). 1971a. Hearings, emergency loan guarantee legislation. 92nd Congress, 1st Sess., June 7–16. Washington, DC: GPO.

—— (Committee on Banking and Currency, House of Representatives). 1971b. Hearings, to authorize emergency loan guarantees to major business enterprises. 92nd Congress, 1st Sess., July 13–15, 19–20. Washington, DC: GPO.

—— (Joint Economic Committee). 1977. "Foundations for a national policy to preserve private enterprise in the 1980s." Washington, DC: GPO.

—— (Joint Economic Committee). 1981. "Monetary policy, selective credit policy and industrial policy in France, Britain, West Germany and Sweden." Washington DC: GPO.

—— (House Committee on Banking, Finance and Urban Affairs). 1982. "US industrial strategy: Hearings before the Subcommittee on Economic Stabilization." September 22. Washington, DC: GPO.

US Dept of Labor. 1980. "Report of the President on US competitiveness." Washington, DC: GPO.

Van Maanen, J. 1991. In P. Frost, L. Moore, M. Louis, C. Lundbert, and J. Martin, eds, *Reframing Organizational Culture*. Beverly Hills: Sage.

Varian, M. 1991. "VM and the VM community: Past, present and future." Princeton, NJ: Office of Computing and Information Technology, Princeton University.

Vernon, R. 1966. "International investment and international trade in the product cycle." *Quarterly Journal of Economics*, 80(2):190–207.

Von Tunzelmann, N. 1981. "Britain 1900–45: A survey." In R. Floud and D. McCloskey, eds, *The Economic History of Britain Since 1700. Vol. 2: 1860 to the 1970s*. Cambridge: Cambridge University Press.

Walker, R. 1985. "Is there a service economy? The changing capitalist division of labor." *Science and Society*, 49:42–83.

Wall Street Journal. 1992. "A swollen GM finds how hard it is to stick with its crash diet." September 9:A1.

Waxman, R., L. Saunders, and H. Carter. 1989. "VHDL links design, text, maintenance." IEEE *Spectrum*, May:40–4.

Webb, D. 1991. "Don't just lay an egg – hatch a profit center." *Electronic Business*, December 9:42–6.

Webber, M. 1984. *Industrial Location*. Beverly Hills: Sage.

Williams, R. 1977. *Marxism and Literature*. Oxford: Oxford University Press.

Williamson, O. 1975. *Markets and Hierarchies*. New York: Free Press.

—— 1985. *The Economic Institutions of Capitalism*. New York: Free Press.

Womack, J.P., D.T. Jones, and D. Roos. 1990. *The Machine that Changed the World: The Story of Lean Production*. New York: HarperPerennial.

Wood, A. 1991. "How much does trade with the south affect workers in the north?" *World Bank Research Observer*, 6(1):19–36.

Wood, S., ed. 1989. *Work Transformed?*. London: Unwin Hyman.

Woods, G.B. 1946. *The Aircraft Manufacturing Industry: Present and Future Prospects*. New York: White Weld.

Wright, E.O. 1985. *Classes*. London: Verso.

Yenne, B. 1987. *Lockheed.* New York: Crescent Books.
York, H.F. and G.A. Greb. 1977. "Strategic reconnaissance." *Bulletin of the Atomic Scientists*, April:33–42.

Index